THE ROUGH GUIDE

Website
Directory

There are more than two hundred Rough Guide travel,
phrasebook and music titles, covering destinations from
Amsterdam to Zimbabwe, languages from Czech to
Vietnamese, and musics from World to Opera and Jazz

www.roughguides.com

ROUGH
GUIDES

Rough Guide Credits

Series editor: Mark Ellingham

Design and layout: Peter Buckley and Duncan Clark

Production: Julia Bovis

Proofreading: Tamara Colloff-Bennett

Publishing Information

This fourth edition published October 2004 by
Rough Guides Ltd, 80 Strand, London WC2R 0RL.

Distributed by the Penguin Group

Penguin Books Ltd, 80 Strand, London WC2R 0RL
Penguin Putnam, Inc., 375 Hudson Street, New York 10014, USA
Penguin Books Australia Ltd, 487 Maroondah Highway,
PO Box 257, Ringwood, Victoria 3134, Australia
Penguin Books Canada Ltd, 10 Alcorn Avenue,
Toronto, Ontario, Canada M4V 1E4
Penguin Books (NZ) Ltd, 182–190 Wairau Road,
Auckland 10, New Zealand

Printed in Italy by LegoPrint.

© Peter Buckley and Duncan Clark, 2004
368 pages; includes index
A catalogue record for this book is available from the British Library.
ISBN 1-84353-344-8

THE ROUGH GUIDE

Website
Directory

written and updated by
Peter Buckley and Duncan Clark

created by
Angus J Kennedy

Contents

contents

contents

contents

FIND IT

Find it

the fine art of searching

Barring total deforestation of the world, it would be impossible to list, let alone review, every website currently floating around the ether. Indeed, this book lists less than one-hundredth of one percent of the sites on the Web. So before proceeding with the directory, here's a quick tutorial about how to find things in the other 99.99% (including webpages which are listed in this book, but which may have moved to a new address since it went to print). The art of finding things online quickly and efficiently is, without doubt, a life-changing skill. Still, most people, including many Net veterans, simply bumble their way around, using the wrong search tools and using them badly. If that's you, the following section could revolutionize your Internet experience. But even if you're already a proficient searcher, you'll doubtless learn something – see p.12 for advanced Google tips.

part 1

How it works

The Net is massive. Just the Web alone houses many billions of pages, with millions more added daily. So you'll need some serious help if you want to find something. Thankfully there's a wide selection of **search tools** to make the task relatively painless. The job usually entails keying your **search terms** into a form on a webpage and waiting a few seconds for the results.

Over the next few pages, we'll introduce you to search tools that can **locate almost anything**: on the Web; linked to from the Web; or archived into an online Web database, such as email addresses, phone numbers, program locations, newsgroup articles and news clippings. Of course, first it has to be put online and public access granted. So just because you can access US government servers doesn't mean you'll find a file on DEA Operative Presley's whereabouts.

Your weapons

There are three main types of Web search tools: **search engines, hand-built subject directories** and **search agents**. Apart from the odd newspaper archive, they're usually free. Because they're so useful and popular, a few years ago there was a trend towards tacking other services onto the side and building so-called **portals, communities** and **hubs**. More recently, that trend has begun to reverse, with the launch of several skeletal search tools free of fancy overheads. Irrespective of which you use, ignore the quantity of froufrou and concentrate on the quality of the results. The next few pages discuss each category in detail and show you how to torture them for answers.

Search engines

The best way to find just about anything online is to start with a **search engine**. The good thing about search engines is they can search through the **actual contents** of webpages (and file servers), not just descriptions. The better search engines can riffle through **billions of**

webpages in a fraction of a second. You simply go to the search engine's website and submit **keywords** – search terms to you and me. It will query its database and, almost instantly, return a list of results or "hits". For example, if you were to search on the expression "Rough Guides", here's what might come up on top:

Rough Guides Travel
Click here. **ROUGH GUIDES**.COM features online coverage of thousands of travel destinations, plus music reviews of every genre. Read ...
www.roughguides.com/ - 33k - <u>Cached</u> - <u>Similar pages</u>

In this case the top line tells us the name of the page or site, and it's followed by some text excerpted from the page and some more info including a description and the page's address. If it suits, click on the link to visit the site.

The reason it's so quick is that **you're not actually searching billions of webpages**. You're searching a **database** of webpage extracts stored on the search engine's server. This database is compiled by a program that periodically "crawls" around, or "spiders", the Web looking for new or changed pages. Because of the sheer size of the Net and a few factors relating to site design, it's not possible for the crawlers to find every site, let alone every word on every page. Nor is it possible to keep the database completely up to date. That means you can't literally "search the Web"; you can only search a snapshot taken by a search engine. So, naturally, different search engines will give you different results depending on how much of the Web they've found, how often they update, how much text they extract from each page and how well they actually work.

tip

Especially if you have a slow connection, don't just click on a search result then hit the Back button if it's no good. Instead, run down the list and open the most promising candidates in new browser windows. It will save you tons of time, as you can read one while the others are loading. Do this by holding down the Shift key as you click (or the Apple key on Macs), or by using the right-click mouse menu.

part 1

So, which search engine?

There are dozens of search engines, but only a few are worth trying. In fact, you'll rarely need more than one. But, since you'll be using it often, make sure it's up to speed. You'll want the **biggest, freshest database**. You'll want to **fine-tune your search** with extra commands. And you'll want the most hits you can get on one page with the most **relevant results on top**. Right now, that's **Google**:

Google www.google.com

This excellent search engine has an uncanny knack of getting it right in the first few hits, and also it provides access to "**caches**" of pages that have disappeared or changed since its crawl, or which are otherwise unavailable. This is great when you can't get a link to load (click on "cached" under a search result to see how this works). Google has become so popular that "to google" something is now a commonly used verb. But most users hardly scratch the surface of what it can do – see p.12 for lots of **tips**. Many users also don't realise that Google has regional versions, such as Google UK, which will give the same results but offers a button to search UK pages:

find it

Google UK www.google.co.uk
Google Australia www.google.com.au
Google Canada www.google.ca
Google New Zealand www.google.co.nz

If Google falls short, try **Yahoo!**. For years its search was driven by other other engines (including Google for a while), but it now has its own technology and the results are impressive. Still no luck? You could try **Teoma**. It has a smaller database than the above two, but it is often praised for the relevancy of its results.

Yahoo! www.yahoo.com **(also .co.uk, .ca, .com.au, etc)**
Yahoo! UK www.yahoo.co.uk
Teoma www.teoma.com

As for the rest, many of them are essentially the same as the above three but in different clothes. For example, at the time of writing (this is a fast-changing area), **AOL** search results come from Google; **AllTheWeb**, **AltaVista** and **MSN** results come from Yahoo!; and **AskJeeves**'s are from Teoma. However, even those that license the same search technology often give slightly different results, present them differently or offer different tools and services. **Lycos**, for example, is currently based on Yahoo!, but it draws on a human-edited directory for commonly search terms and also allows you to preview search results without leaving the main results page. So you may want to try them out.

All The Web www.alltheweb.com
AltaVista www.av.com
AskJeeves www.ask.com
Lycos www.lycos.com
MSN www.search.msn.com

But there are also many search engines not based on one of the big three. **Turbo 10** promises to search bits of the "deep net" that others can't reach. **A9** lets you search both the Web and inside thousands of books, courtesy of Amazon (who own the engine); it also lets you save your search history. **GigaBlast**, meanwhile, has a relatively small index of sites, but offers a host of interesting features (and, remarkably, is entirely the work of one man).

A9 www.a9.com
GigaBlast www.gigablast.com
Turbo10 www.turbo10.com

Or if you seriously need **lots of results**, download an agent such as **Copernic** (see p.21) to query all the engines simultaneously.

More info

For more info than you could possibly ever want about the mirky world of search engines, see:

Search Engine Showdown www.searchenginesshowdown.com
Search Engine Watch www.searchenginewatch.com
Search Engine World www.searchengineworld.com

These sites keep tabs on all the finer details, such as who owns what, how they tick and who's currently biggest – essential reading if you have your own site and want to generate traffic. They also report on technologies that are in the pipeline. To see what Google are experimenting with, go straight to the source:

Google Labs http://labs.google.com

Limitations

Search engines aren't the be-all and end-all of what's on the Web.

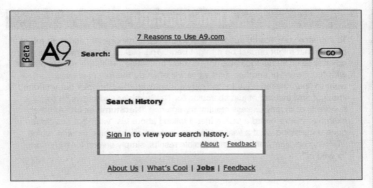

They're only as good as their most recent findings, which might be just a small proportion of what's actually there – and which could be months old. So, just because you can't find it through a Web search doesn't mean it's not there. If you're after something brand-new, for instance, they're not always the best choice. You might be better off searching **Usenet** (see p.25) or a news service.

How to use a search engine (properly)

OK – this is important. Get searching right and your whole relationship with the Internet will improve tenfold. The trick is to think up a **search term** that's unique enough to get rid of junk results, but broad enough not to miss anything useful; it will depend entirely on the subject, so be prepared to think laterally. But first of all you need to know the basic tricks

A typical search

Suppose we want to search for something on the esteemed author, Angus Kennedy. Let's see how you'd do it in most of the major search engines.

A few years ago, if you entered **angus kennedy** you would get a list

Think logically

To increase your search success and efficiency, think logically about an **exact phrase** that might appear on a target page. This makes finding facts and other specific things incomparably quicker and easier. Making a simple phrase with "is", "was" or another short word will often do the trick. Let's say you want to find an alternative for the network software NetStumbler but you don't know of any. Instead of just searching for NetStumbler and browsing through hundreds of mostly useless results, try entering **"NetStumbler or"**. Another example: you've heard a techie friend talking about his "wiki" but you don't quite understand what a wiki actually is. Instead of searching for wiki, which will bring up plenty of incomprehensible results, simply search for the phrase **"a wiki is"**.

of pages that contained the words "angus" or "kennedy", or both. Fine, but it meant you'd get loads of pages about "Angus cattle" and "JFK". These days most search engines will automatically look for pages containing both words.

Unfortunately, there's no guarantee that the two words will be found next to each other. What we really want is to **treat them as a phrase**. A simple way to do this is to enclose the words within quotes:

"angus kennedy"

Now we've captured all instances of Angus Kennedy as a phrase, but since it's a **person's name** we should look for *Kennedy, Angus* as well. However, we want to see pages that contain either of these terms, rather than only those that contain both. We usually do this by inserting an upper-case "OR" between the terms (or, at All the Web, by inserting the terms in brackets). So let's try:

"angus kennedy" OR "kennedy angus"

You may have noticed that we left out the comma of "kennedy, angus", and that we haven't bothered using capital letters. This is because most search engines ignore such details.

By now we should have quite a few relevant results, but they're bound to be mixed up with lots of irrelevant ones. So we should narrow the search down further and exclude some of the excess, such as pages that contain a different person with the same name. Our target writes books about French literature, so let's start by getting rid of that pesky Rough Guide author. To **exclude** a term, place a minus sign (-) in front of it. Let's ditch him, then:

"angus kennedy" OR "kennedy angus" -"rough guide"

Know your engine

That's about all you need to know in most instances, but there are scores of extra tricks – see overleaf for Google tips. Also, there are exceptions to these rules, so you might have to adjust your search terms slightly, depending on the engine, to get the best results. There are still search engines, for example, that require you to use a **plus sign** ("+") to state that the page must contain a word (eg **+angus +kennedy**).

The same applies to online stores, encyclopedias, newspaper archives and anything else you can search. So at some point it's worth reading the instructions. You should find a link to a "FAQ", "Search Tips" or "Help" section on the front page. A few minutes' study could save hours of weeding through poor results.

Observe how the engine interprets **capitals**, **dashes** between words, **brackets**, **wild cards**, **truncations** and **Boolean operators** such as AND, OR, NEAR and NOT.

Also watch out for "**stop words**". These are words that are normally ignored. In Google, for example, common words like "the" and "it" are not included in your search unless they're part of a phrase (eg **"the beatles"**). If for some reason you want to include a common word in a non-phrase search, place a plus sign in front of it (eg **+the beatles**).

tip

You'll be using your favourite search engine often, so drop its address onto your browser's Links bar or set it as your browser's homepage. Consider whether you'd rather have the front search page (for fast loading) or the advanced search page (slower loading, but with a wide assortment of boxes for fine-tuning). Alternatively, use a search toolbar or "deskbar" for even quicker access to your engine of choice (see p.17).

Google Search Wizardry: A Guide

Though Google is the world's most popular search engine, most of its users don't make the most of its many special commands. So here's a tutorial in the finer points of Google searching. It may just change your life...

BASIC SEARCHES

Googling: thomas clark
finds pages containing both the terms "thomas" and "clark".

Googling: "thomas clark"
finds pages containing the exact phrase "thomas clark".

Googling: thomas OR clark
finds pages containing either "thomas", "clark" or both.

Googling: thomas -clark
finds pages containing "thomas" but not containing "clark".

All these commands can be mixed and doubled up so, for example:

Googling: "thomas clark" OR "tom clark" -economist
finds pages containing either name but not the word "economist".

FIND A SYNONYM

Use ~ before a word to search for synonyms and related words. For example:

Googling: ~mac
will find pages containing "macintosh" and "Apple" as well as "mac".

FIND A DEFINITION

Googling: define:calabash
finds definitions from various sources for the word "calabash". (You can also get to a definition (from www.dictionary.com) of a search term by clicking the link in the right of the top blue strip on the results page.)

FIND A FLEXIBLE PHRASE

Use an asterisk as a substitute for any word in a phrase. For example:

Googling: "tom * clark"
finds "tom frederick clark" as well as just "tom clark".

SEARCH FOR A PAGE THAT NO LONGER EXISTS

Let's say you visit **www.roughguides.com**, a page you looked at the other day so you know it exists, but, to your horror, it doesn't seem to be there. Fear not, Google probably has a copy.

Googling: **cache:www.roughguides.com**
> finds Google's "cached" (saved) snapshot of the page, if it has one. (You can reach the same page by searching for **www.roughguides.com** and then clicking the "cache" link underneath the relevant result.)

SEARCH WITHIN A SPECIFIC SITE

Use the **site:** command to search within a specific website. This usually gives more, better and more clearly presented results than the site's internal search would (if it has one at all). For example:

Googling: **site:www.guardian.co.uk "thomas clark" OR "tom clark"**
> finds pages containing either version of Thomas Clark's name within the website of The Guardian newspaper.

SEARCH URLS (WEB ADDRESSES)

The commands **inurl:** and **allinurl:** let you specify that some or all of your search terms appear within the address (url) of the page. This can be very useful if you remember only part of a web address you want to revisit. It's also good for limiting your search to certain types of websites. For example:

Googling: **"arms exports" inurl:gov**
> finds pages containing the phrase "arms exports" in the webpages with the term "gov" in the address (ie. government websites).

SEARCH TITLES

The commands **intitle:** and **allintitle:** let you specify that one or all of your search terms should appear in the title of a webpage (the text that appears on the top bar of your browser window when viewing a page). This can be useful if you're getting lots of results that mention your terms but don't specifically focus on them. For example:

Googling: **train bristol intitle:timetable**
> will find pages with "timetable" in their titles, and "train" and "bristol" anywhere in the page.

NUMBER & PRICE RANGES

Google lets you search for a range of numbers – especially useful for dates. You can also search for a range of prices, though at the time of writing, only the dollar sign can be used.

Googling: **1972..1975 "snooker champions"**
> finds pages containing the term "snooker champions" and any number (or date) in the the range 1972–1975. Googling **numrange:1972-1975** has the same effect.

Googling: **$15..30 "snooker cue"**
> finds pages containing the term "snooker cue" and any price in the range $15–30. Googling **pricerange:15-30** has the same effect.

SEARCH SPECIFIC FILE TYPES

The command **filetype:** lets you specify that your search terms should appear in a specific file, such as pdf format. For example:

Googling: **filetype:pdf climate change statistics**
> would find pdf documents (likely to be more "serious" reports than web-pages) containing the terms "climate", "change" and "statistics".

FIND LINKING PAGES

Links are usually one-way: you can see links from a page, but not links to a page. In Google, though, you can find out. For example:

Googling: **link:www.roughguides.com/music/index.html**
> finds pages which have a link to the Rough Guides' music homepage.

CALCULATIONS & CONVERTIONS

OK, so it's not exactly searching, but Google can act as an excellent calcula-tor. It can cope with standard mathematical functions – such as * (multiply), / (divide), + (add), - (subtract) and ^ (raise to the power) – as well as hundreds of units of measurement, from farenheit to hectares. For example:

Googling: **3465*34223**
> will give you the answer 118,582,695.

Googling: **(24-9)% of (36^4 - 3)**
> will give you the answer 251,941.95.

Googling: **51 fahrenheit in celsius**
> will give you the answer, 10.55 degrees Celsius

Googling: 5 gallons in teaspoons
will give you the answer "5 US gallons = 3840 US teaspoons"!

IMAGES AND OTHER SPECIAL SEARCHES
Besides images, groups and news searches, Google can also do searches focusing on Apple Macs, Linux and Microsoft. Just click on Advanced Search.

REGIONAL GOOGLE
If you're outside the US, don't forget to use your regional branch of Google (see p.18) so you have the option to search only pages from your country.

AND MORE...
Though they're mostly limited to the US, Google can retrieve relevant information if you search for a flight number, an express delivery tracking number, a vehicle ID number and many other such things.

For a full list of Google tools and shortcuts, see www.google.com/help. And if you don't fancy remembering the special commands listed above, many of them can be inputted via a form on Google's Advanced Search page.

Or for answers about every Google-related question you could ever want to ask, see www.geocities.com/googlepubsupgenfaq, the comprehensive FAQ from google.public.support.general newsgroup. More Google news, views, gossip, tips, history and the rest at:

Elgoog www.elgoog.nl
Unofficial Google Weblog http://google.weblogsinc.com
Watching Google Like A Hawk www.watchinggooglelikeahawk.com

Welcome at Elgoog.nl, an ode to Google
This Google info page about
Elgoog,Googlemania,google,pageranking,groups,dance,tools,filtering,add,url,viewer,logo's,adwords,answers,
froogle,compute,dance,toolbar,forums,blogs,tools,api's,francais,deutsch,seo,toolbar,searchengine,zoeken,zoek,nederlands

Links to/from Google itself
Sitemap, Google Add Urls Google
viewer...

More Google's
Domains, Fake and Parody...

Googlemania
Funny logo's, Google history...

Other Google services
Adwords-Answers, Froogle-Compute...

Pageranking
Pagerank, Toolbar...

Groups
Forums, Blogs...

Google in articles
Persons-Research, News-articles...

The Dance
Dance check tool, Dance 2002
pictures...

Tools
Api's, Ip adresses...

Filtering
Germany, China...

Links in other languages
Deutsch German, Francais
French...

Oldindex
Other Searchengines, SEO...

Advanced searches

Any decent search engine will offer you a whole range of advanced tools. For example, you could look for only those pages that include your search term in their **titles**, **URLs** or **domain names**; pages written in a **specific language**; files with a particular **file format**; or pages **updated within a certain time frame**, such as within the last year. These are very valuable – once you've used them, you'll wonder how you ever found anything before.

Certain engines put some of these tools on **dropdown menus** on the search homepage, but for a full list look for an "**advanced search**" link. These tools can also usually be accessed using codes in your search – in Google, for example, entering **"Jimmy White" site:bbc.co.uk** would bring up pages from **www.bbc.co.uk** containing everyone's favourite snooker star. This is extremely useful considering how many sites have poor internal search engines.

Results per page

There's nothing more annoying than getting loads of results from a Web search but only being shown ten of them per page, which is the default for many search engines. In the advanced search options you should find a "results per page" option – 100 should do the trick – and some engines allow you to **set a new default**. At Google, for example, click on "Preferences", select your preferred options from the lists, and they will be stored in your cookies.

Translations

If your results include pages in certain foreign languages, Google and others can **translate them** (albeit pretty roughly) into English or a different language. Just click on "translate" on the hits.

Seaching for images

Most of the major search engines now offer **image-specific searches**, which can prove very handy. However, they are far less comprehensive than text searches because of the way that pictures are named and so

Search toolbars

Many search engines and other sites offer you the opportunity to download a toolbar add-on for your browser. This can be incredibly useful if you use a site a lot. For example, the **Google Toolbar** (http://toolbar.google.com) puts all the search engine's advanced features close at hand. You can do Web, Usenet (see p.25) and image searches without having to go to Google's homepage. You can even drag text from a webpage straight into the search box, and click from one search result to the next without returning to the list.

The **Groowe Toolbar** (www.groowe.com) has even more features, combining the capabilities of the Google bar with those of Yahoo!, Download.com and lots of other major sites. However, arguably the original search toolbar king is **Dave's Quick Search Taskbar** (free from www.dqsd.net). This one goes on your Windows taskbar rather than in your Web browser, allowing you to drag text into it from anywhere and search without even opening your browser first. It automatically searches Google, but you can use shortcuts to do hundreds of other things: search Amazon, Multimap, Dictionary.com, or even make currency calculations. Google are currently developing a similar "Deskbar".

There are many other toolbar add-ons out there, but bear in mind that they all have the potential to make your system more unstable, so **only download what you really need** – or at least really want. Never install any add-ons from sites you don't trust, and use **Spybot** (www.safer-networking.org) or something similar to check you haven't installed any malicious "adware" or "spyware", which might display ads, spy on your online activities and slow down your PC.

on. So just because a photo of you doesn't appear when you tap your name into an image search, it doesn't mean you're not adorning a webpage somewhere. Try running a normal search too, and browse the hits for relevant photos.

Can't find it?

Just because search engines can't find something doesn't mean it's not on the Web. It just means their trawlers haven't visited that site yet. Which means you'll have to turn to another, maybe fresher, source. Read on.

Subject directories

It's sometimes more useful to browse a range of sites within a topic or region rather than throw darts at the entire Web. For this you should turn to a **subject directory**. These aren't compiled by machines trawling the Web; **they're put together by human beings**. Everything is neatly filed under various categories, like a phone directory or library, making it easy for you to drill down to what you're after. This is particularly useful if you're looking for a listing of services in an area – your home town, say.

You usually have the choice of browsing directories by **subject group** and sometimes by other criteria such as **entry date** or **rating**. And usually you can search the directory itself through a form, just like a search engine. Unlike search engines, though, directories don't keep the contents of webpages but instead store titles, categories and sometimes comments or reviews, so adjust your search strategy accordingly. Start with broad terms and work down until you hit the reviews.

General directories

The Internet doesn't have an official directory, but it does have several broadly focused listings that will help you on your way to most subject areas. The **best general directories** are About.com, **Open Directory** and **Yahoo!**.

Yahoo! is the closest the Net has to a central directory. If the Web had seven wonders, it would be up there near the top. Apart from the massive site directory, it also has loads of added extras such as national and metropolitan directories, regional TV listings, weather reports, kids' guides, seniors' guides, Yellow Pages, sport scores, plus outstanding news and financial services. You should spend at least one session online exploring its reaches. Chances are you'll be back there regularly.

Yahoo! www.yahoo.com

If you're located outside the USA, or looking for country-specific information, then switch to the relevant regional guide, if available. For example:

Yahoo! Asia http://asia.yahoo.com
Yahoo! Australia & NZ www.yahoo.com.au
Yahoo! Canada www.yahoo.ca
Yahoo! UK & Ireland www.yahoo.co.uk

The Open Directory is a more recent project, though it has grown fast, being compiled by tens of thousands of volunteers. While it lacks Yahoo!'s armada of added services, its directory is better maintained in many areas, so it pays to look at both. However, it's best-accessed via Google that through its homepage, which is slower and not as well organized.

Open Directory www.dmoz.org
Google Directory http://directory.google.com

About.com deserves a special mention because, unlike most broad directories, its topics are presented by expert guides. This makes it an excellent jumping-off point.

About.com www.about.com

There's no shortage of alternatives. These might prove useful if the above fail, such as:

AltaVista www.av.com/dir
Excite www.excite.com/directory
Lycos http://dir.lycos.com

But broad subject directories aren't always the best at digging up everything within a category or giving you expert guidance. For that you need a specialist directory – or, as the suits call them, **vortals**.

Specialist directories

Whatever your interest, you can bet your favourite finger it will have
several dedicated sites and another that keeps track of them all. Such
specialized directories are a boon for finding new, esoteric or local
interest pages – ones that the major directories overlook. How do you
find a specialist directory? You could go straight to Google with a very
specific search, but in this case it would make more sense to seek a
helping hand. Try **About.com** first. It maintains specialist directories
on most common interests. Next try **Yahoo!** and the **Open Directory**.
If there's more than a couple of Web directories on the subject, they'll
put them in their own section. You might also glean something from
consulting a directory that specializes in listing specialist directories,
such as:

Complete Planet www.completeplanet.com
Directory Guide www.directoryguide.com
GoGettem www.gogettem.com

Search agents

Search agents, or **searchbots**, gather information live from a limited
number of sites – for example, to find new information, to compare
prices or stock, or combine the results from several search engines.
Shopping agents (p.290) like Shopper.com scan online stores for the
best deals.

"**Metasearch**" sites that query multiple search engines and directories simultaneously – such as Metacrawler, Vivisimo, Dogpile, Mamma
and Ixquick – are generally a waste of time. You'll get better results,
faster, by going directly to Google.

You'll find the same goes for the bewildering layers of **search aids
built into Internet Explorer** and the **Windows Start menu**. These
make a search form appear on the left-hand side of your browser.
Clicking "Customize" lets you choose from an impressive array of
search engines, directories, email databases, maps and more – but

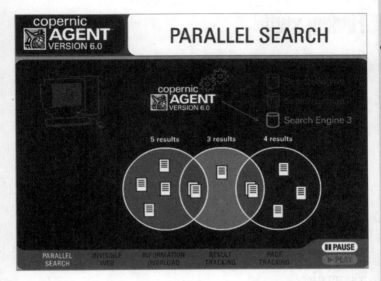

though it looks promising you'll probably get better value at the source. Similarly, only use Apple's OS metasearch agent, **Sherlock**, if you feel you need a handicap.

Instead, for serious research, try **Copernic**. It's a stand-alone program that can query hundreds of search engines, directories, Usenet archives, shops and email databases at once. It filters out the duplicates, displays the results on a single page in your browser, and even retrieves them automatically for offline browsing. And for more on searchbots of all shapes and size, see **BotSpot**.

Copernic www.copernic.com
BotSpot www.botspot.com

part 1

Finding stuff

General search engines and directories are great, but they don't always strike gold first time. As you get more familiar with the run of the Net, you'll gravitate towards specialist sites and directories that shine in specific areas. What's best depends largely on what you're after. When you find a useful site, **store it in your Favorites** so you can return. In the meantime, here's how to:

Find new stuff as it's written

There are many ways to monitor search engines, individual sites and newsgroups for changes. **Tracerlock** (**www.tracerlock.com**), for example, will let you know when your keywords come up on thousands of news sites, trade journals and e-zines – including sites of your own choosing – for a small monthly fee. **Google News Alerts** offers a slightly simpler service for free: enter search terms at **www.google.com/newsalerts** and whenever they appear in one of Google's many newsfeeds, you'll receive an email pointing you to the relevant page.

Find computer help

In many cases, you'll be able to find useful computer help at the websites of the relevant hardware and software manufacturers – including Microsoft (**support.microsoft.com**) and Apple (**support.apple.com**). Otherwise, try a couple of unique phrases from your error or computer problem in Google Groups, followed by a normal Web search if that doesn't work. If your question isn't answered anywhere, join a relevant newsgroup and post it there. See also the Computer section of our Website guide (p.88).

Find local information

You'll sometimes want to find sites that cater to a very specific region. Say, for example, you want to look up film screenings across your hometown, or select a honeymoon suite in Tamanrasset. Although it might seem logical to use a local search engine to find local sites or information, it's often not the most efficient method. Start your searches with Google and then move on if that fails. Most small local search engines simply aren't very good.

Directories, however, can be another matter. Try Yahoo! and the Open (see p.18) and see what's listed in the region. Your target location might be filed under the country, state or province rather than the town or suburb, so start broad and then drill down from there. You should soon find the major specialist directories relevant to your region. For a directory of regional directories, see:

Search Engine Colossus www.searchenginecolossus.com

Find a local business or phone number

Apart from the online residential and business telephone directories from the phone companies, you'll also find a raft of private directories that compete – some even deliver a book as well. While they're not usually as easy to browse as their paper equivalents, online directories can be kept more up to date. Investigate a few of the major services listed below.

192 Enquiries www.192enquiries.com
192.com www.192.com
BT PhoneNet www.bt.com/directory-enquiries
Scoot www.scoot.co.uk
Yellow Pages www.yell.co.uk

Or to find a phone number in almost any country:

World Pages International Directories http://global.wpz.com

Find someone's email address

Not as simple as you might think. By far the best way to find out someone's email address is to **ring up and ask.** Don't know their phone number? Then try one of the online phone directories (see above). Alternatively, if you know where they work, look up their

company's **website.** Still, if this fails, it's worth trying the **email directories.** The biggest directories are:

Yahoo! PeopleSearch http://ukie.people.yahoo.com
Bigfoot www.bigfoot.com
Internet Address Finder www.iaf.net
WhoWhere www.whowhere.com

These get most of their data from Usenet postings (see below) and visitors, so while they're not in any way comprehensive, they're pretty vast
databases – and growing by the day. If these fail, try searching on your
quarry's full name in a search engine or **Google Groups**
(http://groups.google.com).

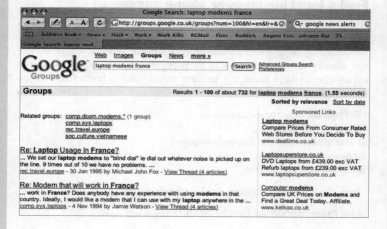

The people-finding features built into Windows, Mac OS, Outlook
Express and Netscape Mail are supposed to tap into these databases, but
rarely work well – if at all. Instead, to query several at once, download
Copernic:

Copernic www.copernic.com

Find out what others think on Usenet

There's no better place to find opinions and personal experiences than **Usenet newsgroups**, online discussion groups where every subject under the sun gets aired. For more on setting up Usenet with a dedicated newsreader, see *The Rough Guide to the Internet*. Alternatively, dive straight in with **Google Groups** (http://groups.google.com) where you can scan close to all Usenet discussions going back two decades. You can pursue entire threads and profile each contributor. Which means you can follow a whole discussion, as well as check out who's who and how well they're respected. On top of that, you can identify which groups are most likely to discuss something, join them and even post messages once registered. You'll get to the bottom of even the most obscure subject.

Find a mailing list

The best place to find mailing lists is through a well-worded Web search (that includes **"mailing list"** and the topic) or through the small-list directories at:

Discussion Lists http://DiscussionLists.com
Topica http://lists.topica.com

Find something you've forgotten

Don't give up if you can't remember at which website you saw that hot tip last week. Just open your browser's History and search your cached pages (see p.30). So long as it hasn't yet been deleted, you should even be able to recall it – even if you're not online.

Find advice

If all else fails – and that's pretty unlikely – you can always turn to someone else for help. Use Google Groups to find the most appropriate newsgroup(s). Summarize your quest in the subject heading, keep your message concise, post, and you should get an answer or three within a few days. Alternatively, try one of the "expert" or community advice services (some free, some not), such as:

Abuzz www.abuzz.com
AllExperts www.allexperts.com
Google Answers http://answers.google.com

When a Web address doesn't work

It won't be long before you come across a Web link or address that won't work; it's very common and usually not too hard to get around. Many of the addresses in this book will be wrong by the time you try them – not because we're hopeless, just because they change. That's the way of the Net. The most useful thing we can do is show you how to find the correct address.

Locate the problem

When a page won't display, the first thing to do is work out where the problem lies. First **check your connection** by trying another site that's very unlikely to be unavailable (such as **www.yahoo.com**). If that works, you know it's not your connection that's causing the problem, and you can continue to try and locate the correct address (read on). If no pages will open, you'll need to locate the problem (see box below).

When one address won't work

There are various reasons why you wouldn't be able to access a specific webpage. But very often there are steps you can take to access the

When no sites will open

If you can't connect to any website, close and then reopen your browser. It might only be a software glitch. Otherwise, it's most likely a problem with your Net connection or proxy server (if you're using one).

Check your mail. If that fails, log off then back on. Check it again. If your mailer connects and reports your mail status normally, you know that the connection between you and your ISP is OK. But there still could be a problem between it and the Net or with your proxy server. Check you have the right proxy settings and, if so, disable them. If it still doesn't work, ring your ISP and see if there's a problem at their end.

Or you can diagnose it yourself. To do this, test a known host – say, **www.yahoo.com** – with a network tool such as Ping or TraceRoute. If this fails, either your provider's connection to the Net is down or there's a problem with your Domain Name Server. Get on the phone and sort it out.

If you've verified that all connections are open but your browser still won't find any addresses, then the problem must lie with your browser setup. Check its settings and reinstall if necessary.

information you're after.

You'll probably be able to work out what the problem is by looking at exactly what happens – such as the error message that your machine may flash up. Here's a run-through of the most likely symptoms you'll encounter.

Symptom: An error message saying "**File not found – 404 error**", or you get directed to another page within the site in question that tells you something like "**The page you requested cannot be found**".
Problem: The host you are trying to access is responding, but the specific file you are trying to access isn't there. It has probably been moved or removed. If **www.roughguides.com/boguspage.html** brought up this message, for example, you'd know the **/boguspage.html** section was the problem.
Solution: If you typed the address in manually, make sure you did it correctly – including uppercase or lowercase letters. Still no luck? Refer to "Finding that elusive page" (p.30).

Symptom: An error message saying "**The server cannot be found**", "**The page cannot be displayed**" or "**DNS lookup error**".

Problem: Unless you typed in the address wrongly, the website you're trying to access probably doesn't exist or is temporarily unavailable. The latter may be due to maintenance on the server where the site lives, or because too many people are trying to access it at once.

Solution: Check the address, and try adding or removing the www part (so try **http://roughguides.com** instead of **www.roughguides.com**, for example). If not, try again later – perhaps even days later – and in the meantime search for a cache of the page (see p.30).

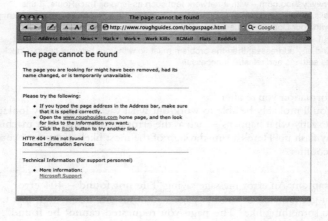

Symptom: A page or frame **instantly comes up blank**.

Problem: Your browser hasn't tried to fetch the page.

Solution: Hit "Refresh". If that doesn't work, reboot your browser and re-enter the address. Failing that, open Internet Options and clear your Temporary Internet Files or browser cache. Finally, if you're still having problems and it appears to be related to Internet Explorer security – such as the acceptance of an ActiveX control at an online banking site – check your security settings within Internet Options/Preferences, disable Content Advisor and consider adding the site to your Trusted Sites.

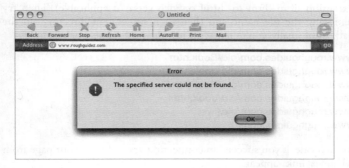

Symptom: You can reach a webpage on another computer but not your own.

Problem: Your **Windows Hosts file** could be the problem – especially if you've ever installed any browser acceleration software.

Solution: Get rid of the offending acceleration program via "Add/Remove" in the Windows Control Panel. Then locate the file called **Hosts** in your Windows folder (it will have no file extension). Open it with Notepad and remove any lines not starting with # except for the **localhost** entry. Save the file and exit.

Symptom: An error message saying: **"Not authorized to view this page"**.

Problem: Some sites, or pages, require a password to be accessed, or can only be reached from certain systems (such as a company network).

Solution: Train to be a cracker.

Finding that elusive page

If you can connect to the host (the website) but the individual page isn't there, there are a few tricks to try. Check capitalization, for instance: **book.htm** instead of **Book.htm**. Or try changing the file name extension from .htm to .html or vice versa (if applicable). Then try removing the file name and then each subsequent directory up the path until finally you're left with just the host name. For example:

www.roughguides.com/old/Book.htm
www.roughguides.com/old/book.htm
www.roughguides.com/old/Book.html
www.roughguides.com/old/book.html
www.roughguides.com/old/
www.roughguides.com

In each case, if you succeed in connecting, try to locate your page from whatever links appear.

Using a search engine

If you haven't succeeded, there's still hope. Try **searching for the problematic address in Google**, and you may find that, though the actual page is no longer available, you can still access Google's **cached copy** – if so a link saying "cache" will appear under the search result. You could even use the shortcut, searching for:

cache:www.roughguides.com/old/Book.htm

If that doesn't work, you could try searching in the relevant domain (website) for a keyword from the name of the file or from what you expect the file to contain. So, continuing the above example, you could search with Google for:

Book.htm site:roughguides.com

Also remember that you can use a search engine to look only within URLs (addresses). So if the elusive file has an unusual name, let's say **worldcupstats.html**, you could search the Web for URLs containing that term. At Google you would enter:

inurl:worldcupstats.html

Get sidetracked

If everything else fails, try searching on related subjects, or scanning through relevant sections of **Yahoo!** or the **Open Directory**. By this stage, even if you haven't found your original target, you've probably discovered half a dozen similar (if not more interesting) pages, and in the process figured out how to navigate the Net more effectively.

Just browsing?

If the only thing you're searching for is something new, cool and generally worth a diversion, then try one of the numerous sites dedicated to listing, ranking or reporting such things. Some of these concentrate on the good...

Cool Site of the Day www.coolsiteoftheday.com
Cool Stop www.coolstop.com
Netsurfer Digest www.netsurf.com/nsd
Yahoo!'s Picks www.yahoo.com/picks

...others focus on the bad and the ugly:

Cruel Site of the Day www.cruel.com
Losers.org www.losers.org
Useless Pages www.go2net.com/useless
Worst of the Web www.worstoftheweb.com

Alternatively, cruise other people's lives, thoughts and links via some weblogs or blogs (see p.66).

But at www.Googlestore.world there...

fanproductssuperstore.html

For Shareholders

If especially a site you are interested in it's related investor-or-relation launch from a page of a site or to the Open Directory for the site, even if you haven't found your original site, you'll probably discovered that it doesn't matter to be seeking great other pages, and use the browser forward-and-back to navigate the site more effectively.

Just browsing?

It the only thing you'll be finding on the Internet that you'll and you actually worth a life time, it's beyond the imagination the delight and worthwhile nature of researching and using. Some of these conveniences in the good...

Designs of the Day – www.one-inspiring.com
   Free toys: www.coolstore.com
   Babylon Object: www.babylon.com/net
   Yahoo prize: www.verkkokauppa.net

Collectibles: Great Ltd. and the U.K.
   Great Site of the New: www.one.com
   Learn here: www.learn.org
   Uphill Colleges: www.helpcourses.net
   Minds of the Web: www.whodoingresearch.net

Alternatively, there's other people – live chatting and things for your webshop or other help.

THE
DIRECTORY

The Directory

the best of the Web

Amusements

Looking for a chuckle or perhaps to extend your lunchbreak into the late afternoon? Click through the following directories to enter a whole new dimension of time-wasting:

Ranks.com www.ranks.com/home/fun/top_humor_sites
Open Directory http://dmoz.org/Recreation/Humor
Yahoo! http://dir.yahoo.com/Entertainment/Humor

If you have a high-bandwidth connection or are blessed with abnormal patience, you might like to investigate the world of online animation. Offerings range from clones of old school arcade games to feature-length Flash cartoons. Peruse the galleries and links from:

the directory

About Animation http://animation.about.com
Animation http://dmoz.org/Arts/Animation
b3ta www.b3ta.com
David Shringley www.mudam.lu/shrigley
Flasharcade www.flasharcade.com
Flashgames www.theflashgames.com
Flashkit www.flashkit.com
Flazoom www.flazoom.com
Shockwave www.shockwave.com

Ali G Translator
www.webdez.net/alig
Make yourself comprehensible to the Staines massive.

Amused.com
www.amused.com
Online headquarters of the easily amused, featuring everything you need to waste
several weeks at work.

Assassin
www.newgrounds.com/assassin
Waste a few excess celebrities.

Bilbana
www.tv4.se/lattjo/kojan/bilbanan.asp
Shockwaved online Scalextric.

Brain Candy
www.corsinet.com/braincandy
Riddles, jokes, insults and general wordplay.

Caption of the Day
www.cdharris.net/dailypics
Prepare for your upcoming appearance on *Have I Got News for You* here.

Cartoon Bank
www.cartoonbank.com
Every cartoon ever published in *The New Yorker*.

Colouring Book
www.geek-boy.com/colorbook.html
For when you really have nothing better to do.

the directory

Comedy Central
www.comedycentral.com
Download full *South Park* episodes, listen to comedy radio and see what's screening across the network. More of a station promo than a source of laughs.

Comic Book Resources
www.comicbookresources.com
www.cartoon-links.com
www.crimeboss.com
www.geocities.com/Area51/Aurora/2510/greatest_comics
Comic and cartoon sites, shops, fanfare – and the hundred greatest? If you're really serious about your comics, check out Sequential Tart, a Webzine about the industry:
www.sequentialtart.com
And for a daily online comic strip, visit:
http://www.reallifecomics.com

Complaint Letter Generator
www.pakin.org/complaint
Punch in a name for an instant dressing-down.

Computer Pranks
www.computerpranks.com
Convince your friend that his new laptop is possessed.

Dean & Nigel Blend In
www.deanandnigel.co.uk
Witness the gentle art of urban camouflage.

the directory

The Elizabethan Curse Generator
www.tower.org/insult/insult.html
Curse with grace and elegance, thou prating fen-sucked rudesby.

Exorcist Bunnies
www.angryalien.com/0204/exorcistbunnies.html
It's short, it's sharp, it's scary and it's got bunnies in it – what more do you want?

Extra Bad
www.extrabad.com
Bitter and twisted cartoons.

The Flash Mind Reader
www.flashpsychic.com
Be amazed. Be very amazed.

Funny Forwards
www.ilovebacon.com
www.collegehumor.com
www.mrjoker.net
www.goofball.com
Most of the sight gags that arrive in your inbox courtesy of your caring friends will wind up in these, or similar, archives sooner or later. Usually before you see them. Don't go near the galleries if you're a bit sensitive.

Gary Duschl's Gumwrapper Chain
www.gumwrapper.com
If only you had so much ambition.

Graffiti The Web
www.yeahbutisitart.com/graffiti
Vandalise websites for fun.

Guimp
www.guimp.com
The world's smallest fully-featured website?

Half Bakery
www.halfbakery.com
Questionable concepts.

Horrorfind
www.horrorfind.com
A helpful hand into the darkness.

the directory

amusements

Hot or Not?
www.hotornot.com
www.ratemyface.com
Post a picture of yourself or
someone else, and passing
chumps will rate your attractive-
ness on a scale of one to ten. So
popular it's spawned a string of
spoofs:
www.gothornot.com
www.amiannoyingornot.com
www.amigeekornot.com
Create your own custom "Am I"
page at:
www.iamcal.com/ami
Or if you'd rather rate buildings
than people, check out:
www.archibot.com/ratings

In the 70s/80s/90s
www.inthe70s.com
www.inthe80s.com
www.inthe90s.com
Re-enter the landscape that wall-
papered your childhood memories.

The Insanity Test
www.knplogic.co.uk/are_u_mad.html
Try not to laugh.

Internet Conspiracy Generator
www.westword.com/extra/conspire.html
Are you really that desperate for pub conversation fodder?

The Internet Squeegee Guy
www.website1.com/squeegee
Your monitor's looking a bit dusty.

Japanese Engrish
www.engrish.com
Copywriters wanted, English not a priority.

Jester: the Online Joke Recommender
http://shadow.ieor.berkeley.edu/humor
It knows what makes you laugh.

Random Name Generators

Generator of Random Bandnamesx
www.irz.com/robin/bandnameprogram

Get a Gangsta Name
www.jasonschock.com/gangsta

Hobbit Name Generator
www.chriswetherell.com/hobbit

Louis Farrakhan African Name Generator
www.fadetoblack.com/namegenerator

Metal Gear Solid Name Generator
www.buzzsite.com/goodies/MGSnamegen

What's Your Pokéname?
http://pizza.sandwich.net/poke/pokemon.html

The Work Nickname Generator
http://users.snip.net/%7Ecbravo/v2/fun.htm

WuName
www.recordstore.com/wuname

Wu Name Generator
www.blazonry.com/scripting/wuname.php

Joke Index
www.jokeindex.com
www.humor.com
www.humordatabase.com
www.humournet.com
www.looniebin.com
www.tastelessjokes.com
www.twistedhumor.com
So many jokes it's not funny.

Misc Games
www.pastor2youth.com/gamesindex.html
An archive of "fun" Christian games.

National Lampoon
www.nationallampoon.com
Daily humour from the satire house that PJ built. Not what it was in the 1970s, as you'll see from the vault.

Newspaper Comic Strips
www.kingfeatures.com
www.comics.com
The entire works of the Phantom, Mandrake and friends.

The Official Rock-Paper-Scissors Strategy Guide
www.worldrps.com
Master such techniques as Speed Play, Rusty and Lowball, then make like Gary Kasparov and play the computer.

The Onion
www.theonion.com
Unquestionably the finest news satire on or off the Net. See also:
www.private-eye.co.uk
www.satirewire.com
www.spin-on-this.com
Or for breaking satire headlines:
www.gagpipe.com

Online Etch-A-Sketch
www.hairytongue.com/etchy
Relive your youth and create square animals to your heart's content.

Perpetual Bubblewrap
www.urban75.com/Mag/bubble.html
Seconds of fun for the whole family.

Pet Fish
www.petfish.com
Turn your monitor into a virtual fish-tank.

Piercing Mildred
www.mildred.com
Tattoo, pierce and scar Mildred to your heart's content – no fuss, no pus.

Planktone
www.planktone.co.uk
Create strange music, zoom in on shapes and find a polar bear.

The Pocket
www.thepocket.com
Gadgets, games, greeting cards, cartoons and more, updated daily.

the directory

The Post-Modernism Generator
www.elsewhere.org/cgi-bin/postmodern
Sprinkle your next essay with "postsemanticist dialectical theory" and fool your teacher.

Prank.org
www.prank.org
Mischief for every occasion. Or for a history of hoaxes, visit:
www.museumofhoaxes.com

Rather Good
www.rathergood.com
See what all the fuss is about. This is one Flash site not to be missed. Kittens as you've never seen them before playing "Independent Women" as you've never heard it before – more fun than you could have with a tennis racket and a bag of rotten apples.

Joel Veitch
rathergood.com

music- elbow
independent woman

Rec.humor.funny
www.netfunny.com/rhf
Archives of the rec.humor.funny newsgroup, updated daily.

The Simulator
http://conceptlab.com/simulator
Put yourself in the shoes of a minimum-wage slave at Mickey D's.

Sissyfight
www.sissyfight.com
Scratch, tease and diss your way to playground supremacy.

The Spam Letters
www.spamletters.com
Jonathan Land is sick and tired of junk email and isn't going to take it anymore.

The Spark.com
www.thespark.com
Most famous for its tests (purity, slut, bastard, etc) which have been taken by some
eight million people, plus numerous other ways to laugh at your friends. Find more
unreliable information about yourself at Emode (www.emode.com).

Star Wars Asciimation
www.asciimation.co.nz
The Star Wars saga rendered in vivid ASCII text – George Lucas would be spinning
in his grave if he were dead.

Stick Figure Death Theater
www.sfdt.com
Stickcity citizens meet their sticky ends.

Superjam
www.super-jam.com
Upload a picture of yourself, paste it on one of the dancing figures and watch
yourself do the Smurf.

The Surrealist Compliment Generator
www.madsci.org/cgi-bin/cgiwrap/~lynn/jardin/SCG
"In caressing your follicles I am only vaguely reminded of the bitter harvest", and
other bon mots.

UnderGround Online
www.ugo.com
Vigilante gang of counterculture sites that's close to the antithesis of AOL.

Universal Translator Assistant Project
http://hometown.aol.com/JPKlingon/uta
Translate the Bible into Klingon, Vulcan, Romulan – even Esperanto! Of course, you
could always just teach yourself Klingon at the Klingon Language Institute:
www.kli.org

Web Economy Bullshit Generator
www.dack.com/web/bullshit.html
Learn how to "leverage leading-edge mindshare" and "incubate compelling interfaces".

Xiaoxiao

www.xiaoxiaomovie.com

The Jackie Chan and Bruce Lee of the stick figure world battle to the death. Head straight for "No. 3".

Antiques and Collectables

Action Figure Collectors

www.actionfigurecollectors.com

Looking for that elusive Lando Calrasian toy? Try here first.

Antique Hot Spots

www.antiquehotspots.com

No-nonsense and very comprehensive set of links to online antique dealerships.

Antiques on the Web

www.bbc.co.uk/antiques

The BBC's superb antiques site includes buying advice from *Antiques Roadshow* experts, feature articles, hints on scoring big at car boot sales, exhibition listings and the latest finds from the *Roadshow*.

Antiques Trade Gazette

www.atg-online.com

The Web home of the *Antiques Trade Gazette* features articles, auction calendars and a page where you can report stolen items.

Antiques UK

www.antiques-uk.co.uk

Similar to most antique portals in that it offers links to dealers and salvage warehouses, but it has an excellent want ads feature – allowing you to post a message if you're after a specific item and a dealer can then get in touch with you through the site.

ANTIQUES-UK
www.antiques-uk.co.uk

Antiques Web
www.antiques-web.co.uk
A comprehensive database of directory information (including the best list of UK antiques fairs on the Net) for the British antiques community.

Cartophilic Society of Great Britain
www.csgb.co.uk
Homepage of the organization devoted to card collecting.

Collectics
http://collectics.com/education.html
A variety of essays on collectable antiques covering Clarice Cliff to Lalique.

Collecting Airfix Kits
www.djairfix.freeserve.co.uk
A shockingly in-depth site devoted to plastic modelling.

Collector Café
www.collectorcafe.com
A portal for the collecting community, with channels for just about every collectable from advertising memorabilia to writing instruments. For a UK-based portal, try Antiques Bulletin, Antiques World or World Collectors Net:
www.antiquesbulletin.com
www.antiquesworld.co.uk
www.worldcollectorsnet.com

Comics International
www.comics-international.com
Perhaps the most useful comics site on the Web, this gateway features a near-definitive directory of UK stockists and dealers, an excellent links page, comics reviews and unusually informative FAQs. See also About's comic book collecting page:
http://comicbooks.about.com

I Collector
www.icollector.com
The eBay of the high-end collector's market, this auction site hosts more than 650 auction houses selling everything from Francis Bacon originals to George II armchairs.

the directory

Invaluable
www.invaluable.com
If you can't get to the *Antiques Roadshow* or you're a serious collector, the online branch of *Invaluable* magazine provides an appraisal service. If you've had an item stolen, it also has a tracer service to improve your odds of recovering it. These don't come cheap, but you can try them for free. A similar, less expensive service used to be offered by the American site, Eppraisals, but this has now been integrated into eBay.

Kitsch
www.kitsch.co.uk
Great British site for collectors of retro-chic featuring *Dukes of Hazzard* items, Presleyana, lava lamps, James Bond paraphernalia, etc. As an added bonus, they belong to the Which? Webtrader code of practice, so you know you can buy that Farrah pencil in confidence.

Labelcollector.com
www.labelcollector.com
Salute the golden era of fruit crates and jars.

LAPADA
www.lapada.co.uk
The homepage of the Association of Art and Antique Dealers features a directory of members, fair and auction listings and advice on buying, selling, taking care and providing security for antiques.

Modern Moist Towelette Collecting
http://members.aol.com/MoistTwl
As opposed to classic moist towelette collecting.

Numismatica
www.limunltd.com/numismatica
With loads of articles, news, listings, FAQs, guides and links, this is the best portal for coin collectors on the Web. For banknote collectors, try Collect Paper Money: www.collectpapermoney.com

Old Bear
www.oldbear.co.uk
Don't throw away that beat-up, stinky old teddy bear – it might be worth a few sovereigns. This site will tell you if you can start a trust fund with your Gund or if you're stuck for life with your Steiff.

Philatelic Resources on the Web
www.execpc.com/~joeluft/resource.html
Joseph Luft's listing of more than 4000 websites devoted to stamp collecting.

Sandafayre
www.sandafayre.com
Auctions and information from the world's largest stamp dealer.

TV Toys
www.tvtoys.com
One of the best sites to explore the ever-expanding world of TV memorabilia with knowledgeable articles about collecting certain shows and links to collectables for sale.

Watchnet
www.watchnet.com
Online hub for the fine and vintage wristwatch collecting community.

World War II Collectibles
www.wwii-collectibles.com
Lame layout, but beneath the clutter and bad interface lies a treasure trove of stamps, coins, posters, propaganda material and military ephemera.

Architecture

Adam
http://adam.ac.uk
Designed for university students, this is a search engine of Internet resources for art, architecture and design.

the directory

Archibot

www.archibot.com

If you're interested in contemporary architecture and design, this very sexy site is the best portal on the Web. It features news and links that are updated daily (you can have them emailed to you), forums and an excellent metasearch engine to weed out all the building code sites.

Architecture.com

www.architecture.com

For anything relating to British architecture, the Royal Institute of British Architects should be your first port of call. It allows you full access to their database of article abstracts; has a find-an-architect function if you're redesigning your garden shed; and has links to more than a thousand sites.

Architecture Mag

www.architecturemag.com

One of the top online architecture magazines. The others include Architectural Review, Architecture Week and Metropolis:

www.arplus.com

www.ArchitectureWeek.com

www.metropolismag.com

Or, if you prefer your magazines on paper, browse the list at:

www.architectstore.com/magazine.html

Arcspace
www.arcspace.com
Excellent Danish site devoted to contemporary architecture, with copiously illustrated exhibits, feature articles and portfolios.

Building Conservation
www.buildingconservation.com
Preserve your palace.

Glass, Steel and Stone
www.glasssteelandstone.com
A fun site, with browsable galleries (including ones devoted to haunted and odd architecture), forums and news stories that are updated daily.

Great Buildings Online
www.greatbuildings.com
An exemplary resource. If you download free Design Lite software you can get three-dimensional models of Stonehenge, Chartres Cathedral, Falling Water and other masterpieces by Alvar Aalto, Le Corbusier and Ludwig Mies van der Rohe. Of course, there are also flat photographs and information on the architects of over a thousand great buildings. The constant pop-up ads are very irritating, though.

National Trust
www.nationaltrust.org.uk
The National Trust's site includes information on all of their properties, news, a gift shop and accommodation details.

Art

If you're an artist, photograph your work (preferably with a digital camera) and post it online: it's cheap gallery space and your disciples can visit at any time without even leaving home. But don't expect them to stumble across it randomly. You'll need to hand out its address at every opportunity, and don't forget to include news of your exhibitions and contact details. Like in the real world, finding art online is very much a click-and-miss affair (**www.glyphs.com/moba**), and of course entirely a matter of taste.

If you're looking for online exhibitions, including those dedicated to individual artists, turn to the Museums and Galleries chapter (p.205). The following section is devoted to portals, art education sites, artist resources and places to buy art.

the directory

A.A. Art
www.1art.com
For budding Constables, this excellent arts education site offers free online painting lessons, video workshops and forums on technique.

Aliens and UFO Art
www.wiolawapress.com
Defy the Government by becoming as one with alien sculptures.

AllPosters.com
www.allposters.com
www.allaboutart.com
www.postershop.co.uk
Plaster over the cracks in your bedroom walls. Also try Barewalls (www.barewalls.com), but beware of the massive shipping charge on European orders.

Amico.org
www.amico.org
Thumbnails from the top North American galleries.

Art Advocate
www.artadvocate.com
Check out and buy work by emerging artists selected by knowledgeable folks from the Big Apple. To buy affordable work from British artists try Art Connection, New British Artists and Red Dot:
www.art-connection.com
www.newbritishartists.co.uk
www.reddotart.com

Art Capital Group
www.artcapitalgroup.com
Borrow posh pictures to hang in your snooker room.

Art.com
www.art.com
With an address like that, you've got to deliver, and the site does. With its huge catalogue of reproductions, limited editions, posters, photos, animation and *Mona Lisa* mugs, this American site (which ships to the UK) is effectively an art shopping mall.

Artchive
www.artchive.com
Featuring critical biographies, links to images of art works on the Web, excerpts from the art-theory canon and art CD-ROM reviews, this site may be the best jumping-off point for art experts. There are also self-portrait and landscape "tours" for those unfamiliar with art history.

Art Crimes
www.graffiti.org
The first and still the best graffiti site on the Web. Art Crimes features an amazing array of burners, interviews with the most well-known writers, a good FAQ page and an untouchable set of graf links.

Art Cult
www.artcult.com
Find out how much serious pictures are worth, as well as what's selling where, when and for how much. Or if you're really planning on spending some money, try the (not free) service at Art Price:
www.artprice.com

Art Deadlines List
www.xensei.com/users/adl
A bulletin board and host page of an email newsletter that alerts artists to competitions, scholarships, grants and employment opportunities.

ArtLex
www.artlex.com
This visual arts dictionary is a truly superb resource for students, experts and bluffers alike. Containing extensively cross-referenced definitions of over three thousand terms and examples (reproductions appear either below the definition or are linked to another site hosting one), this is one of the most useful art sites on the Web.

Art Net
www.artnet.com
With its frighteningly comprehensive artists' index, excellent exhibition listings and articles both breezy and dense, the homepage of Art Net magazine probably serves as the best art portal on the Web.

Arts Council of England
www.artscouncil.org.uk
For information on everything from National Lottery funding to online exhibition spaces, this is the first place to check. Also see the Arts Council of Northern Ireland (www.artscouncil-ni.org), the Arts Council of Wales (www.ccc-acw.org.uk) and the Scottish Arts Council (www.sac.org.uk).

Arts Wire
www.artswire.org
This site from the New York Foundation for the Arts is geared to the US, but it's probably the best artist resource on the Web, with news, job openings, tutorials, workshops and a database of other arts resources.

the directory

Core 77
www.core77.com
Get a hand with industrial design.

D'Art
http://dart.fine-art.com
A giant online art marketplace with more than five thousand participating sites and tens of thousands of works.

Elfwood
www.elfwood.com
Sketches and tales from a gaggle of junior fantasy and sci-fi buffs.

Find Stolen Art
www.findstolenart.com
Make sure your new Botticellis weren't lifted from the Vatican.

Grove Dictionary of Art Online
www.groveart.com
Freeload for a day on the definitive work of art reference.

Interactive Collector
www.icollector.com
Bid for art and collectables like celebrity cast-offs. Then, of course, there's always eBay: www.ebay.co.uk

Internet Design & Publishing Center
www.graphic-design.com
Portal for the graphic design and DTP communities featuring articles, tips, reviews, forums and plenty of goodies to download. Also check out About's excellent graphic design channel (http://graphicdesign.about.com) or Graphic Design Gate (www.graphicdesigngate.com) for links.

Stelarc
www.stelarc.va.com.au
No artist has given his body to the Net like Prof. Stelarc. More hanging around at:
www.suspension.org

3D Artists
www.raph.com/3dartists
Art that looks too real to be real.

Web Museum
www.southern.net/wm
A treasure of the Net, the Web Museum hosts a fantasy collection of art – like having the Louvre, the Metropolitan Museum of Art, the Hermitage and the Prado all right around the corner. There is also an extensive glossary of terms, artist biographies and enlightening commentary on each of the works displayed.

World Wide Arts Resources
www.wwar.com
Its URL may lead you to believe that this is a site for military enthusiasts, but this list bank is probably the most comprehensive art search engine, with links to just about everything from art supplies and atelier services to gallery spaces and arts education courses. Also worth a gander is:

www.artcyclopedia.com
And, for a more academic perspective:

http://adam.ac.uk

Asian Interest

BBC Asian Life
www.bbc.co.uk/asianlife
A good, if relatively small, Asian site from the Beeb. Strong on news, sport and music – and has streaming TV and radio.

British Born Chinese
www.britishbornchinese.org.uk
Articles, humour, links, a newsletter and more for the British Chinese population.

Click Walla
www.clickwalla.com
Probably the most wide-ranging site serving Britain's Asian community, Click Walla is comprised of sections devoted to music, film, news, students, weddings, food, listings, beauty and fashion, health and Asian businesses. Other UK portals worth

asian interst

checking out include:
www.auntieg.com
www.netasia.co.uk
www.redhotcurry.com

India Abroad
www.indiaabroad.com
The focus here is largely on the US and Canada, but this huge site is a model portal in terms of both content and design, with extensive news coverage, a broad array of channels, immigration advice, in-depth interviews and shopping facilities.

Lankaweb
www.lankaweb.com
A virtual community for Sri Lankans across the world.

Sada Punjab
www.sadapunjab.com
Devoted to keeping Punjabi culture alive. The site's features include a literature archive of folktales, ghazals and poems; a Punjabi jukebox; an archive of Sikh religious texts; language tutorials; and a magazine. See also Punjab Online and Punjabi Network:
www.punjabonline.com
www.punjabi.net

South Asia Network
www.southasia.net
This portal features the South Asia search engine and serves as a useful gateway to information on Bangladesh, Bhutan, India, The Maldives, Nepal, Pakistan and Sri Lanka.

Tehelka
www.tehelka.com
A very influential Internet newsletter from India, which has had a role in exposing corruption in politics and helped to break cricket's match-fixing scandal.

Auctions

You know how auctions work: the sale goes to the highest bidder, as long as it's above the reserve price. Or, in the case of a Dutch auction, the price keeps dropping until a buyer accepts. Well, it's the same online. You simply set a starting bid and then leave an instruction to raise it in preset increments (if and when you get outbid) up to a ceiling. If you're the highest bidder when the auction ends, the deal is struck.

Once the deal's been settled, it's up to the buyer and seller to arrange delivery and payment, though both can be arranged through trusted third parties. There are millions of goods for sale in thousands of categories across hundreds of online auctions. These are but a few of the best auction sites on the Web.

A1 Auctions
www.bullnet.co.uk/auctions
Service allowing you to run auctions from your own site.

BidXS
www.bidxs.com
A brilliant tool allowing you to search across hundreds of auction sites simultaneously.

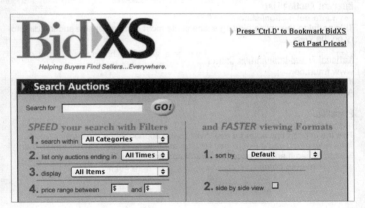

the directory

eBay

www.ebay.co.uk

The granddaddy of all auction
sites. The pages may be hectic
and distracting, but underneath the
clutter eBay has millions of items
for sale – everything from scuzzy
Def Leppard t-shirts to Scottish
Masonic kilt pins to the original
Robert E. Lee car from *The Dukes
of Hazzard*. With features like
scorecards on buyers and sellers,
round-the-clock customer support,
chat-rooms and automatic insurance on items up to £120, eBay is

the prototype on which all other auction sites are based. Some of the biggest sites
to follow its path are: Amazon, Bid-Up TV, eBid, Freeserve Auctions and QXL:
www.amazon.co.uk/auctions
www.bid-up.tv
www.ebid.co.uk
http://auctions.freeserve.com
www.qxl.com

I Collector

www.icollector.com

Home to over 650 auction houses, this American site aims to be a high-end eBay
with an emphasis on art and antiques. One for the serious collector.

Internet Auction List

www.internetauctionlist.com

This portal to the online bidding scene is the most comprehensive auction directory on the Web.

National Fraud Information Center

www.fraud.com

If you're worried about getting swindled by an online auctioneer, this excellent
American site has all the information you need to protect yourself.

Priceline

http://travel.priceline.co.uk

This travel giant has added a new twist to the auction game by allowing you to
state how much you'd like to pay for airplane tickets, hotels and car rental, then
waiting to see if anyone accepts. LastMinute.com offers a similar service:
www.lastminute.com

Sotheby's

www.sothebys.com

You won't find that S Club 7 signed photo disc here, but if you've got money to burn, sites don't come any classier than this online home of the august auction house. You can bid on live auctions as well as specialist Internet bidding wars, and there are also chat rooms to make art novices feel more at home. For similar, if not quite so grand, service, try Bonham's or Christie's:

www.bonhams.com

www.christies.com

Vendio

www.vendio.com

Tools and services for the serious online auction seller.

What the Heck

www.whattheheck.com/ebay

Your guide to the bizarre stuff people try to unload on eBay. Want to see the legendary listing of the person who auctioned their kidney for $2.5 million? It's here, as are listings for partially used packs of cigarettes, old toilet paper and all sorts of inappropriate ephemera. Alternatively, go straight to the source:

http://listings.ebay.com/pool3/plistings/list/all/category1466

Aviation and Aircraft

Aeroflight

www.aeroflight.co.uk

One of the best aviation resources on the Web, Aeroflight has comprehensive listings of air shows and museums, a detailed bibliography, photos and a wealth of information on the world's air forces.

Aeroseek

www.aeroseek.com

If it takes off and lands, you'll find it on this aviation search engine and portal. Also try:

www.airlinerphotos.com

www.airliners.net

the directory

Airchive
www.airchive.com
Shiny online museum of commercial aircraft.

Airdisaster.com
www.airdisaster.com
http://planecrashinfo.com
Way more goes wrong up in the air than you realize. Here's why you should be frightened to fly. For firsthand tales of terror, see:
www.pprune.com

Airport City Codes
www.airportcitycodes.com/aaa
A quirky site that has details on nine thousand airports, plus cheat sheets on the world's commercial aircraft, funny airplane stories and a crucial section on airplane etiquette. Alternatively, watch some airports live:
www.webcamlocator.com/airports/airframe.html
Or listen in on their air traffic control:
www.faa.gov/ats/at/index.html

Airsafe
www.airsafe.com
Overcome your fear of plummeting (or perhaps make it worse).

Air Sickness Bag Virtual Museum
www.airsicknessbags.com
Bring up some treasured memories.

All the World's Rotorcraft
http://avia.russian.ee
The 'copter spotter's guide to the universe.

Aviation Forum
www.theaviationforum.com
Shout about the awful food on your last flight.

Hot Air Ballooning
http://hotairballooning.com
More than just a load of hot air.

Babies and Parenting

Aware Parenting Institute
www.awareparenting.com
A garish site, but an excellent resource for those interested in child-centred parenting.

Babycare Direct
www.babycare-direct.co.uk
Although ordering could be made a lot easier, this is nevertheless one of the better UK sites specializing in nursery goods. The range of their stock is very extensive and they offer some good discounts.

BabyCentre
http://www.babycentre.co.uk
Probably the most complete baby site on the Web, with advice on everything from conceiving to lullaby lyrics to sleep routines to coping with your kid bursting into tears on a plane.

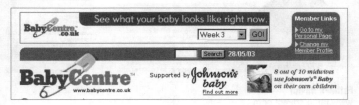

BabyNamer
www.babynamer.com
Why not give your babe a cutesy name like Adolph? It apparently means "noble hero". More suggestions to scar it for life at:
www.babynames.com
www.baby-names-meanings.com
www.go.to/babynames
www.indiaexpress.com/specials/babynames

The Baby Registry
www.thebabyregistry.co.uk
No, not a who's who of the baby world or a baptism gift-list but an "advice directory" of helpful organizations and websites.

the directory

Babyworld
www.babyworld.co.uk
The homepage of *Babyworld* magazine offers all the usual chat rooms, shopping facilities and pregnancy diaries, plus one of the most detailed health sections around.

Dr Greene
www.drgreene.com
If your baby gets sick and you can't get to a doctor, try pediatrician Dr Greene for advice.

Fathers Direct
www.fathersdirect.com
A good site aimed at working dads, with news on the latest child development research, articles on fatherhood by Red Or Dead's Wayne Hemingway and Laurence Llewellyn-Bowen, information on the paternity leave scheme and other parental resources.

Homebirth
www.homebirth.org.uk
Lots of advice for parents choosing to give birth at home, including birth stories and pain relief options as well as recommended books, videos and articles.

Mothers Who Think
www.salon.com/mwt
As with just about everything else on Salon, this section is funny, informative, engaging and well written, and a perfect antidote to all the sites and publications that treat mums as scarcely more intelligent than their babies.

National Childbirth Trust

www.nctpregnancyandbabycare.com

The NCT's official site is a good place to find out about antenatal classes, breast-feeding counsellors, mothers' groups and the NCT's own books on pregnancy and childbirth.

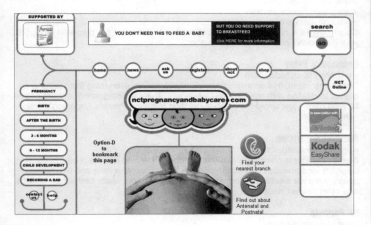

Need a Nanny?

www.dfee.gov.uk/nanny

A guide for parents looking for a nanny. It's not the most exciting site in the world, but it does offer plenty of sensible advice for those seeking childcare. For more general information on childcare options, try the Day Care Trust or the National Childminding Association:

www.daycaretrust.org.uk

www.ncma.org.uk

Net Doctor

www.netdoctor.co.uk/children

Certainly among the best UK health sites, Net Doctor's specialist pages are filled with largely jargon-free information for mother and child. The children's health area is particularly useful as it details the symptoms and treatments of common child-hood ailments and illnesses.

Parents.com

www.parents.com

Unlike many sites linked to paper publications, the homepage of the American magazine *Parents* doesn't skimp on online content, and because of its ties to a respected publication, the advice and information is authoritative.

Pregnancy Calendar
www.pregnancycalendar.com
www.parentsoup.com
www.parenthoodweb.com
www.babycenter.com
Count down the nine months from conception to birth and get prepared to juggle your life around your new family member.

Pregnancy Today
www.pregnancytoday.com
Despite its name, this enormous American site covers everything from pregnancy diaries to dealing with troublesome teenagers. There's a staggering amount of useful stuff here – just avoid the celebrity section featuring Pamela Anderson's pregnancy.

SheilaKitzinger.com
www.sheilakitzinger.com
Sheila Kitzinger is one of the gurus of childbirth. Her site may be a bit too campaigning for some, but beneath the occasionally hectoring tone and ill-advised poetry there's a wealth of information on breast-feeding, water births, home births and other related issues.

UK Parents
www.ukparents.co.uk
A comprehensive parenting e-zine written in plain and largely unpatronizing language, covering pretty much everything from pre-conception to sending the young 'uns off to school.

Betting and Gambling

It's tempting to say that online betting is for those who like that extra added element of risk, but if you stick to well-known bookmakers who've invested heavily in their security systems and avoid the casinos (which are often pretty dodgy and sometimes require you to buy a CD-ROM or download fifteen megabytes of software) you should be fine. To find a bookie, try Bookies Index (**www.bookiesindex.com**) or go straight to one of the big names:

BlueSQ www.bluesq.com
Coral Eurobet www.eurobet.co.uk
Ladbrokes www.ladbrokes.com and www.bet.co.uk
Littlewoods www.bet247.com
Paddy Power www.paddypower.com
Sporting Index www.sportingindex.com
Tote www.totalbet.com
Victor Chandler www.victorchandler.com
William Hill www.williamhill.co.uk

Fantasy Racing
www.fantasy-racing.co.uk
If you're nervous or just like betting for the sport rather than the money, try this risk-free site.

National Lottery
www.national-lottery.co.uk
It could be you ... but it probably won't.

Oddschecker
www.oddschecker.co.uk
Useful site that allows you to view the odds that all the bookies are offering, linking directly to their sites so you can place a bet.

The Racing Post
www.racingpost.co.uk
The online home of the venerable tip sheet.

Settle-a-Bet
www.settle-a-bet.co.uk
How to beat the odds.

Sports Betting
www.sportsbetting.com
Tired of UK sports? Put a nickel on a baseball game.

24 Dogs
www.24dogs.com
Comprehensive, Wembley-owned greyhound resource and betting service. Also see The Dogs (www.thedogs.co.uk).

UK Betting Guide
www.ukbettingguide.co.uk

Pretty comprehensive portal that will give you hundreds of ways of parting with your cash online. For even more, try Bet Info:
www.betinfouk.net

Win 2 Win
www.win2win.co.uk
One of the very few free horseracing tipster services on the Web, it also has a section devoted to different betting systems.

World of Gambling
www.gamble.co.uk
News, reviews and advice on everything from baccarat to slot machines.

Black Interest

Africa Online
www.africaonline.com
This bilingual (French) portal features some of the most comprehensive African news coverage on the Web. Other African portals worth a look are Africa Guide, All Africa and Africa Homepage:
www.africaguide.com
http://allafrica.com
www.africahomepage.org

Africana
www.africana.com
This American site is most likely the best black culture portal on the Web. In addition to the expected channels covering lifestyle, the arts, heritage and the homefront, Africana features columns by journalists like Nelson George and Amy Alexander; radio channels playing jazz, blues, Afro-Cuban, Afro-Brazilian, gospel and R&B; and an excellent, searchable encyclopedia of the African diaspora. Also check The Black World Today:
www.tbwt.com

Black Search
www.blacksearch.co.uk
Search engine and directory for "Black Orientated" sites.

Black Britain

www.blackbritain.co.uk

Although less authoritative than Africana (see above), this site is nevertheless an extensive gateway to black British culture, with a friendly, inclusive feel. Also try Black Net:

www.blacknet.co.uk

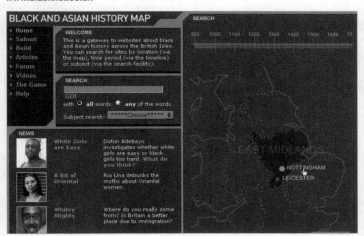

Black History Map

www.blackhistorymap.com

In essence, this site from Channel 4 is a black history search engine accessed through a map of Britain or a timeline. But it also includes features and videos on topics like the Black Irish in the Caribbean.

Black Information Link

www.blink.org.uk

The 1990 Trust's bulletin board for the UK's black community serves two functions: it provides news, events listings and links; and it serves as a forum for political advocacy.

Black Presence

www.blackpresence.co.uk

A forum and resource for researchers and other people interested in the history of black culture in Britain. Also includes news, features on music and articles on contemporary figures like Chris Ofili.

the directory

Windrush
www.bbc.co.uk/history/community/multicultural/windrush
The BBC's celebration of fifty years of Afro-Caribbean culture in Britain, with a
heavy slant towards education: timelines, achievements, first-person remembrances, poetry and a literature guide.

Blogs

Blogs, or Weblogs, are essentially diaries – logs of a person's thoughts,
what they did, what's interesting them, and news. They are getting a lot
of coverage at the moment because they represent one of the latest
development in the Web's democratization of culture: due to their
immediacy and their liberation of the means of production, blogs are
being hyped as the new publishing revolution. Here are some blogging
resources and some of the best blogs on the Net:

Adam Curry's Weblog
http://live.curry.com
Blog of former MTV VJ; go straight to the MTV Chronicle for all the dirt.

Apparently Nothing
www.apparentlynothing.com
Regular photographic postings and commentary.

Belle de Jour
http://belledejour-uk.blogspot.com
"The diary of a London call girl"; but is it fact or fictional?

Bert – The Evil One
http://neuromantics.net/bert
Not a happy bunny – please excuse his bad language.

Beyond Nothern Iraq
http://stuarthughes.blogspot.com
A fantastic and intelligent blog that follows daily events in the Gulf; written by a
BBC reporter who lost his leg to a landmine in Iraq. Also see:
http://iraqblogcount.blogspot.com

Blogger.com
www.blogger.com
Links, news and everything you need to create your own blog.

BlogSearchEngine
http://blogsearchengine.com
In case you hadn't guessed, this is a blog search engine. It also boasts loads of articles and blog news features.

The Big Smoker
www.thebigsmoker.co.uk
Award-winning blog covering all sorts of stuff, from news and reviews to cinema and culture. The site is beautifully laid out, well-written and funny.

Boom Selection
http://boomselection.info
The headquarters of the British bootleg mix scene.

The Bunker
http://neuromantics.net/bunker
Pitching itself as "an outboard brain", this genius blog of Paul Cleghorn.

Call Centre Confidential
http://callcentrediary.blogspot.com
The gripping diary of a call centre team leader.

the directory

Coolfer
www.coolfer.com
The definitive Big Apple blog, covering "for the most part" music and the music industry, and, of course, NYC.

The Daily Report
www.zeldman.com/coming.html
Web guru Jeffrey Zeldman dishes up tech advice and links, and the wickedly funny "If the great movies had been websites".

The Diary of Samuel Pepys
www.pepysdiary.com
Every day brings an entry from the renowned 17th century diarist. If you've missed his exploits to date, there's a very useful "story so far" page.

Eatonweb Portal
http://portal.eatonweb.com
A huge list of blogs.

Forbes Best Blog Guide
www.forbes.com/personaltech2003/04/14/bestblogslander.html
This list should help you wade through the ever-rising tide of blog sludge.

FourOnTour
http://geocities.com/fourontour
There are thousands of travel blogs out there, and many of them are profoundly

dull. This is one of the better ones: it follows the adventures of four Brits trying to make their way around the globe without getting on a plane.

Going Underground
http://london-underground.blogspot.com
Adventures below the streets of London.

Librarian.net
www.librarian.net
A model blog, with a crucial insight on the subterranean world of the librarian.

Magnetic Kid Liv
http://adscond.org/olivia
Quirky teenage ramblings.

MetaFilter
www.metafilter.com
Long-standing community weblog.

nyclondon
www.nyclondon.com/blog
Stunning photoblog.

Pixelsurgeon
www. pixelsurgeon.com
Easy to navigate blog of oddities and observations from and of the world wide web. As well as the regular posts, there are interviews, features and reviews, and lots of lovely pictures too.

Pop Culture Junk Mail
www.popculturejunkmail.com
Your guide to the flotsam of post-industrial society.

PubSub
www.pubsub.com
Subscribe to this service, enter a few keywords and PubSub will let you know when there are new blog posts that match your interests.

Shiny Shiny
http://shinyshiny.tv
What the world has been waiting for – a girls' guide to gadgets.

Talking Points Memo
www.talkingpointsmemo.com
All the dirt from the Washington DC Beltway.

the directory

Vagabonding
www.vagabonding.com
Great travel blog by Mike Pugh.

Weblogs: A History and Perspective
www.rebeccablood.net/essays/weblog_history.html
A history of the phenomenon.

Books and Literature

If a squillion Web pages aren't enough to satisfy your lust for the written word, maybe you should use one to order a book. You'll be spoilt for choice, with hundreds of shops offering millions of titles for delivery worldwide. That includes many web-only superstores such as Amazon as well as most of the major high-street chains (many of which operate their sites "in partnership" with Amazon or another online retailer). These superstores typically lay on all the trimmings: user ratings, reviews, recommendations, sample chapters, author interviews, bestseller lists, press clippings, publishing news, secure ordering and gift-wrapping. They also generally offer serious reductions, though these are usually offset by shipping costs. The UK big boys are:

Amazon www.amazon.co.uk
Blackwell's http://blackwell.co.uk
BOL www.uk.bol.com
Bookzone www.bookzone.co.uk
Country Books www.countrybookshop.co.uk
Heffers www.heffers.co.uk
Tesco www.tesco.com/books
Waterstone's www.waterstones.co.uk
WHSmith www.bookshop.co.uk

You can search across many stores simultaneously for availability and the best price by going to:

AddAll www.addall.com
BookBrain www.bookbrain.co.uk
Kelkoo http://uk.kelkoo.com

Can't find it online? Try searching by specialism in directories of book-sellers in the UK (**www.booksellers.org.uk/search**) or worldwide (**www.bookweb.org/bookstores**). Or browse the following selection of the best book and literature sites…

Abe Books
www.abebooks.com
www.alibris.com
www.bibliofind.com (now combined with Amazon)
Millions of old, used and rare books from sellers worldwide. To search UK out-of-print specialists, try:
www.clique.co.uk
Or to swap your savings for a manuscript or first edition, go straight to:
www.bibliopoly.com

Audio Book Collection
www.audiobookcollection.com
Thousands of audio book titles for sale. A larger selection can be found at the American sites, Talking Book World and Audible:
www.talkingbooks.com
www.audible.com

Banned Books Online
http://onlinebooks.library.upenn.edu/banned-books.html
Extracts from books that riled the righteous.

Bartleby

www.bartleby.com

Online versions of such classic reference texts as Gray's *Anatomy*, Strunk & White's *Elements of Style*, the King James Bible and works of fiction and verse by HG Wells, Emily Dickinson and many others.

Bibliomania

www.bibliomania.com

Houses the digital versions of some eight hundred classic literary works. However, Bibliomania also features study aids as well as digital versions of reference books, plus a shopping facility if you'd prefer the real thing.

Bodleian Library

www.bodley.ox.ac.uk

The homepage of Oxford's university library houses such digital library projects as the Broadside Ballads Project, the Internet Library of Early Journals, Allegro Catalogues of Japanese and Chinese books, the Toyota City Imaging project plus an array of images from Medieval texts.

Book-A-Minute

www.rinkworks.com/bookaminute

Knock over the classics in a lunch hour.

BookCloseouts

www.bookcloseouts.com

Millions of books slightly past their shelf life.

Book Crossing

www.bookcrossing.com

Print out a unique ID label, stick it on your finished-with book and then leave it on a train or park bench. If someone finds it and likes it, they'll follow the instructions on the label, go to the site, leave a message and review and then "release" it again. Some books have now changed hands more than twenty times.

The Bookseller

www.thebookseller.com

UK book trade news, bestseller lists and more. For US publishing news, complete with author road schedules and content from *Publisher's Weekly* and *Library Journal*, see: www.bookwire.com

The British Library

www.bl.uk

The British Library's site is more use to academics and researchers than to most ordinary Joes, but bookworms will delight in the ability to search the entire catalogue online as well as view select exhibits from the library's collection. There are also some beautifully presented, fully interactive versions of classic texts, com-

plete with turning pages and a magnifying glass:
www.bl.uk/collections/treasures/digitisation4.html

Carol Hurst's Children's Literature Site
www.carolhurst.com
Reviews of books for kids, as well as ideas on how to incorporate them into the curriculum.

Classic Novels – In Five Minutes a Day
www.classic-novels.com
Get masterworks like *Oliver Twist* or *Huckleberry Finn* emailed to you in free bite-sized installments.

The Electronic Labyrinth
http://eserver.org/elab
An exploration of the implications that the hyperlink has for literature.

The Electronic Text Center
http://etext.lib.virginia.edu
The University of Virginia's digital archive project is similar to the others but it includes more foreign language texts than any of the competition, so if you're after esoterica like Mescalero Apache texts or just Voltaire's *Candide* in the original French, this is the place to look.

Everything Romantic: Romance Novel Central
http://mrsg.lunarpages.com
Funny and opinionated news and reviews for fans of romance novels. For more broad-chested heroes, check out All About Romance and The Romance Reader:
www.likesbooks.com
www.theromancereader.com

E Server
www.eserver.org
Over 30,000 online works, including classic novels, academic articles, journals, recipes and plays.

Gallery of "Misused" Quotation Marks
www.juvalamu.com/qmarks
A proofreader's revenge on the world. Not to be confused with the Apostrophe Protection Society:
www.apostrophe.fsnet.co.uk

Global Books in Print
www.globalbooksinprint.com/GlobalBooksInPrint
The bible of the publishing industry online: the most comprehensive database of English books anywhere. It'll set you back a few bob to use it though.

the directory

ebooks

As if the Internet hadn't already sparked enough publishing, along comes the electronic book or ebook. At the moment, most ebooks are simply regular books converted into a special ebook format – or plain old Acrobat .pdf format – so you can read them either on a computer, a pocket PC, a palmtop or a dedicated ebook device.

Once you have the necessary software:

eBook Reader
www.adobe.com/products/ebookreader
Microsoft Reader www.microsoft.com/reader

You can choose titles from a specialist ebookshop:

eBooks www.ebooks.com
eBookstore www.gemstar-ebook.com
Peanut Press www.PeanutPress.com

Or from someone offering free ebooks:

Black Mask www.blackmask.com
Free eBooks www.free-ebooks.net

Or from the ebook departments of the major book retailers:

Amazon www.amazon.co.uk/ebooks
Barnes and Noble http://ebooks.barnesandnoble.com

For news, reviews and info on ebook hardware and software, visit:

Planet eBook www.planetebook.com
eBook Web www.ebookweb.org

Or to try and get your own ebook published, go to:

Authors Online www.authorsonline.co.uk
Online Originals www.onlineoriginals.com
Mushroom eBooks www.mushroom-ebooks.com

the directory

The Internet Public Library
www.ipl.org
Browse online books, magazines, journals and newspapers.

January Magazine
www.januarymagazine.com
Dissecting books and authors.

Journal Storage
www.jstor.org
Organization devoted to digitally archiving scholarly journals.

JournalismNet
www.journalismnet.com
Tips and tools for tapping into the big cheat sheet. More facts for hacks at:
www.facsnet.org
www.usus.org

Literary Criticism on the Web
http://start.at/literarycriticism
Links to literary criticism organized both by author and subject, as well as a list of
general sites.

Literary Marketplace
www.literarymarketplace.com
Find publishers and literary agents to pester with your manuscript.

London Review of Books
www.lrb.co.uk
Everything you'd expect from the paper version of this literary institution, including
a good – if not complete – archive of articles from writers like Christopher
Hitchens, Iain Sinclair, Edward Said and Marjorie Garber. See also *The New York
Review of Books*:
www.nybooks.com

MysteryNet
www.mysterynet.com
Hmm, now what could this be?

Online Book Pages
http://onlinebooks.library.upenn.edu
Searches and links to around 20,000 free online books.

the directory

Perseus Digital Library
www.perseus.tufts.edu
Hundreds of translated Greek and Roman classics. For more ancient and Medieval literature, see Tech Classics Archive and Classical Library:
http://classics.mit.edu
http://sunsite.berkeley.edu/OMACL

Poetry.com
www.poetry.com
Your complete poetry resource, featuring literally millions of poets, plus advice on rhyming and technique, online poetry slams, the hundred greatest poems and love poems. If you're good enough, they'll even publish your own.

Poetry Society
www.poetrysociety.org.uk
www.poets.org
Halfway-houses for budding poets and their victims. Give it a go – you won't be the worst in the class:
www.nylon.net/poetry

Powerpoint Hamlet
www.myrtle.co.uk/art/hamlet
The Bard's greatest work remade as a Powerpoint presentation.

Project Gutenberg
www.gutenberg.net
Copyrights don't live forever; they eventually expire. In the US, that's seventy-five years after first publication. In Europe, it's some seventy years after the author's death. With this in mind, Project Gutenberg is gradually bringing thousands of old texts online, along with some more recent donations.See also:
http://digital.library.upenn.edu/books

Pure Fiction
www.purefiction.com
For pulp worms and writers alike. Not a word of it is true.

Random Access Memory
http://randomaccessmemory.org
A truly wonderful concept: this vast repository of memories (of anything at all) is the embodiment of what the Web is meant to be all about. Simple, compelling, about real people and real lives, with no corporate intrusion.

Religious and Sacred Texts
http://davidwiley.com/religion.html
Links to online versions of the holy books of many of the world's major religions – everything from the Bhagavad Ghita to the Zand-i Vohuman Yasht.

Science Fiction Weekly
www.scifi.com/sfw
The first portal of call for both Isaac Asimov and Gene Rodenberry fans.

Shakespeare
http://the-tech.mit.edu/Shakespeare
The Bard unbarred online. To get the plays as PDFs, go to:
www.hn.psu.edu/faculty/jmanis/shake.htm
Or for lots more, try:
www.opensourceshakespeare.com
http://absoluteshakespeare.com
http://shakespeare.palomar.edu

The Slot: A Spot For Copy Editors
www.theslot.com
Soothing words of outrage for grammar pedants.

Text files
www.textfiles.com
Chunks of the junk that orbited the pre-Web Internet. For a slightly more modern
slant, see:
www.etext.org

Urban Legends
www.urbanlegends.com
www.snopes.com
Separate the amazing-but-true from the popular myths.

Vatican Library
www.ibiblio.org/expo/vatican.exhibit/exhibit/a-vatican_lib/Vatican_lib.html
The Library of Congress's online exhibit of artefacts from the Pope's library.

Village Voice Literary Supplement
www.villagevoice.com/vls
The online version of *The Village Voice*'s literary supplement is the complete printed
version for non-New York residents and includes writing from major new voices
and insightful reviews.

the directory

Web Del Sol
http://webdelsol.com
A portal for small literary reviews and journals, hosting such prestigious American names as *Kenyon Review*, *Mudlark*, *Sulfur* and *Prairie Schooner*.

Word Counter
www.wordcounter.com
Paste in your composition to rank your most overused words.

The Word Detective
www.word-detective.com
Words never escape him. See also:
www.quinion.com/words

Business

These homepages of prominent business magazines offer much of the same content as their paper versions, but often at a cost:

Advertising Age www.adage.com
Adweek www.adweek.com
Barrons www.barrons.com
Campaign www.campaignlive.com
Fast Company www.fastcompany.com
Financial Times www.ft.com
Forbes www.forbes.com
Upside www.upside.com
Wall Street Journal www.wsj.com

See also News, Newspapers and Magazines (p.230) and Money and Banking (p.197).

AccountingWeb
www.accountingweb.co.uk
Safe playpen for British
beancounters.

Setting Up Shop Online

Freemerchant.com
www.freemerchant.com
www.bigstep.com
www.bizfinity.com
www.jumbostore.com
www.clickandbuild.com
http://store.yahoo.com
Set up an online shop for next to nothing.

Cafepress
www.cafepress.com
Refab a kit commerce site in your own name.

WorldPay
www.worldpay.com
www.bidpay.com
www.paypal.com
Organize credit card payment.

Adbusters
www.adbusters.org
Headquarters of the world's culture jammers, dedicated to declaring independence
from the ever-encroaching corporate state. More culture jamming to be found at
®TMArk and Blow the Dot Out Your Ass:
www.rtmark.com
www.blowthedotoutyourass.com

Ad Critic
www.adcritic.com
www.superbowl-ads.com
Make a cuppa while you wait for this year's best US TV ads. For the best of the
past twenty, see:
www.usatvads.com
For "Badvertising", go to:
www.bad-ad.org

Ad Forum
www.adforum.com
www.sourcetv.com
Gateway to thousands of agencies, their ads and the humble creatives behind
them.

the directory

Annual Report Gallery
www.reportgallery.com
View the annual reports of over two thousand publicly traded companies for free.

The Biz
www.thebiz.co.uk
A business-to-business portal for British companies.

Bizymoms
www.bizymoms.com
Crafty ways to cash up without missing the afternoon soaps.

Business.com
www.business.com
Attempting to become the Yahoo of business sites.

Business Advice Online
www.businessadviceonline.org.uk
Information and advice on taxes, regulations, e-commerce and consultations from the
Small Business Service. For more resources see:
http://home3.americanexpress.com/smallbusiness/tool/interactive_tools.asp
www.businesslink.org

Business Ethics
www.business-ethics.com
Apparently it's not an oxymoron.

BVCA
www.bvca.co.uk
Homepage of the British Venture Capital Association, offering basic advice for businesses seeking funding.

City Wire
www.citywire.co.uk
Probably the best place to come for UK financial news. City Wire also contains
research reports on what the directors are up to.

Clickz
www.clickz.com
The Web as seen by the marketing biz.

Cluetrain Manifesto
www.cluetrain.org
Modern-day translation of "the customer is always right". Read it or perish.
Alternatively, if you'd prefer an update on "never give a sucker an even break" consult the Ferengi Rules of Acquisition:
www.dmwright.com/html/ferengi.htm

the directory

business

CommerceNet
www.commerce.net
It may be US-heavy, but this is the main source for e-commerce news and an essential bookmark for any company doing business online.

Confederation of British Industry
www.cbi.org.uk/home.html
Tomorrow's public policy today.

Customers Suck!
www.customerssuck.com
Grumbling dispatches from the retail front.

Delphion Intellectual Property Network
www.delphion.com
Sift through a few decades of international patents plus a gallery of obscurities. Ask the right questions and you might stumble across tomorrow's technology long before the media. For UK patents see:
www.patent.gov.uk

DTI
www.dti.gov.uk
The homepage of the Department for Trade and Industry offers policy news and resources that affect every UK business.

Entrepreneur.com
www.entrepreneur.com
Get rich now, ask us how.

Flame Broiled
www.geocities.com/capitolhill/lobby/2645
The disgruntled ex-Burger King employee homepage. If only every company had one.

Flounder's Mission Statement Generator
www.giantflounderpenis.com/mission.html
It is this site's "business to holistically re-engineer economically sound resources to exceed customer expectations".

81

the directory

The Foundation Center
http://fdncenter.org
Companies who might happily spare you a fiver.

Fucked Company
http://fuckedcompany.com
Join the rush to gloat over startup shutdowns.

Garage.com
www.garage.com
Matchmaking agency for entrepreneurs and investors founded by Apple's Guy
Kawasaki. For more help milking funds to feed your online white elephant, see:
www.moneyhunter.com

Guerilla Marketing
www.gmarketing.com
Get ahead by metaphorically butchering your competitors' families and poisoning
your customers' water supply.

Inc
www.inc.com
Online presence of American magazine for entrepreneurs and small businesses;
includes advice and services like assistance with creating business and marketing
plans, health insurance quotes and financing.

InfoUSA
www.infousa.com
Find likely Americans to bug with your presentation.

International Trademark Association
http://inta.org
Protect your brand identity.

Internal Memos
www.internalmemos.com
Leaked.

Killer Internet Tactics
www.killertactics.com
How to murder brain-dead Web surfers with HTML.

Mondaq
www.mondaq.com
Regulatory information and financial commentary on over eighty world economies.

Disgruntled Customer Sites

The Web may be the most important business tool ever invented, but it just may be the most important consumer tool ever invented as well. This is what happens when companies don't follow the "customer is always right" rule, or just get too big for their boots.

BTopenwoe
www.btopenwoe.co.uk
Chronicling incompetence along the information superhighway.

Ford Really Sucks
www.fordreallysucks.com
A cautionary tale for businesses which try to prevent anyone from buying domain names even remotely connected to them.

Microsuck
www.fuckmicrosoft.com
Yes, someone actually hates Bill Gates more than you.

Fuck McDonald's
www.fuckmcdonalds.co.uk
Here's where to go when the chips are down.

Patent Café
www.patentcafe.com
Protect your crackpot schemes and see them through to fruition.

Planet Feedback
www.planetfeedback.com
Let US companies know what you think of their service.

The Prince's Trust
www.princes-trust.org.uk
Learn new skills thanks to Charlie.

Statistical Data Locators
www.ntu.edu.sg/library/stat/statdata.htm
Links to economic and demographic data of just about every world economy.

Super Marketing: Ads from the Comic Books
www.steveconley.com/supermarketing.htm
The ads that kept you lying awake at night wishing you had more money.

The Wonderful Wankometer
www.cynicalbastards.com/wankometer
Measure corporate hyperbole. Couple with:
www.dack.com/web/bullshit.html

Cars and Motor Bikes

Before you're sharked into signing for a new or used vehicle, go online and check out a few road tests and price guides. You can complete the entire exercise while you're there, but it mightn't hurt to drive one first. Start here:

Autobytel www.autobytel.com
Autolocate www.autolocate.co.uk
Autotrader www.autotrader.co.uk
BBC Top Gear www.topgear.beeb.com
Car Importing www.carimporting.co.uk
Car Shop www.carshop.co.uk
Carseekers www.carseekers.co.uk
DealerNet www.dealernet.com
Exchange & Mart www.exchangeandmart.co.uk

4 Car www.4car.co.uk
Kelly Blue Book www.kbb.com
Oneswoop www.oneswoop.com
Upgrade Your Car www.upgradeyourcar.com
What Car? www.whatcar.com

WHATCAR? For expert, impartial advice
Monday, 02 June 2003
Home | **News** | Road tests & Research | Advice | Use

>Home >News Story
Latest news
Model news
The best news for UK car buyers

Automobile Association
www.theaa.com
Not merely an online rest stop trying to hawk you memberships, the AA's site has useful free features like a cheap petrol finder and route planner. See also The RAC or National Breakdown:
www.rac.co.uk
www.internationalbreakdown.com

Bike Trader
www.biketrader.co.uk
Part of the Autotrader group, this site offers the same services as its parent site: good search tool, advice on buying and selling motor bikes and links to insurance and finance companies.

Breath Testing
www.copsonline.com/breath_test.htm
Slurring your swearwords, wobbling all over the road, mounting gutters and knocking kids off bikes? Pull over and blow into this site.

Car Net
www.carnet.co.uk
Massive automotive portal, including advice and information on collecting, research facilities, trivia, forums, links, classifieds, want ads, rallying news and more.

the directory

Circuit Driver
www.circuitdriver.com
This e-zine for speed junkies includes racing information (with online booking facilities), car and gear reviews, rallying and drag racing advice, car databases, photos and driving technique guides.

Classic Car Directory
www.classic-car-directory.com
Good resource for classic car enthusiasts, with price guides, dealer directories, events listings, classifieds and links.

Full Pull
www.fullpull.com
All the latest from the American tractor-pulling scene.

The Highway Code
www.highwaycode.gov.uk
Fail your driving theory test online first.

Layover
www.layover.com
Long, wide loads of truckin' stuff for prime movers and shakers.

Lowrider.com
www.lowrider.com
Online community for vatos locos and other connoisseurs of barely-street-legal motor vehicles with the lowest clearance known to man.

MOT
www.ukmot.com
Let Malcolm the mechanic help you make
sure your car is road worthy.

Motorcycle News
www.motorcyclenews.com
Everything on two wheels ... plus the
obligatory bikini babes. Also see
BikersWeb:
www.bikersweb.co.uk
Or for a more measured approach, the Motorcycle Action Group:
www.mag-uk.org

Mudpuppy's CB Radio Page
www.angelfire.com/wi/citizensband
That's a 10-4 good buddy, this here's the Rubber Duck and I'm about to put the hammer down.

Parkers Online
www.parkers.co.uk
Car price and specs database going back twenty years. For new models and insurance quotes, try New Car Net:
www.new-car-net.co.uk

Speedtrap.com
www.speedtrap.com
A great resource for drivers who want to know, umm, where traffic flashpoints might occur. See also UK Speed Traps:
www.ukspeedtraps.co.uk

Street Trucks Magazine
www.streettrucksmag.com
Custom trucking bible for fans of bags, grilles, rims, souped-up air intake manifolds and other things they could only dream up in the States.

Woman Motorist
www.womanmotorist.com
The demographic group that motor vehicle insurers prefer.

World Parts
www.world-parts.com
If you're seeking a hubcap or an entire engine, tell this site the car's make and model and the country in which you live, and it will tell you who stocks your part.
Also try Find a Part:
www.find-a-part.com

Making our roads safer...

Motoring online isn't just about wide-wheels and horsepower:

Brake www.brake.org.uk
Roadweb www.roadweb.org.uk
S.P.E.E.D. kills www.safespeed.org.uk/s.p.e.e.d.html
SpeedLIMIT www.speedlimit.org.uk
Think Road Safety www.thinkroadsafety.gov.uk

classifieds

Classifieds

Online classifieds need no explanation. They're like the paper version, but easier to search and possibly more up to date. In fact, most papers are moving their classifieds to the Net, though you might have to pay to see the latest listings. Here's a small selection:

Ad-Mart www.ad-mart.co.uk
Ad Trader www.adtrader.co.uk
eDeluxe http://deluxe.trader.com
Exchange And Mart www.exchangeandmart.co.uk
Excite Classifieds http://classifieds.excite.com
Friday-Ad www.friday-ad.co.uk
Its Bazaar www.itsbazaar.com
London Classifieds www.londonclassified.com
Loot www.loot.com
Net Trader www.nettrader.co.uk
Photo Ads www.photoads.co.uk
Preloved www.preloved.co.uk
Reel Exchange www.reelexchange.co.uk
Sell It Net www.sellitnet.com

Computing and Tech News

Every decent PC brand has a site where you can download the latest drivers, get support and find out what's new. It won't be hard to find. Usually it's the company name or initials between a www and a com.

So you'll find Dell at: **www.dell.com**, Compaq at: **www.compaq.com**, Gateway at: **www.gateway.com**, and so forth. Most of the big names also have international branches, which will be linked from the main site. Consult Yahoo! if that fails. If you're in the market for new computer bits, check out the best price across online vendors:

AnandTech www.anandtech.com/guides.html
FindComp www.findcomp.com/uk
Price Watch www.pricewatch.com
StreetPrices.com http://Europe.StreetPrices.com

Popular package software vendors include:

Buy.com www.buy.com
Chumbo.com www.chumbo.com
Jungle.com www.jungle.com

Bear in mind that if you buy from US sites, imports might be taxed upon arrival.

Apple
www.apple.com
Essential drop-in to update your Mac, pick up QuickTime and be hard-sold the latest hardware. To top up with news, software, and brand affirmations, see:
www.macaddict.com
www.appleinsider.com
www.tidbits.com
www.macintouch.com
www.macnn.com
www.macslash.com
For the latest applications, hints and news on OSX, seek out:
www.macosxapps.com
www.macosxhints.com
If you're still desperately clinging on to your old Quadra or Performa, try:
www.lowendmac.com

the directory

And to diagnose your ailing Mac:
www.macfixit.com

And if iPods are what float your boat, take a trip to:
www.apple.com/ipod
www.ipodlounge.com
Alternatively, pick up a copy of The Rough Guide to The iPod, iTunes and Music Online. If, however, this desirable piece of white plastic is a little out of your price range, consider the paper alternative, at:
http://users.macunlimited.net/kieranbaxter/ipod

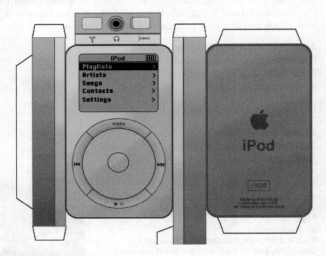

Bastard Operator from Hell
http://bofh.ntk.net
www.theregister.co.uk
If you work in a big office, you know this man.

Chankstore FreeFont Archive
www.chank.com/freefonts.htm
Download a wacky Chank Diesel display font free each week. If there's still space in your font sack, arrive hat in hand at:
www.printerideas.com/fontfairy
www.pizzadude.dk/fonts.html
www.fontface.com
www.flashkit.com/fonts

Clip Art
http://webclipart.about.com
Bottomless cesspit of the soulless dross used to inject life into documents.

CNET
www.cnet.com
Daily technology news and features plus reviews, shopping, games, and downloads, along with schedules, transcripts and related stories from CNET's broadcasting network.

Desktop Publishing
http://desktoppub.about.com
http://desktoppublishing.com
Get off the ground in print.

Dingbat Pages
www.dingbatpages.com
For when you just can't get enough symbol fonts.

Easter egg archive
www.eeggs.com
A racing game in Excel 2000, a basketball game in Windows 95 and a raygun-wielding alien in Quark Xpress? They're in there all right, but you'll never find them on your own. Here's how to unlock secrets in scores of programs.

Electronic Privacy Information Center
www.epic.org
Since 1994, EPIC has been at the vanguard of the campaign to protect privacy over the Internet. For a withering attack on the UK's Regulation of Investigatory Powers Act, go to:
www.fipr.org/rip
For coverage of free speech issues on the Net, go to:
www.eff.org

Extra Web Space
www.myspace.com
www.xdrive.com
www.kturn.com
www.mac.com
Storage space on the Net that's perfect for backups and file transfers. For free services, check out the directory at:
www.freewebsiteproviders.com/virtual-disk-drives.htm
If you want the files stored on your virtual disk drive burned on a CD-ROM and sent to you, try:
www.XBurn.com

the directory

Forward Garden
www.forwardgarden.com
The resting place of every piece of junk email you've ever received. True
masochists should also tune their browser into:
www.spamradio.org

Ghost Sites: The Museum of Failure
www.disobey.com/ ghostsites
A chronicle of the rise and fall of the cyber empire.

Gibson Research Corporation
http://grc.com
If you're at all interested in computer security or are a raving paranoiac, you owe it
to yourself to check out this site.

The GNU Project
www.gnu.org
The homepage of Richard Stallman's efforts to create a free operating system. You
might know it better as Linux, named after Linus Torvald's kernel. For more on
GNU/Linux, try:
www.linux.org

Guide to Flaming
www.advicemeant.com/flame
Learn how to win friends and influence people on newsgroups, forums and chat
rooms.

Hackers' Homepage
www.hackershomepage.com
Everything you shouldn't do to your computer or someone else's. More at:
www.attrition.org
www.cultdeadcow.com
www.2600.com
Just make sure you run every antivirus utility you've got after stopping by.

InfoAnarchy
www.infoanarchy.org
All the latest news and views from the battle to keep information free.

Internet Speed Test
www.zensupport.co.uk/speedtest
Wallow in the grim truth about the speed of your connection. More at
www.dslreports.com/stest
www.beelinebandwidthtest.com

ISP Review
www.ispreview.co.uk
Compare your Internet Service Provider with the rest and get the latest broadband news. Also try:
www.net4nowt.com
And for UK Broadband Help:
www.broadband-help.com/home.asp

IT Reviews
www.itreviews.co.uk
Independent, jargon-free reviews of hardware, software, games, etc. For more reviews, try About's Computer Reviews:
http://compreviews.about.com/compute/compreview
And also Review Finder:
www.reviewfinder.com

Microsoft
www.microsoft.com
If you're running any Microsoft product (and the chance of that seems to be approaching 100 percent), drop by this disorganized scrapheap regularly for upgrades, news, support and patches. That includes the latest free tweaks to Windows, Office and all that falls under the Internet Explorer regime.

Modem Help
www.modemhelp.org
Solve your dial-up dramas for modems of all persuasions including cable, ISDN and DSL. And be sure to check your modem maker's page for driver and firmware upgrades.

the directory

computing and tech news

The Museum of Counter Art
www.counterart.com
"THE showcase for over 500 sets of counter digit artwork".

Need to Know
www.ntk.net
Weekly high-tech wrap-up with a sarcastic bite.

Newslinx
www.newslinx.com
Have the top Net technology stories, aggregated from around fifty sources,
delivered to your mailbox daily.

Old Computers
www.old-computers.com
Relive the days when your Sinclair ZX81 or Commodore Vic 20 could barely play
solitaire. More at HCM:
www.homecomputer.de

Old English Computer Glossary
www.u.arizona.edu/~ctb/wordhord.html
All your favourite computer terms translated into Arthurian dialect.

Palmgear
www.palmgear.com
Know your palm like the back of your hand. For the PocketPC, see:
www.pocketmatrix.com

PC Mechanic
www.pcmech.com/byopc
www.tweak3d.net
http://arstechnica.com/tweak/hardware.html
How to build or upgrade your own computer.

PC Tweaking
www.anandtech.com
www.arstechnica.com
www.pcextremist.com
www.pureperformance.com
www.sharkyextreme.com
www.shacknews.com
www.tweaktown.com
www.ugeek.com
How to overclock your processor into the next millennium, tweak your bios and
upgrade your storage capacity to attract members of the opposite sex.

PC Tyrant
www.pctyrant.com
A useful corrective to the relentless optimism and gung-ho futurism of most online
computer zines.

PCWebopedia
www.pcwebopedia.com
Superb illustrated encyclopedia of computer technology.

Peer to Peer Central
www.peertopeercentral.com
News on peer-to-peer systems like Napster and Gnutella.

The Register
www.theregister.co.uk
Punchy tech news that spins to its own tune.

SafeWeb
www.safeweb.com
Originally designed for surfers in countries with repressive regimes, SafeWeb is a
service that encrypts all data sent from and received by your computer while surfing the Net so that all of your downloads are safe from prying eyes. For more
anonymous surfing, try The Anonymizer:
www.anonymizer.com

the directory

PC Help

The best place to find an answer to your computer problems is usually on Usenet. Chances are it's already been answered, so before you rush in and post, search the archives through Google Groups.

Google Groups http://groups.google.com

That's not to say you won't find an answer on the Web. You probably will, so follow up with a Web search. You'll find a choice of engines at the very bottom of the results page. If you click on Google, for example, it will perform the same search in the Web database. Apart from Usenet, there are several very active computing forums on the Web, such as:

Computing.net www.computing.net
Tek Tips www.tek-tips.com

And there are hundreds of troubleshooting and Windows news sites, such as:

ActiveWin www.activewin.com
Annoyances www.annoyances.org
Common Problems www.users.qwest.net/~careyh/fixes.htm
Virtual Dr http://virtualdr.com
WinOScentral www.winoscentral.com

Don't forget to keep your hardware installation drivers up to date. You'll find the latest files for download direct from the manufacturer's website, or at driver guides such as these:

Driver Forum www.driverforum.com
Driver Guide www.driverguide.com
Drivers HQ www.drivershq.com
Windrivers www.windrivers.com

Scantips
www.scantips.com
Become a scan-do type of dude.

Slashdot.org
http://slashdot.org
News for those who've entirely given up on the human race.

Tech Dirt
www.techdirt.com
Keeping tabs on the dark underbelly of the Internet economy.

Techtales
www.techtales.com
Customers – they might always be right but they sure do ask the darndest things.

Tom's Hardware Guide
www.tomshardware.com
One of the most important sites on the Net, at least for the hardware industry.
Tom and his reporters are credited with the delayed release of Pentium's 1GHz
Pentium III processor because the site gave it a thumbs down. This is the best
source for bug reports and benchmark tests.

WebReference
www.webreference.com
If you don't know your HTML from your XML or DHTML, try this reference and
tutorials site. For more tips and tricks, try Webmonkey:
http://hotwired.lycos.com/webmonkey
And for streaming video tutorials, try Virtual Dr:
www.virtualdr.com

Windrivers
www.windrivers.com
Driver file updates and hardware reviews compiled by a Windows fanatic of such
maniacal proportions he even named his son "Gates".

Wired News
www.wired.com
The Net's best source of breaking technology news plus archives of Wired magazine. For more, try Geek.com:
www.geek.com

Woody's Office Portal
www.wopr.com
Beat some sense out of Microsoft Office. For Outlook, see:
www.slipstick.com/outlook

Yahoo! Computing
www.yahoo.com/Computers
The grandpappy of all computing directories.

ZDNet
www.zdnet.com
Computing info powerhouse from Ziff Davis, publisher of *PC Magazine*, *MacUser*, *Computer Gaming World* and scores of other IT titles. Each magazine donates content such as news, product reviews and lab test results; plus there's a ton of prime Net-exclusive technochow. The best place to start researching anything even vaguely computer-related.

Play it safe

Unless you're 100 percent certain that a download or attachment is safe, even if it's been sent by your best friend, DON'T OPEN IT! Instead, save it to your Desktop or a quarantine folder and examine it carefully before proceeding. That should include running it past an up-to-date antivirus scanner such as AVG (www.grisoft.com). You'll find everything you need to know about viruses at:

About.com http://antivirus.about.com
Alt.comp.virus FAQs www.faqs.org/faqs/computer-virus
AVG Anti-Virus www.grisoft.com
Symantec www.symantec.com/avcenter

Crafts

About Hobbies
www.about.com/hobbies
Your first portal of call for any crafts search should be About's impressive hobbies page which contains links to their basketry, beadwork, candle-making and wood-working sites as well as twenty other crafts sites that they host.

Allan's Wood Miser's Workshop
http://members.aol.com/woodmiser1
Great site full of tips and advice for the thrifty woodworker. For more carpentry tips, try About's woodworking site:
http://woodworking.about.com
and Woodweb if you're a pro:
www.woodweb.com

The original home of the sawboard.

Classic Stitches
www.classicstitches.com
The homepage of *Classic Stitches* magazine includes some 150 downloadable charts to set your needles working.

Crafts Council
www.craftscouncil.org.uk
News on and listings of craft shows, events, exhibitions, seminars and workshops. The Crafts Council also provides a regional list of shops selling contemporary crafts as well as buying guides.

Crafts Unlimited
www.crafts-unlimited.co.uk
Over 1100 cross-stitch patterns to buy, plus downloadable beginner's and advanced guides to cross-stitch technique. Also check out Cross-Stitch Design: www.maurer-stroh.com

Home Sewing Association
www.sewing.org
An essential bookmark for budding Gallianos and hopeless bachelors alike. The site is packed with sewing lessons for absolute beginners and tips and trends and advanced techniques for more experienced seamstresses.

Internet Craft Fair
www.craft-fair.co.uk
Put a stitch in time at this massive online community for the UK's crafts scene.

Planet Patchwork
www.planetpatchwork.com
Blocks and vectors of information devoted to the mystique of quilting.

Popular Crafts
www.popularcrafts.com
The digital home of *Popular Crafts* magazine includes event listings, book reviews, forums, news and online crafts projects with step-by-step instructions on decorating flower pots and making birthday party cards.

Wool Works
www.woolworks.org
Containing an archive of more than 250 patterns, an extensive hints and tips section on making socks and knitting for dolls, and a comprehensive links page – this is a darn good knitting site.

Education

This chapter is perhaps a bit of a misnomer as the entire Internet is potentially the greatest single educational resource that's ever been invented: the latter-day equivalent of the library at Alexandria. Here you'll find educational resources (for students, teachers and parents), general homework sites, information on distance learning and admissions guides. For other study tools, try the Reference chapter or other subject headings (Art, Politics, History, etc.).

About Education
http://education.about.com
They may be geared towards the US, but, as usual, About's education pages are an excellent source of information and news. Having trouble with times tables or conjugating Latin verbs? Try About Homework:
http://homework.about.com

Academic Info
www.academicinfo.net
Research directory for students and teachers.

Ask an Expert
www.cln.org/int_expert.html
Links to hundreds of experts who will happily answer your homework question or offer you careers advice. There are also teaching experts awaiting questions from harried pedagogues.

Best websites for Students
www.unn.ac.uk/~iniw2/bestsite.htm
Links to help you write your next essay.

Channel 4: Homework High
www.homeworkhigh.co.uk
Channel 4's homework site allows you to ask experts questions and browse the archive of responses. Much better than the BBC's similar site because it's not linked to the station's programmes.

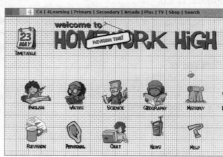

the directory

Click Teaching
www.clickteaching.com
A site for primary school teachers largely written by primary school teachers.

EduFind
www.edufind.com
Massive education resource site, with a TEFL slant.

Evil House of Cheat
www.cheathouse.com
Thousands of college essays, term papers and reports. But beware, teachers can check for traces of plagiarism:
www.turnitin.com

Good Schools Guide
www.goodschoolsguide.co.uk
Unfortunately, in order to gain full access to this very useful site, you need to buy the paper version of the popular book, which then lets you get to the weekly updates and the school reviews written by parents for parents.

Guide to Grammar and Style
http://andromeda.rutgers.edu/~jlynch/Writing
Handy online guide to English language usage. It won't replace Strunk & White or the *Chicago Manual of Style*, but if you're in a pinch, could be worth a try. For more basic grammar instruction, try Pop-Up Grammar:
www.brownlee.org/durk/grammar

International Centre for Distance Learning
http://www-icdl.open.ac.uk
The Open University's distance learning resource centre contains a huge database on courses and organizations as well as abstracts of journal articles and research papers pertaining to distance education. Also check out its related site, The Learning Network:
www.netlearn.co.uk
And the International Distance Learning Course Finder:
www.dlcoursefinder.com

Internet Public Library
www.ipl.org
Browse the catalogue of some 16,000 online texts, utilize the original resources and ask homework questions – all without a horn-rimmed librarian telling you to down your Discman.

the directory

ISIS

www.isis.org.uk

The homepage of the Independent Schools Information Service allows parents and teachers to search their database for information on prospective schools and employers.

Learn.co.uk

www.learn.co.uk

A huge resource for both students and teachers, with dowloadable sample SATs, lesson plans, an online community for teachers, revision advice and information on the national curriculum.

Learning Alive

www.learningalive.co.uk

It claims to be the largest educational resource on the Net, but to access its Living Library (where most of these resources are stored), you have to subscribe – at £50 a year.

Maths Help

www.maths-help.co.uk

Send this site's boffins a question and they'll email back an answer. For more help with numbers, try Maths Net:
www.mathsnet.net

National Curriculum Online

www.nc.uk.net

The government's definitive national curriculum site for teachers, with outlines, goals and FAQs. For the Scottish curriculum, go to the Scottish CCC Homepage: www.sccc.ac.uk

National Grid for Learning

www.ngfl.gov.uk

This site is the centrepiece of the Government's plans to harness the Net as the future of education. As you might guess, it's a bit of a sprawling mess, but there are sections devoted to just about every educational issue you can think of, as well as tons of links, a virtual teacher centre and so on.

National Union of Students
www.nus.org.uk
How to buy a pint if your grant runs out.

Profquotes
www.profquotes.com
They sure do say the darndest things.

SearchEdu
www.searchedu.com
Search millions of university and education pages.

Sova (Sleep)
http://sova.lulea.org
Pictures of your tuition fees hard at work.

Study Abroad
www.studyabroad.com
Hop grass that's greener.

StudyWeb
www.studyweb.com
An absolutely enormous education portal, with links to some 160,000 resources, all organized by grade level (some translation from American English required).

The Teacher Network
www.theteachernet.co.uk
Resources, links, job search for teachers.

Thesis
www.thesis.com
Online version of the Times Higher Educational Supplement.

Topmarks Education
www.topmarks.co.uk
This excellent and very easy-to-use site searches the Web for educational sites pertaining to your subject and appropriate age level, so if you're searching for sites to help you with GCSE revision it will weed out all the sites aimed at Key Stage 1 students. See also Schoolzone:
www.schoolzone.co.uk

UCAS
www.ucas.co.uk
Information on university courses, including admissions requirements and general facts and figures, from the University and Colleges Admissions Service.

the directory

Unofficial Guides
www.unofficial-guides.com
Get the real dope on the unis from the students themselves, not the marketing boards.

Up My Street
www.upmystreet.com
Type in your postcode and get quick access to the performance tables of local schools.

Web66: International School Web Site Directory
http://web66.coled.umn.edu/schools.html
Add your school's Web page if it's not already listed.

Word Central
www.wordcentral.com
A site designed to broaden kids' vocabulary by introducing them to the joys of wordplay. There's also a section for teachers with lesson plans and a history of the English language.

Employment

If you're looking to move on up, beware that if you post your CV online your boss could find it – embarrassing at the very least. The same situation could also arise if you leave it online once you're hired. Most job agencies have sites these days, and the better ones update at least daily, so there are far too many to attempt to list here. What's best for you will depend on what field you're in and where you want to work. Bigger isn't always better, as you'll find yourself competing with more applicants. On the other hand, your prospective employer isn't likely to restrict their job search to a site that isn't well known. Whether you're looking for a job or to fill a vacancy, try:

Fish4Jobs www.fish4jobs.co.uk
Go Job Site www.jobsite.co.uk
Gradunet www.gradunet.co.uk
Guardian Jobs Unlimited http://jobs.guardian.co.uk
Job Search www.jobsearch.co.uk
Monster www.monster.co.uk
Overseas Jobs www.overseasjobs.com
People Bank www.peoplebank.com
Personnel Net www.personnelnet.com
Reed www.reed.co.uk
Stepstone www.stepstone.com
Total Jobs http://totaljobs.com

All Jobs UK
http://alljobsuk.com
This recruitment portal claims to give access to every job vacancy on the Internet – all two million of 'em.

A–Z Guide to British Employment Law
www.emplaw.co.uk
Get the upper hand on your boss.

The Best Resumes on the Net
http://tbrnet.com
Helpful advice on building the perfect CV, featuring a software program – the Resume Creator 3.1 – for the lazy.

the directory

Brilliant Careers
www.channel4.com/brilliantcareers
Channel 4's employment site is a no-nonsense guide to the job market, with advice, support, vacancies and personality tests.

Buzzword Bingo
www.progress.demon.co.uk/Fun/Buzzword-Bingo.html
When your boss says something like, "proactive" or "quality management system", check it off on your card – you're a winner if you complete a row.

Cool Works
www.coolworks.com
Seasonal jobs in US resorts, national parks, camps, ranches and cruise lines.

Despair Inc.
www.demotivators.com
Take the mickey out of your boss and colleagues with a range of bitter and twisted calendars and mugs.

DEMOTIVATION

SOMETIMES THE BEST SOLUTION TO MORALE PROBLEMS IS
JUST TO FIRE ALL OF THE UNHAPPY PEOPLE.

Expat Network
http://www.expatnetwork.co.uk
Subscription placement and settling service for working globetrotters.

FT Career Point
http://career.ft.com/careers
Advice from the suits at the *Financial Times*.

Hungry and Homeless
www.hungryandhomeless.co.uk
No, not another site mocking yesterday's dotcom millionaires, but one that houses pictures and histories of homeless people looking for work.

Integrity Based Interviewing
www.interviewing.net
Ex-federal agents show you how to get to the truth without drawing any blood.

Internet Career Guide
www.careerguide.net
This directory functions as a portal for both jobseekers and employers. Included are links to headhunters, CV writing services, recruitment and outplacement services.

I-resign.com
www.i-resign.com
Quit now while you're ahead.

Mindless Jobs of America
www.geocities.com/Area51/Vault/9932/mja.html
Think your job sucks?

The Riley Guide
www.rileyguide.com
Messy but massive directory of job-hunting resources.

Salary Info
www.salary.com
http://jobsmart.org/tools/salary
See what you're worth stateside, and then how much you'd need in another town:
www.homefair.com/homefair/calc/salcalc.html

Temp 24-7
http://jobsearch.about.com/cs/tempjobs
Share the pain of temporary work at this online community for temps.

the directory

UK Jobs Sites
www.transdata-inter.co.uk/jobs-agencies
An excellent resource for the jobseeker, this directory lists and ranks all the major British online headhunters and ranks them by number of vacancies, services, regions and industries they serve.

Washington Alliance of Technology Workers
www.washtech.org
This American homepage of the first dotcom union is an excellent source of news, rumours and advice for the largely unorganized technology sector.

Working Wounded
www.workingwounded.com
Get back at your boss and your co-workers without getting fired.

Yahoo! Careers
http://careers.yahoo.com
As ever, Yahoo is in on the act, and as ever, does it superbly. This arm, however, handles only US placements. But key "employment" as a search term or click on "international" and you'll be awash with options spanning the globe.

Environment

Earth Systems Virtual Library
www.earthsystems.org/virtuallibrary/vlhome.html
Probably the most complete set of environmental links on the Net.

eNature.com
www.enature.com
Vibrant field guides to North American flora and fauna.

Envirolink Network
http://envirolink.netforchange.com
Online community for the environmentally aware, containing links to articles on sustainable energy sources and pesticides, daily news updates, a green marketplace and forums on topics like genetic engineering. See also EcoNet: www.igc.org/igc/gateway/enindex.html

Environmental Organization Directory
www.eco-portal.com
Find primary production and green-minded sites.

ForestWorld

www.forestworld.com
http://forests.org
Timber tales from both sides of the bulldozer.

Friends of the Earth

www.foe.co.uk
The homepage of the environmental pressure group features information on local, national and international campaigns, and information on the issues involved.

Greenpeace

www.greenpeace.org
In addition to the charity's campaigns, the Greenpeace homepage covers genetic engineering, ocean preservation, toxic waste and the transport of nuclear materials.

Lycos Environment News

www.ens-news.com
The Web's best source for unbiased environmental news.

Rainforest Information Portal

www.rainforestweb.org
News from the frontline against deforestation. For more Amazonia try the Rainforest Alliance:
www.rainforest-alliance.org
And the Tropical Rainforest Coalition:
www.rainforest.org

Subsea Explorer

www.subseaexplorer.com
This site for scuba divers may force you to subscribe, but if you do you could win a diving expedition to the Titanic – plus there are excellent educational resources for kids, articles on the subaquatic environment, underwater webcams and cheap diving equipment from the shop. To explore the sky as well as the sea, try the equally excellent Sky and Sea:
www.seasky.org

UK National Air Quality Information Archive
www.airquality.co.uk
Worried about chemical factories or diesel emissions? Check the air quality for your
area here. To feel guilty about the amount of carbon dioxide you are responsible for,
check out the Carbon Calculator:
www.clearwater.org/carbon.html

Events and Entertainment

Aloud
www.aloud.com
Book music, festival and event tickets online from this member of the Which? Code
of Practice. See also Ticketmaster:
www.ticketmaster.co.uk

Ananova - Going Out
www.ananova.com/whatson
Comprehensive and nationwide general entertainment listings which you can have
sent to your WAP phone.

British Arts Festivals
www.artsfestivals.co.uk
Keep tabs on the UK's highbrow festivals from Brighton to Edinburgh on this comprehensive site.

eFestivals
www.efestivals.co.uk
If you can't get enough of playing your bongos in the mud, point your virtual cara-
van to this site which contains ticket information, line-ups, rumours and reviews of
festivals like Homelands, T in the Park, Glastonbury, Creamfields and the Essential
Festival.

London Theatre Guide
www.londontheatre.co.uk
This venerable site boasts not only excellent theatre listings but regularly updated cast news and seating plans. See also What's On Stage for regional as well as London listings:
www.whatsonstage.com

Nightclubbin UK
www.nightclubbinuk.com
Listings and links for a large majority of Britain's clubs.

Planit4Kids
www.planit4kids.co.uk
Listings and events information organized by region for the most demanding audience of them all.

Scene One
www.sceneone.co.uk
UK-wide entertainment guide covering music, film, theatre and comedy with an excellent search facility.

This Is London
http://www.thisislondon.co.uk
The *Evening Standard*'s site includes, film, theatre, comedy and clubbing listings for the capital, as well as a visitor's guide and reviews of pubs and restaurants.

Time Out
www.timeout.com
Definitive London listings from the venerable magazine, as well as global city guides if you're planning to venture abroad.

fashion and beauty

Regional Listings

Most UK events sites can seem like a Big Smoke screen with all the emphasis on London. Here are a few that attempt to redress the balance:

Bournemouth	www.bournemouth.co.uk
Brighton	www.whatsonguide.co.uk
Cardiff	www.metroplex.co.uk/WhatsOn/cardiff
Chester	www.chestercc.gov.uk/asp/events
Coventry	www.cwn.org.uk/whatson
Edinburgh	www.edinburghguide.com
Hampshire	www.hants.gov.uk/whatson
Manchester	www.manchesteronline.co.uk
Newcastle	www.tyne-online.com/whatson.asp
Sheffield	www.sheffnet.co.uk/events/events.asp

Webflyers
www.webflyers.co.uk
Guide to clubbing in Edinburgh and Glasgow.

Yack
www.yack.com
Perhaps the best guide to online events, Yack lists the webcasts, chats, film, animation and other events occurring on the Internet everyday.

Fashion and Beauty

Unless it entirely erodes your reading time, the Net isn't likely to cut your guilty expenditure on glossy mags. While there's a spree of fledgling style zines and something from nearly all the big rack names, nothing compares to getting it in print. Nonetheless it will certainly supplement your vice. What you will find the Net better for is researching products, checking out brands and saving money on consumables like cosmetics at stores such as:

Drugstore www.drugstore.com
Gloss www.gloss.com

iBeauty www.ibeauty.com
Perfumania www.perfumania.com
Reflect www.reflect.com
Sephora www.sephora.com
HQ Hair www.hqhair.com (UK)
Think Natural www.thinknatural.com (UK)
Perfume Shop www.theperfumeshop.com (UK)

Buying clothes online is tough but popular nonetheless. They're out there, if you know what you're doing, but you'll soon see why Boo.com failed. Label sites are sometimes interesting for new season looks, stockists and direct ordering.

Afro Hair and Beauty
www.afrohairandbeauty.co.uk
Links to, and resource pages for, black haircare and beauty products.

Bad Fads Museum
www.badfads.com
Revisit your past fashion mistakes.

the directory

BK Enterprises
www.b-k-enterprises.com
The only place to get that authentic 1970s Elvis jump suit. Prices range from $900 to $5000. Also has links to boot dealers, glasses shops and the place to get show scarves to complete the look.

Cosmetic.org
www.cosmetic.org
www.ienhance.com
Adjust your imperfection without pills or creams.

Debenhams
www.debenhams.com
Do some etail therapy at the site of everyone's favourite department store.

Diesel
www.diesel.co.uk
Browse their latest catalogue, hear music, and lots more – a very cool site. Also find time to check out the DieselKids games site, at: www.protokid.com

Enoki World
www.enokiworld.com
All the accessories you need for that vintage lifestyle: Pucci dresses, jadeite juicers, Pierre Cardin pink tweed skirts, 1960s Gucci handbags.

FashionBot
www.fashionbot.com
Search several UK high-street retailers' catalogues.

Fashion Icon
www.fashion-icon.com
Irreverent New York fashion zine.

Fashion Information
http://www.fashioninformation.com
Pay for trend-forecasting reports.

FASHION NET
Your Guide to Fashion on the Net

SEARCH THE WEB'S TOP FASHION SITES

SITES DESIGNERS ONLINE FASHION SHOPPIN
CONTENT FASHION NEWS RUNWAY SHOWS DE
WORK JOB LISTINGS HOW-TO

SS-03

Giorgio Armani

Fashion Net
www.fashion.net
Handy shortcut to the highest-profile shopping, designer, magazine, modelling and fashion industry sites, with enough editorial to warrant an extended stopover.

Fashion Live
www.fashionlive.fr
Splashy, sexy Parisian e-zine covering both *haute couture* and more achievable fashion trends. They've taken over the Place de Mode shopping site, allowing you quick access to the looks you see on its pages.

Fashionmall.com
www.fashionmall.com
www.brandsforless.com
Mail-order familiar, and mostly American, labels.

Fashion UK
www.fuk.co.uk
Minimal but fresh vanity monthly from London.

Figleaves.com
www.figleaves.com
Online underwear superstore for both men and women.

Firstview
www.firstview.com
See what's trotting the catwalks – sometimes at a price. For more previews, seek out Virtual Runway:
www.virtualrunway.com

Fragrance Direct
www.fragrancedirect.co.uk
It may look like a site for kids, but this etailer offers tremendous bargains on a good range of perfumes, cosmetics and skincare products.

The Lipstick Page
www.thelipstickpage.com
Cosmetic appliances for fun and profit.

Moda Italia
www.modaitalia.net
Patch through to the Italian rag traders.

Net-à-Porter
www.net-a-porter.com
Can't get to Harvey Nick's? Try here for posh frocks and accessories: Bottega

the directory

Veneta, Clements Ribeiro, Missoni, Fake London and Paul & Joe are some of the cult labels this site stocks. Plus there's no snooty attitude. For Marc Jacobs, Fendi and Louis Vuitton, try:
www.eluxury.com
www.yoox.com

Organization for the Advancement of Facial Hair

www.ragadio.com/oafh

Includes an archive of classic beard styles and a library of grooming tips. For more advice on beard trimmers and how to keep your hulihee at its best (or just to see pics of guys who look like 1970s country singers), try these other hirsute sites:
www.badburns.com
http://members.aol.com/beardguy
www.menwholooklikekennyrogers.com

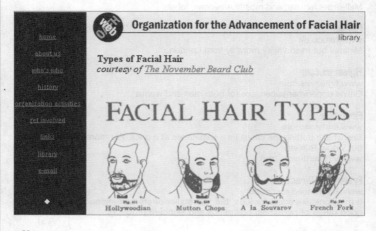

osMoz

www.osmoz.com

They haven't invented scratch'n'sniff technology for the Web yet, but this French site (in English) is the next best thing. A fragrance test will tell you whether floral or hesperide scents suit you best, and if you register they will send you free samples.

Salonweb

www.salonweb.com

Frizzy, fly-away, mousy, permed hair? Try this haircare portal for all the tips and advice you'll ever need.

Mullets

The Kentucky Waterfall, the Soccer Rocker, the Missouri Compromise, Business Up Front/Party In The Back, Neck Blanket, Ape Drape, the Tennessee Top Hat – whatever you want to call it, no hairstyle in the history of the civilized world has generated so much scorn, derision or passion as the mullet. Here are a few sites where you can mull over "the hairstyle of the gods":

Dan's Mullet Haven
www.fortunecity.co.uk/southbank/pottery/3
Wrestlers, musicians and footballers.

Mullet Junky
www.mulletjunky.com
Homepage of the mullet hunters.

Mullet Lovers
www.mulletlovers.com
Galleries, galleries, galleries.

Mullet Madness
www.mulletmadness.com
The official haircut of the Salt Lake City Winter Olympics.

Mullets Galore
www.mulletsgalore.com
The most comprehensive mullet site.

Rate My Mullet
www.ratemymullet.com
Heap even more scorn on the poor sods.

the directory

Solemates: The Century in Shoes
www.centuryinshoes.com
Stepping out in the 20th century.

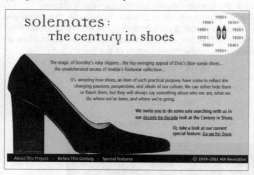

Studs And Spikes
www.studsandspikes.com
Trick out your leather jacket.

Style.com
www.style.com
With an impressive archive of images from all the major catwalk shows of the past two years, the online home of American *Vogue* is one of the best resources for fashionistas. If you're after a more standard magazine approach, try the British equivalent:
www.vogue.co.uk

Style Maven
www.stylemaven.com
Your guide to hip boutiques in London, New York, LA and San Francisco.

Textile Dictionary
www.ntgi.net/ICCF&D/textile.htm
Don't know your buckram from your qiviut? Check here.

Victoria's Secret
www.victoriassecret.com
Order online or request the catalogue preferred by nine out of ten teenage boys.

Wellbeing.com
www.wellbeing.com
Boots' revamped site has everything you'd expect from the high-street pharmacy.

Zoom
www.zoom.co.uk
Portal for the Arcadia group shops (Dorothy Perkins, Top Shop, Principles, Burton Menswear, etc), allowing you to recreate your high-street experience on the information superhighway.

Film

When it comes to movies, one site clearly rules:

The Internet Movie Database www.imdb.com

To say that it's impressive is an understatement. You'll be hard-pressed to find any work on or off the Net as comprehensive as this exceptional relational database of screen trivia from over 100,000 movies and a million actors. It's all tied together remarkably well – for example, within two clicks of finding your favourite movie you can get full filmographies of anyone from the cast or crew and then see what's in the cooker. Still, it's not perfect, or without competition. You'll find a similar service with superior biographies and synopses at the colossal:

All Movie Guide www.allmovie.com

Or for more Chan, Li and Fat:

Hong Kong Movie Database www.hkmdb.com

For cinema listings:

Cinemas Online www.cinemas-online.co.uk
Cineworld www.cineworld.co.uk
Odeon www.odeon.co.uk
Picture House www.picturehouses.co.uk
Teletext-Cinema www.teletext.co.uk/bigscreen
UCI Cinemas www.uci-cinemas.co.uk

the directory

Ain't It Cool News
www.aintitcool.com
The movie news and gossip site that has Hollywood execs quaking in their boots. Founder Harry Knowles has been blamed several times when movies have tanked at the box office, and *Premiere* magazine has ranked him as one of Hollywood's most powerful people. Receive the wisdom of Harry here, along with whispers of what's in production and interviews. More production gossip can be overheard at:
www.chud.com
www.corona.bc.ca/films
www.darkhorizons.com
www.imdb.com/Sections/Inproduction

asSeenonScreen
www.asseenonscreen.com
Buy stuff you've seen on TV or in movies. For more, try:
www.movieprop.com
www.propstore.co.uk

The Astounding B Monster
www.bmonster.com
Excellent resource for fans of Mamie Van Doren, Rondo Hatton and other cult 1950s and 1960s drive-in/late-show fodder. For fans of more modern fare like *Cannibal Women in the Avocado Jungle of Death*, there's:
www.badmovieplanet.com
www.stomptokyo.com/badmoviereport
www.badmovies.org
www.ohthehumanity.com
http://members.aol.com/shockcin
If your critical faculties are so deadened that you might actually like to own one of these celluloid atrocities, try Science Fiction Continuum:
www.sfcontinuum.com
Just make sure you've got a NTSC-compatible VCR.

Atom Films
www.atomfilms.com
Watch entertaining short films. For sixteen-colour silliness see:
www.pixelfest.com

Bad Movie Night

www.hit-n-run.com

Invite a couple of mates over to your house, get in a few beers, rent an aggressively mediocre movie and hurl invective at the screen. More snide remarks available at:

http://bigempire.com/filthy

www.mrcranky.com

www.thestinkers.com

But to really unveil box office evil, try:

www.capalert.com

www.screenit.com

Blaxploitation.com

www.blaxploitation.com

Superfly guys and gals stickin' it to the man. More Afros and dashikis at BadAzz Mofo:

www.badazzmofo.com

Blooper Files

www.blooperfiles.com

Archive of screw-ups and inconsistencies from Hollywood's finest. More continuity errors at:

www.movie-mistakes.co.uk

www.nitpickers.com

Bollywood World

www.bollywoodworld.com

Massive portal for the Indian film industry, with everything from production news to ringtones for your mobile.

British Film Institute

www.bfi.org.uk

Reviews, features, and loads of great content.

Brutesquad Movies
www.brutesquad.com/MOS/movie_body.htm
Preview movies like *Schindler's List II* (starring Arnold Schwarzenegger) and *Titanic: Horror of the Deep* (Jeff Goldblum saving the world against a pack of marauding blue whales).

Carfax-Abbey Horror Film Database
www.carfax-abbey.com
Splatter-flick Central, with loads of info on gore masters like Dario Argento and Wes Craven. More zombies and fake blood at:
www.joblo.com/arrow
www.dune12.demon.co.uk
www.sexgoremutants.co.uk
www.zombiegirls.net
Fans of Christopher Lee and Peter Cushing should grab some garlic and head to:
www.edhouse.clara.net/ghoul.html

Dogme95
www.dogme95.dk
Homepage of the Danish film movement led by Lars Von Trier, including the manifesto, a how-to page and the latest news from the film vanguard.

Drew's Script-O-Rama
www.script-o-rama.com
www.scriptshack.com
Hundreds of entire film and TV scripts. Need help writing or selling your own? Try:
www.scriptfly.com

DVD Debate
www.dvddebate.com
All the latest UK DVD release news and reviews, plus a mighty useful section on the codes that enable you to change the regional setting on your DVD player. For more on DVD hardware and software:
www.dvdfile.com
www.dvdtimes.co.uk
www.dvdweb.co.uk

E! Online
www.eonline.com
Daily film and TV gossip, news and reviews.

Empire Magazine
www.empireonline.co.uk
Reviews of every film showing in the UK.

555-LIST
http://home.earthlink.net/~mthyen
Catalogue of fake telephone numbers used in TV and film.

Gil*galad's Martian Theaethyr
www.televar.com/~gnostran
Applying AstroTarotry to old movies makes them so much clearer.

Golden Raspberry Award Foundation
www.razzies.com
The Oscars in an alternate universe.

Hollywood Reporter
www.hollywoodreporter.com
Tinseltown tattle, previews and reviews daily, plus a flick biz directory.

Home Cinema Choice
www.homecinemachoice.com
In-depth reviews of DVD players.

In-Movies
www.in-movies.com
If you've got broadband access you can watch trailers and short films. For shorts from closer to home, try Brit Shorts:
www.britshorts.com
For more trailers, pull up to The Trailer Park:
www.movie-trailers.com
For specially commissioned full-length features, point your ADSL hookup to here:
www.sightsound.com

film

the directory

Melon Farmer's Video Hits
www.dtaylor.demon.co.uk
Challenges British screen censorship.

Movie Cliches
www.moviecliches.com
Nothing unfamiliar.

MovieFlix
www.movieflix.com
Download hundreds of movies, some free but most require a monthly subscription of $6.95.

MovieLens
http://movielens.umn.edu
Become a member of this site and it will give you movie recommendations based on your tastes. It may be a bit of a behavioural research exercise, but it's still a pretty neat way of avoiding video shop malaise. Another site plays it safe: www.filmsite.org

Moviemags.com
www.moviemags.com
Directory of film print and e-zines.

Movie Review Query Engine
www.mrqe.com
This specialist search engine, dedicated to finding film reviews on the Web, has a database of more than 25,000 titles and does an excellent job of finding info on obscure movies. But perhaps you'd prefer a summary:
www.rottentomatoes.com
www.filmreview.co.uk
www.filmunlimited.co.uk

Movies.com
www.movies.com
www.universalstudios.com
www.film.com
Preview box office features and trailers direct from the major studios.

The Movie Shelf of Apartment 304
www.compusmart.ab.ca/kroyea/movie.htm
Cool martial arts and Yakuza flick site, with good features on Sonny Chiba and cover art.

Mr Kiss Kiss Bang Bang

www.ianfleming.org

An outrageously complete and obsessive guide to the shaken, not stirred universe of James Bond, with daily news and rumour updates.

A Bond-type girl poses in the same style outfit as was seen on the famous poster from *Casino Royale*

My Movies

www.mymovies.net

Huge film site with production news, gossip, reviews, competitions, shopping, trailers and, if you've got broadband, movies on demand.

SciFi.com

www.scifi.com

http://scifi.ign.com

www.cinescape.com

Science fiction news, reviews and short films.

Sendit

www.sendit.com

This is perhaps the best British DVD and video shop on the Net: good selection, excellent search facility and great prices. Other video and DVD etailers worth checking out are:

the directory

www.dvdworld.co.uk
www.bensonsworld.co.uk
www.videoshop.co.uk
To compare prices:
www.dvdpricesearch.com
www.formovies.com

Share Reactor

www.sharereactor.com
Find out quite how many films – from classics to current releases – are available via the eDonkey file-sharing network and then download the eDonkey software to start plundering. It's illegal, of course, to download anything protected by copyright (not that that seems to stop anyone).

Shooting People

http://shootingpeople.org
In their own words, "the fastest growing UK online filmmakers'community"; whether you're a director without a crew, or runner with nowhere to run, look here first.

Showbizwire

www.showbizwire.com
Entertainment newsbreaks from about fifty major sources.

The Silents Majority

www.silentsmajority.com
This great online journal devoted to silent film is certainly one of the best film sites on the Web, even if you don't know Fatty Arbuckle from ZaSu Pitts.

Smoking List Movie Reviews

http://SmokingSides.com/asfs/m
A history of smoking on the silver screen. Non-smokers might want to try Soup at the Movies:
www.soupsong.com/imovies.html

Variety

www.variety.com
Screen news fresh off the PR gatling gun.

VCR Repair Instructions

www.fixer.com
How to take a VCR apart and then get all the little bits back in so it fits easier into the bin.

Warning6
www.cinepad.com/warning6.htm
If you don't want to know the twists at the end of *The Usual Suspects* or *The Crying Game*, don't you dare visit this site.

Westerns.com
www.westerns.com
A great site for fans of classic oaters. They've got streaming videos of some obscure low budget shoot-'em-ups like *Fury* and *Can Be Done...Amigo*, plus MP3s of Roy Rogers and Gabby Hayes, bios and filmographies of your favourite cowboys and cow-girls, and, of course, a tradin' post.

Lo-tech Film Recreations

Who needs a £20 million special effects and pyrotechnics budget when you've got a couple of Lego sets?

Being Puffy
www.urbanentertainment.com/2
Being John Malkovich becoming P. Diddy.

The Fountainhead – A Parody
www.jeffcomp.com/faq/parody
Ayn Rand's capitalist parable starring Skull Force.

Kevin's Custom Star Wars Minifigs
http://members.aol.com/jmacroy/update/legos/customs.html
But it's so lifelike.

Lego Star Wars Trilogy
www.tanukikoji.or.jp/yes/lsw
Thankfully, there's no Jar Jar Binks.

Monty Python & the Holy Grail
www.lego.com/eng/studios/screening/movie.asp?title=montypython
Even funnier than the real thing.

Shark Attack
www.exposure.co.uk/eejit/3act/sharkattack.html
Jaws in Lego vision.

Titanic Legos at Sea
www.prtc.net/~kisspr/index2.htm
At least there's no Celine Dion soundtrack.

the directory

Flowers

About Flowers
www.aboutflowers.com
The meanings of flowers and the right ones for various occasions.

Clare Florist
www.clareflorist.co.uk
A Which? Webtrader offering a good range of bouquets, from classic to funky.

Daisys2Roses
www.daisys2roses.com
Despite a slight design flaw, this site allows you to create your own bouquet, a service which almost no other online florist offers. On top of that, this site has a special offer of half-a-dozen roses for £10 plus delivery.

First Flowers Direct
www.firstflowers.com
The flowers from this site come straight from the Covent Garden Flower Market and because of that they offer a better, less old-fashioned, range of bouquets. They also belong to the Which? Webtrader Code of Practice.

Flowers2Send
www.flowers2send.com
"The UK's first virtual florist" offers an impressively wide range of bouquets, although you can't create your own.

Interflora
www.interflora.co.uk
Interflora may be the biggest name in flowers, but their site is pretty run-of-the-mill. Aside from reliability and name recognition, its main feature is a personal organizer that will remind you of anniversaries and birthdays.

Teleflorist
www.teleflorist.co.uk
Like most of the big players, Teleflorist's site seems to offer a fairly limited range of bouquets and arrangements. It does, however, feature Internet exclusives and a percentage of proceeds from certain orders are donated to charity.

Food and Drink

About French Cuisine
http://frenchfood.about.com
Everything you need to become the next Escoffier. To become the next Fanny Craddock, go to the Great British Kitchen:
www.greatbritishkitchen.co.uk/gbk

African Studies Cookbook
www.sas.upenn.edu/African_Studies/Cookbook
A frighteningly comprehensive database of African recipes.

Al Mashriq
http://almashriq.hiof.no/general/600/640/641/recipes/misc.html
No-nonsense list of Middle Eastern recipes.

The Alternative to Food and Drink UK
www.alternative-food-and-drink.co.uk
Bachelors' paradise: ratings of supermarket booze, a guide to "dehydrated things in pots" and other essential aspects of single life.

BBC Food
www.bbc.co.uk/food
A very branded site (there are lots of familiar faces) but with a good database of solid recipes that you can be sure will have been tested properly.

Beershots
http://micro.magnet.fsu.edu/beershots
Beers of the world put under a microscope.

BEERSHOTS
microscopic views of beers from around the world

the directory

Berry Brothers & Rudd
www.bbr.co.uk
Although the site looks a little intimidating, don't be put off: this is one of the country's best wine-ordering services. You can pick up bottles for around £6, although at the other end the sky's the limit. Try also:
www.oddbins.co.uk
www.virginwines.com

Bevnet
www.bevnet.com
Know your New Age beverages.

Cheese
www.cheese.com
Excellent cheese information site with an exhaustive list of cheeses and detailed info on composition.

Cheeseburger in Paradise
www.fdu.com/cburger.htm
Stranded in Alabama or Helsinki and jonesing for a cheeseburger? Check here for your nearest vendor.

Chile-Heads
www.exit109.com/~mstevens/chileheads.html
www.ringoffire.net
Get 'em while they're hot.

Chinatown
www.chinatown-online.co.uk/pages/food
Good site for Chinese recipes, information on ingredients and contextual stuff.

Chocolate Lover's Page
http://chocolocate.com
The good gear: where to find recipes and dealers.

Cigar Aficionado
www.cigaraficionado.com
Archives, shopping guides, and tasting forums from the US glossy that sets the benchmark in cigar ratings. Modelled on:
www.crackaficionado.com

Cocina Mexicana
http://cocinamexicana.com.mx/ingles/menu/frame.html
A great site devoted to authentic Mexican cuisine...unfortunately, it's in Spanish.

Cocktail Time

www.cocktailtime.com
http://cocktails.about.com
www.webtender.com
www.barmeister.com
www.drinkboy.com
Guzzle your way to a happier home. Yes, do buy the book.

Coffee Geek

http://coffeegeek.com
Everything caffeinated. For essential espresso links, see:
more www.espressotop50.com
And for even more of the brown stuff:
www.coffeeuniverse.com
www.coffeefest.com

Cook's Thesaurus

www.foodsubs.com
Find substitutes for fatty, expensive or hard-to-find ethnic ingredients.

Cooseman's Specialty Produce Guide

www.1webblvd.com/coosemans/guide.htm
An excellent guide to all the weird and wonderful things at your greengrocers.

Cucina Direct

www.cucinadirect.co.uk
Excellent online kitchen equipment site with a solid bricks-and-mortar business behind it.

Curryhouse

www.curryhouse.co.uk
Make the perfect vindaloo or look up your nearest balti house if you're too lazy. For more masala matters, try:
http://rubymurray.com

Delia Online

www.deliaonline.com
A double-header of a site: lots of good recipes and useful tips plus the alarming Delia diary for true fans who really want to know about her life. And to see where all the site's ideas came from, go to:
www.marthastewart.com

Dolce Vita

www.dolcevita.com/cuisine
Life is sweet at this Italian cookery site.

the directory

food and drink

Specialist Shopping Sites

Club Chef Direct www.clubchefdirect.co.uk
Suppliers of restaurant-quality meat, fish and produce.

Cyber Candy www.cybercandy.com
Brilliant site for exploring candy from all over the world – great for US and Japanese expats looking for a sugary flavour of home.

Fifth Sense www.fifthsense.com
An excellent site if you want to experiment a bit with spices or sauces from around the globe – mostly dry or bottled goods, though.

Fortnum & Mason www.fortnumandmason.com
Excellent luxury food shopping site sensibly separated into goods that can be sent in the UK only and those worldwide.

Marchents www.marchents.com
A good site that offers food delivery on everything from meat to veg, plus there's kitchen kit to buy too.

Real Meat www.realmeat.co.uk
A decent site that sells very good products - the firm behind the site is well known in foodie circles for producing top-notch flesh.

Thornton's www.thorntons.co.uk
Yummy chocolates and the site ain't bad either: easy to shop, with lots of gift ideas.

The Empty Bowl
www.emptybowl.com
"The definitive source for all your cereal needs."

Epicurious
www.epicurious.com
The best food website there is. Online marriage of Condé Nast's *Gourmet*, *Bon Appetit*, and *Traveler* magazines, crammed with recipes, culinary forums and advice on dining out worldwide.

Fair Trade on-line
www.fairtradeonline.com
Buy ethically traded food and drink from this site run by Traidcraft and Oxfam. For more on Fairtrade in the UK, see:
www.fairtrade.org.uk

132

Famers' Markets
www.farmersmarkets.net
Find your nearest farmers' market and start buying local food.

Final Meal Requests
www.linuxkungfu.com/finalmeals.html
Sobering reading from Bush's Land of the Free.

Food Allergy and Anaphylaxis Network
www.foodallergy.org
All the news and developments from the peanut intolerance frontline.

Foodlink
www.foodlink.org.uk
Your complete guide to food safety. See also:
www.foodpres.com
But if you can't remember anything about food safety unless it's set to music, go to:
http://foodsafe.ucdavis.edu/music.html

Eating Out

The AA www.theaa.co.uk
Decent search engine for nationwide restaurants and pubs.

Grabameal www.grabameal.co.uk
A database of over 23,000 restaurants and take-aways in the UK.

Square Meal www.squaremeal.co.uk
One of the better restaurant finders, plus news and views from the dining world.

This Is London www.thisislondon.co.uk
The Evening Standard site is the best site for searching for bars and pubs and restaurants in London: comprehensive and with good-length reviews so you get an idea of exactly what you'll be getting.

Time Out http://eatdrink.timeout.com
Frequently updated rundown of London eateries, searchable by area or cuisine.

Toptable www.toptable.co.uk
No-nonsense site that covers London and some surrounding areas.

Zagats www.zagats.com
Excellent search engine for restaurant reviews the world over, plus restaurant news.

FoodnDrink
www.foodndrink.co.uk
A useful site with an online version of Harden's restaurant guide (created by people rather than food critics) and a restaurant booking facility, through:
www.5pm.co.uk
Plus links to shopping sites, gourmet bookshop and a good cookery school directory.

Fruitarian Site
www.fruitarian.com
The joys of chomping on raw fruit and the chance to make new fruitarian friends.

Generic Mac and Cheese Gallery
www.geocities.com/macandcheesebox
Gawp in wonder at the diet of the American student.

Good Pub Guide
www.goodguides.com
Offers a good pub locator for the UK, as if you needed help.

Internet Chef
www.ichef.com
Over 30,000 recipes, cooking hints ("Ground Beef Meals"), kitchen talk and more links than you can jab a fork at.

Jamie Oliver
www.jamieoliver.net
The most overexposed man in European media – but he makes a great salad.

Lakeland
www.lakelandlimited.co.uk
Everything you could and couldn't possibly need in the kitchen.

Leaping Salmon
www.leapingsalmon.com
Quality prepared food that you simply assemble according to instructions – barely a chopping board required, and excellent food to boot. If you get the munchies in the middle of the night and need food cooked to order delivered to your door, try Room Service:
www.roomservice.co.uk

Meals For You
www.mealsforyou.com
A decent American recipe search engine – each listing includes the details of the fat and cholesterol present in each recipe.

the directory

New York Seafood
www.nyseafood.org
Great site for loads of piscine information. For cod and haddock delivered to your door, try The Fish Society:
www.thefishsociety.co.uk

An Ode to Olives
www.emeraldworld.net/olive.html
You'll never look at an olive ambivalently again.

Oreo Stuff
www.jeffmajor.com/oreos
Someone with way too much time on his hands.

Our Food
www.ourfood.com
An excellent collection of scientific articles pertaining to food science and food safety.

Porkrind.com
www.porkrind.com
Everything you wanted to know about deep-fried pork fat and more.

Ray's List of Weird and Disgusting Foods
www.andreas.com/food.html
How many have you tried?

Real Beer
www.realbeer.com
None of the usual beer yarns like waking up in a strange room stark-naked with a throbbing head and a hazy recollection of pranging your car. Here beer is treated with the same dewy-eyed respect usually reserved for wine and trains. Like to send your chum a virtual beer? Stumble over to:
www.pubworld.co.uk

Recipe Link
www.recipelink.com
Points to more than 10,000 galleries of gluttony.

Recipe Search
www.birdseye.com/search.html
Cast your line into the fish finger king's own recipe database or trawl through hundreds of other Net collections. See also:
http://recipes.alastra.com
www.mealsforyou.com

Restaurant Row
www.restaurantrow.com
Key in your dining preferences and find the perfect match from hundreds of thousands of food barns worldwide.

Scope GM Food
http://scope.educ.washington.edu/gmfood
Forums, FAQs, email lists and reference library concerning mutant seeds.

ScotchWhisky.com
www.scotchwhisky.com
Excellent site with loads of info on whisky, plus a shopping facility.

Spice Advice
www.spiceadvice.com
Encyclopedia of spices covering their origins, purposes, recipes and tips on what goes best with what.

Switcheroo
www.switcheroo.com
Seriously clever and useful site that offers you both an encyclopedia of ingredients and help if you're missing an ingredient when cooking. For example, if you're making a cake but there's no fat in the house, substitute mashed banana. Yes, really.

Tasty Insect Recipes
www.ent.iastate.edu/misc/insectsasfood.html
Dig in to such delights as Bug Blox, Banana Worm Bread, Rootworm Beetle Dip and Chocolate Chirpie Chip Cookies (with crickets).

Tea & Sympathy
http://pages.ripco.net/~c4ha2na9/tea
For more, try the Tea Council:
www.teacouncil.co.uk
To buy tea, try The English Tea Store:
www.englishteastore.com

the directory

Thai Recipes
www.importfood.com/recipes.html
Just click if you don't have an ingredient.

Tokyo Food Page
www.bento.com
Where and what to eat in Tokyo, plus recipes. More help packing sushi at:
www.thesushibar.com
www.sushilinks.com

Top Secret Recipes
www.topsecretrecipes.com
www.copykat.com
At least one commercial recipe, such as KFC coleslaw, revealed each week. Many are surprisingly basic.

Tudocs
www.tudocs.com
Rates cooking links across the web. Search under "fruit", for instance, and get linked to such ever-useful sites as 104 Things to Do With a Banana.

Buying Groceries Online

Buying food online is a very real option these days, even in most rural areas. You might even find that delivery is free if you place a sizeable order. Many of the big supermarkets offer online shopping:

Asda www.asda.co.uk
Iceland www.iceland.co.uk
Ocado www.ocado.com
Sainsbury's www.sainsburys.co.uk
Tesco www.tesco.co.uk
Waitrose www.waitrose.com

Or you could go for an organic delivery – which you'll find surprisingly good-value compared to the organic offerings in the supermarkets. There are nationwide schemes such as Simply Organic and Organic Shop, and the Soil Association has a directory of local schemes and suppliers.

Organic Delivery Company www.organicdelivery.co.uk
Planet Organic www.planetorganic.com
Simply Organic www.simplyorganic.net
Soil Association www.soilassociation.org

The Ultimate Cookbook
www.ucook.com
Pinch recipes from hundreds of popular cookbooks. More food porn unplugged at:
www.cook-books.com

Vegetarian Society of the UK
www.vegsoc.org
Support for veggies.

Wine Spectator
www.winespectator.com
Research your hangover.

Zack's Bug Eating Page
http://eat.bees.net
You better get used to it, because it'll be your diet soon.

Furniture and Interiors

BBC Good Homes
www.beeb.com/goodhomes
The BBC's interiors magazine has all the features you've come to expect, offering
advice on everything from Moroccan living rooms to the good flooring guide.

DesignBoom
www.designboom.com
Massive site with details of loads of design events worldwide. There's also a wealth
of articles and potted histories.

Design Gap
www.design-gap.co.uk
Directory of work by three hundred contemporary British designers and furniture
makers that includes everything from tchotchkes to chests-of-drawers.

Design-Online
www.design-online.co.uk
A database of British interior designers, feng shui consultants, building services,
soft furnishing companies and other providers of interiors essentials.

Furniture Guide
www.furnitureguide.com
Very impressive site covering all aspects of furniture, with glossaries, buying
guides, shop locator, articles, style guide, etc.

the directory

furniture and interiors

Furniture Wizard
www.furniturewizard.com
Tips on how to restore your Louis XIV chair after your cat pees on it.

Geomancy.Net – The Centre for Applied Feng Shui Research
www.geomancy.net
Harmonize Qi and recreate the ambience of a Chinese restaurant. For more wizard assistance, try Qi Whiz and Feng Shui Fanzine:
www.qi-whiz.com
www.fengshui-fanzine.co.uk

History of Furniture Timeline
http://maltwood.finearts.uvic.ca/hoft
Detailed history of furniture, with glossary and links.

Illustrated History of Furniture
www.cwru.edu/UL/preserve/stack/Furniture.html
Complete text of an 1893 historical study of furniture in PDF format.

Let's Go Retro
www.letsgoretro.com
Relive your youth and get a Space Invaders machine for your living room.

Nubold.com
www.nubold.com
Home of lighting, glass, ceramics and tableware from contemporary designers like Bodo Sperlein and Nic Wood. They even offer a wedding list service for couples with impeccable taste.

On-Line Furniture Style Guide
www.connectedlines.com/styleguide
Detailed guide to styles from Jacobean to Scandinavian contemporary.

Sotheby's Collecting Guides
www.sothebys.com/connoisseur/guides
The venerable auction house's guides to collecting ceramics, furniture, prints, rugs, clocks and silver.

StyleSource Design
www.stylesource.co.uk/design
The peach colour-scheme and the face of Laurence Llewelyn-Bowen might suggest otherwise, but this site is a good source of information and advice on everything from frosted mirrors to colour trends and period design.

Tribu-Design
www.tribu-design.com/en
A fascinating database of twentieth-century furniture and design.

Wallpaper Online
www.wallpaperonline.co.uk
Apparently wallpaper hasn't been this trendy since the 1970s, so stock up at this easy-to-use site, featuring a database of 20,000 papers, borders and fabrics.

The Work of Charles and Ray Eames
http://lcweb.loc.gov/exhibits/eames
The Library of Congress's online exhibition of the work of the most influential designers of the twentieth century.

the directory

Games

Most multiplayer games can be played across the Net. There are also thousands of simple table, word, arcade and music games as diverse as Chess, Blackjack, Connect 4, and Frogger that can be played on the Web courtesy of Java and Shockwave. In some cases you can even contest online opponents for prizes. Peruse the selection on offer at:

Coffee Break Arcade www.coffeebreakarcade.com
Flash Kit www.flashkit.com
Flazoom www.flazoom.com
Flipside www.flipside.com
FreeArcade.com www.freearcade.com
Gamesville www.gamesville.com
Playsite www.playsite.com
Pogo.com www.pogo.com
Shockwave.com www.shockwave.com
The Station www.station.sony.com
Yahoo! Games http://games.yahoo.com
Web Games www.happypuppy.com/web

Al Menconi Ministries
www.gospelcom.net/menconi/topics/games
Videogame reviews from a Christian perspective.

The Atari Time Machine
http://homepage.eircom.net/~morrikar
Museum and homage to the videogame console that just about started it all. For fans of its chief rival, there's:
www.intellivisionlives.com

Blues News
www.bluesnews.com
Keep up with what's Quakin'.

Cheat Station
www.cheatstation.com
Get Sonic to do what you want him to do. For more devious tricks, try The Codebook:
www.codebook.se

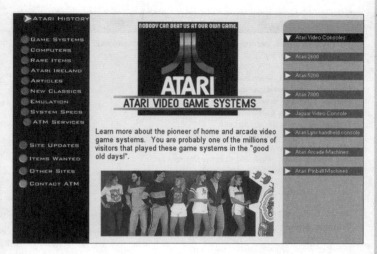

NOBODY CAN BEAT US AT OUR OWN GAME.

ATARI
ATARI VIDEO GAME SYSTEMS

Learn more about the pioneer of home and arcade video game systems. You are probably one of the millions of visitors that played these game systems in the "good old days!".

- Atari History
- Game Systems
- Computers
- Rare Items
- Atari Ireland
- Articles
- New Classics
- Emulation
- System Specs
- ATM Services
- Site Updates
- Items Wanted
- Other Sites
- Contact ATM

- Atari Video Consoles
- Atari 2600
- Atari 5200
- Atari 7800
- Jaguar Video Console
- Atari Lynx handheld console
- Atari Arcade Machines
- Atari Pinball Machines

ContestGuide
www.contestguide.com
www.contestlistings.com
http://home.iwon.com/index_gen.html
www.uggs-n-rugs.com.au/contests
Get junk-mailed for life by entering loads of competitions.

Croft Times
www.cubeit.com/ctimes
More news about the Tomb Raider bombshell than you could ever want. For the truly smitten, you can download a customized version of Internet Explorer featuring Lara's likeness everywhere.

Freeloader
www.freeloader.com
Download free games (like *Grand Theft Auto* and *Hidden & Dangerous*) for your PC. The catch: you have to look at ads ... lots of ads.

Game Downloads
www.fileplanet.com
Stock up on even more gaming software.

the directory

Games

For reviews, news, demos, hints, patches, cheats, downloads, and other PC game necessities try:

Adrenaline Vault www.avault.com
Gamers.com www.gamers.com
Games Domain www.gamesdomain.co.uk
Gamespot www.gamespot.com
GameSpy www.gamespy.com
Happy Puppy www.happypuppy.com
Mac Gamer www.macgamer.com
Old Man Murray www.oldmanmurray.com
Total Games www.totalgames.net

Console Games

Absolute Playstation www.absolute-playstation.com
Console Domain www.gamesdomain.co.uk
Hotgames.com www.hotgames.com
Psx Extreme www.psxextreme.com
Total Games www.totalgames.net
Videogame Strategies http://vgstrategies.about.com
XBox http://xbox.ign.com

GameFAQs
www.gamefaqs.com
Stuck on a level or just want to know more?

Game Girlz
www.gamegirlz.com
Team up with other game grrls and prepare to kick dweeb-boy butt right across their own turf. More reinforcement at:
www.womengamers.com

Gameplay
www.gameplay.com
Fifteen years old and still going strong, this is certainly the best British gaming portal, with an excellent magazine, shop and loads of online gaming options. For cheats, lotsa links and lower prices check out:
www.ukgames.com

the directory

Gaming Age
www.gaming-age.com
All the latest news from the gaming frontline, plus interviews with designers and previews of big games before they hit the shops.

Kasparov Vs. The World
http://classic.zone.msn.com/kasparov
Take tips from the Russian master. Then play chess online:
http://chess.about.com

The Odyssey Resource
www.run.to/odyssey
Relive those halcyon days when Pong seemed like the greatest thing since striped toothpaste.

PC Game Finder
www.pcgame.com
Search the leading game lairs.

Scoring: **Large Rocks = 10pt. -- Med. Rocks = 20pt. -- Small Rocks = 50pt.**
Scores will only last for two weeks... wanna give everyone a shot at glory.

SPACE ROCK SHOOTING THING

Score: 0
Ships: 2

the directory

Pointless Games
http://pointlessgames.com
Believe it or not, a selection of games that are actually worse than Pong.

Popex
www.popex.com
Similar to Fantasy Football or Fantasy Shares, but with pop bands.

RPG Vault
http://rpgvault.ign.com
Role Playing Gamers' heaven.

Text-Based Pong
www.karber.net/textbased/pong/default.htm
Pong – the first and greatest computer game. This is the oddest version you'll ever play.

Vintage Gaming
www.vg-network.com
www.emuunlim.com
www.download.net
Revive old school arcade games like Xevious on your home PC. For more 1980s fun, try Smilie Games:
www.smiliegames.com

Gardening

About gardening
http://gardening.about.com
About's home gardening guide.

The Botanical Dermatology Database
http://bodd.cf.ac.uk
Why you should wear gardening gloves.

British Trees
www.british-trees.com
Dedicated to the preservation of British woodland, including an excellent guide to native trees.

The Carnivorous Plant FAQ
www.sarracenia.com/faq.html
Novel solutions for garden pests.

Crocus
www.crocus.co.uk
The main draw of this online garden centre is that plants are delivered by trained gardeners who will help bolster your borders. There are also sections devoted to plant finding, jargon busting and news and advice on organic gardening.

Dig It
www.dig-it.co.uk
Comprehensive gardening site, including a shopping service where everything is allegedly sourced from environmentally friendly companies, a good magazine section and a facility to email the site's experts. For more, see Just Gardeners: www.justgardeners.com

E-Garden
www.e-garden.co.uk
Initially this large site appears to be heavy on the hard sell, but lurking beneath the commerce are a well-organized magazine section, a Latin translator and very useful problem-solvers on subjects like diseases, climbers and herbaceous perennials.

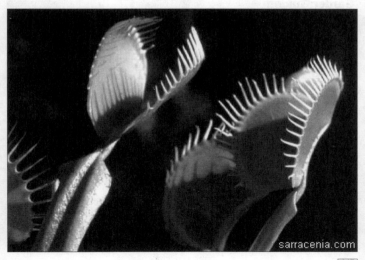

sarracenia.com

the directory

English Country Gardening
www.suite101.com/welcome.cfm/english_country_gardening
Jane Hollis's site devoted to the grand old art of English country gardening includes discussion groups, articles, virtual tours and flower show and garden reports.

Expert Gardener
www.expertgardener.com
Has the usual features, with the added extra of Charlie Dimmock calendars available for purchase.

Garden Forum
www.gardenforum.co.uk
All the latest news, views, advice, job postings and gossip from the gardening community.

Garden Guides
www.gardenguides.com
Has most of the features you should expect from the better general gardening sites (plant guides, discussion forums, advice), but this site sets itself apart with its lengthy book extracts on topics like choosing bulbs and designing herb gardens.

Garden Visit
www.gardenvisit.com
Maps of gardens open to the public around the world and a history of garden design.

Garden Web
www.gardenweb.com
One of the best horticultural resources on the Web, this site hosts a multitude of regional and specialist forums (roses, wild flowers, kitchen gardens), plus a glossary, plant database, calendar of events, plant and seed exchange, plenty of articles and shopping areas.

Growing Lifestyle
www.growinglifestyle.com
A dedicated home-and-garden search engine.

Kitchen Gardener
www.taunton.com/finegardening
Online presence of *Kitchen Gardener* magazine, dedicated to foodies who grow their own produce. For a more organic perspective, check out: www.thevegetablepatch.com

Open Directory Gardens
http://dmoz.org/Home/Gardens
The Open Directory Project's comprehensive set of links.

Postcode Plant Database
www.nhm.ac.uk/science/projects/fff
This excellent resource from the Natural History Museum allows you to find the right native trees, shrubs and flowers for your area.

Royal Botanic Gardens
www.rbgkew.org.uk
Featuring access to its enormous academic database, the homepage of Kew Gardens is one for the real horticulturalist.

Royal Horticultural Society
www.rhs.org.uk
The online presence of the RHS includes plant databases, seasonal advice and a garden finder.

The Vine Weevil Advice Centre
www.vine.weevil.org.uk
Dedicated to combating Britain's number-one garden pest.

Gay and Lesbian

AEGIS
www.aegis.com
Claiming to be the largest HIV/AIDS related site on the Web, AEGIS is an amazing resource filled with the latest news from the treatment front, bulletin boards, a law library of judicial cases and an archive of publications from organizations like Gay Men's Health Crisis, Act Up and the Government. For more news, advice and dispatches from the activist front, try:

the directory

Gay Men's Health Crisis www.gmhc.org
Act Up New York www.actupny.org

The AIDS Memorial Quilt
www.aidsquilt.org
View the quilt online, find out how to become involved with the project, and contribute to the memory book.

Gay.com UK
http://uk.gay.com
The British version of the enormous American portal has a huge array of channels for everyone from scene queens to those not yet out of the closet. Other portals of call are Planet Out, Queer Theory and Queery:
www.planetout.com
www.queertheory.com
www.queery.com

the directory

Gay Britain Network
www.gaybritain.co.uk
Homepage of the network that hosts sites like UK Gay Shopping, UK Gay Guide and Gay Video Shop.

Gay & Lesbian Alliance against Defamation
www.glaad.org
Stand up against media stereotyping and discrimination against those deviating from the heterosexual norm.

Gayscape
www.gayscape.com/gayscape
Probably the best gay search engine on the Web. See also the Queer Resource Directory:
www.qrd.org
For more Brit-specific links, try The Gay Index:
www.gayindex.co.uk
And for less mainstream links, go to Larry-bob's Queer Hotlist:
www.io.com/~larrybob/hotlist.html

Gay to Z
www.gaytoz.com
Directory of gay-friendly hotels, bars, clubs, builders, plumbers, electricians and erotica in London, Manchester and Brighton. Give them your email address and they'll send you more complete guides on the above cities plus Paris. For more hotels in the UK and abroad, try:
UK Gay Hotel Guide:
www.gayhotel.co.uk

Gay Travel Guide
www.gaytravel.co.uk
This excellent site has detailed guides to destinations such as Mykonos, Benidorm, Ibiza, New York and Amsterdam, plus a good search facility for gay-friendly hotels in more exotic locales.

Holy Titclamps
www.holytitclamps.com
Homepage of San Francisco's fab queer zine which features fiction by the likes of Sarah Schulmann and Steve Abbot plus comics, poetry, rants and humour from some of the best writers and artists on the scene.

Lesbian UK
www.lesbianuk.co.uk
A database of resources, both on- and offline, for Britain's lesbian community.

the directory

The Old Dyke
www.rowfant.demon.co.uk
Essays devoted to lesbian and women's history.

OUTintheUK
www.outintheuk.com
Fantastic, non-profit networking site for gay men who want to meet other gay men socially.

OutRage!
http://outrage.nabumedia.com
Peter Tatchell's organization fighting for equal rights and against assimilation into straight society.

Pink Passport
www.pinkpassport.com
A site with all the usual features, but it does have one of the best gay venue selectors on the Web, covering the entire world.

Rainbow Network
www.rainbownetwork.co.uk
As its name suggests, this site covers pretty much the entire spectrum of gay and lesbian life, from the Eurovision Song Contest to rallying the pink vote in the General Election.

Stonewall
www.stonewall.org.uk
The homepage of the lesbian and gay rights organization may strike some as dull and worthy, but it's a good source of information on British activism and issues like the age of consent.

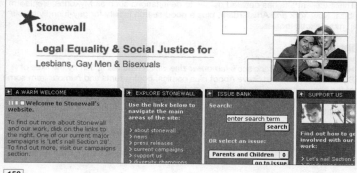

Stonewall

Legal Equality & Social Justice for

Lesbians, Gay Men & Bisexuals

A WARM WELCOME

Welcome to Stonewall's website.

To find out more about Stonewall and our work, click on the links to the right. One of our current major campaigns is 'Let's nail Section 28'. To find out more, visit our campaigns section.

EXPLORE STONEWALL

Use the links below to navigate the main areas of the site:

> about stonewall
> news
> press releases
> current campaigns
> support us
> diversity champions

ISSUE BANK

Search:

enter search term

search

OR select an issue:

Parents and Children

go to issue

SUPPORT US

Find out how to get involved with our work:

> Let's nail Section 28

Techno Dyke
www.technodyke.com
Part of the Indie Gurl Network (www.indiegurl.com) of zines, this fun e-zine has drag king galleries, horoscopes, articles on sex and relationships and a "Biosphere" section.

UK Gay Guide
www.gayguide.co.uk
The design is slightly irritating, but this site features excellent guides to gay-friendly services throughout the UK plus advice and personals.

Genealogy

Don't expect to enter your name and produce an instant family tree, but you might be able to fill in a few gaps.

Ancient Faces
www.ancientfaces.com
Picture your ancestors.

Cyndi's List
www.cyndislist.com
Twenty million users can't be wrong. With just about 100,000 links, the genealogy resource you're after is undoubtedly here. For Brit-specific links, try Suzy's Genealogy Page:
www.geocities.com/heartland/3934/britain.htm

Ellis Island Records
www.ellisislandrecords.org
If your family had a stopover in the US in the past 150 years or so, their records will be here.

the directory

Family History
www.familyhistory.com
This site, a section of the massive Ancestry.com umbrella, hosts some 130,000 message boards organized by surname or location. You can also set up your own family website here for free.

FamilySearch
www.familysearch.org
If you're going to be doing family research on the Web you'll come here at one stage or another. This site (also known as the LDS Resource) is run by the Mormons, who believe it is their duty to record the ancestry of every living soul. The religious aspect is played down in favour of sheer information, and what they have collated is nothing short of astonishing: some 450 million family names.

Genuki
www.genuki.org.uk
This should be your first stop on your search for your family roots. They have an excellent section for beginners, offering advice on how to search and how to use the Internet's resources. More beginner's advice can be found at Starting English Research:
www.xmission.com/~nelsonb/starte.htm

Historical Text Archive
http://historicaltextarchive.com
A very useful resource for people with Caribbean and African ancestry, including a Caribbean ancestry newsletter and a database of slave names. Also check the Christine's Genealogy site:
http://ccharity.com

Public Record Office
www.pro.gov.uk
Not a great resource in itself, but if you need to approach the Public Record Office or National Archive for materials this site gives you the lowdown on how to go about it. More information can be found on the Government's Family Records site:
www.familyrecords.gov.uk

RootsWeb
www.rootsweb.com
The oldest, largest and probably the best free genealogy site on the Net. It features a very good search engine, links to resources and lots of humour preventing things from getting too dull. More gene gardening can be done at:
www.ancestry.com
www.familytreemaker.com
www.genhomepage.com
www.genealogytoday.com

Surname Listings
www.surnameweb.org
Dig up dirt on your family name.

Gossip and Celebrities

Every celebrity has at least one obsessive fan site in their honour, but finding them can sometimes be tricky. If they're not listed in Yahoo, try:

Celebhoo www.celebhoo.com
CelebSites www.celebsites.com
Celebrity Site Of The Day www.csotd.com
Webring www.webring.org
Google Directory http://directory.google.com/Top/Arts/Movies

Search engines tend to find porn scuttlers who've loaded their HTML meta tags with celebrity names – easy bait, when you consider that most fans would be more than happy to catch a glimpse of their idol in various states of undress:

the directory

Celebrity Nudity Database www.cndb.com

If they succeed in catching your attention, at least have the sense not to pull out your credit card. Adding **-naughty -naked -nude** to your search term, or enabling an adult filter such as Google's SafeSearch (under Preferences), might help weed them out.

ABC News Entertainment
http://abcnews.go.com:80/sections/entertainment
Rumours and legit showbiz news from one of America's big three TV networks.

Beat Box Betty
www.beatboxbetty.com
Gossip and industry news "with a twist of blonde".

Bizcotti
http://bizcotti.com
Attempting to be *The Onion* of the gossip world.

Celebrity Babies
http://celebritybabies
.webjump.com
What would the offspring of your favourite celebrity couple look like?

Celebstatus

www.celebstatus.com
One of the Web's greatest games, this is fantasy football for celeb spotters with a cast of A, B and C list "stars" accumulating points for tabloid appearances.

Chic Happens

www.hintmag.com/chichappens/chichappens.php
Horacio Silva and Ben Widdicombe's superb gossip page.

Cinescape

www.cinescape.com
The latest insider industry news. Not as good as *The Hollywood Reporter*, but you don't have to subscribe.

Coat Hangers of the Rich and Famous

www.geocities.com/hangmycoat
A revealing look inside the closet of some of the world's biggest stars. For those who prefer to give their object of desire some TLC, there's Stars auf Krücken: www.fortunecity.de/spielberg/quincy/28

Donna's Long and Short of It

www.metal-sludge.com/LongShort.htm
The skinny (or the chubby) on the members of the heavy metal fraternity.

Drudge Report

www.drudgereport.com
Rumours from inside the Washington Beltway with a right-wing slant, from the online columnist who almost brought down a president.

E! Online

www.eonline.com
The latest from the States courtesy of the homepage of the American cable TV channel.

Famous Birthdays

www.famousbirthdays.com
http://us.imdb.com/OnThisDay
See who shares your birthday.

Famous Name Changes

www.famousnamechanges.com
The truth behind celebs trying to give themselves some personality.

Fanzine

www.fanzine.co.uk
The official addresses of stars and pop groups. For more direct access, try Chip's

the directory

Celebrity Home E-mail Addresses:
www.addresses.site2go.com
Reach out to more stars at Celebrity Addresses and Celebrity Email:
www.writetoaceleb.com
www.celebrityemail.com

Filth2Go
www.filth2go.com
Outrageous, scandalous, rude gay gossip zine. Unfortunately, you have to subscribe.

Find a Grave
http://www.findagrave.com
See where celebrities are buried.

FIND A GRAVE

Find Famous Graves
See the graves of thousands of
famous people from around the
world.
- Search by **name**
- Search by **location**
- Search by **claim to fame**
- Search by **date**
- **Most popular** searches
- New listings
- New photos

Find Graves
Find the graves of ancestors,
create virtual memorials, add
'virtual flowers' and a note to a
loved one's grave, etc.
- Search **4.3 million** grave records
- Search for a cemetery
- Add burial records
- Stroll through our online cemetery
- Top 50 Contributors
- Surname index

The Gossip Lowdown
www.mindspring.com/%7Ealexfan/lowdown.html
Click here to subscribe to Simone Sentral's crucial newsletter.

Hello!
www.hellomagazine.co.uk
All the jet trash and desperate celebs you expect from the glossy, only with lower
production values. For an American version of the same without the minor royalty, try:
People http://people.aol.com

Hollywood Gossip
www.jtj.net/jtj/gossip.shtml
Is Keanu gay? Fading stars and other matters of international import.

National Enquirer
www.nationalenquirer.com
All the news that's not fit to print elsewhere. Even less believable "news" can be found at Weekly World News:
www.weeklyworldnews.com

New York Post
www.nypostonline.com/gossip/gossip.htm
The latest dish from the columnists of the Big Apple's most notorious tabloid. For even more tittle-tattle, try their sister site:
www.pagesix.com

PeopleNews
www.peoplenews.com
Who did what, where and when, updated twenty times a day. As recommended by Tara Palmer-Tomkinson.

Popbitch
www.popbitch.com
Scurrilous, rude, fun and yes, downright bitchy, this is without question the best British pop gossip site. Their weekly mailing lists have brought down careers and halt work all over the capital every Thursday.

Pop Justice
www.popjustice.com
Fabulously bitchy site taking aim at the teen pop hordes.

The Smoking Gun
www.thesmokinggun.com
Tom Cruise's petition for divorce, Linda Fiorentino's nudity rider and other documents of celebrity misbehaviour.

TeenHollywood.com
www.teenhollywood.com
All the latest dirt and news on Tinsletown's pretty young things.

Variety
www.variety.com
Screen news fresh off the PR gatling gun.

Who Would You Kill?
www.whowouldyoukill.com
So who would you toss into *Dawson's Creek*?

Greetings Cards

If stretching the bounds of good taste doesn't bother you, you'll find thousands of sites that will gladly speckle your message with multi-media tutti-frutti. Rather than forward your "card" directly, your victim will generally receive an invitation to drop by and collect it from the site. And of course being masked by a third party makes it perfect for harassing valentines and sending ransom notes. The above directories list hundreds of virtual card dispensers, but check out the most popular ones first:

Blue Mountain www.bluemountain.com
eGreetings www.egreetings.com
Hallmark www.hallmark.com
Pulp Cards www.pulpcards.com
Regards.com www.regards.com
Tackymail http:/www.tackymail.com
Virtual Insults www.virtualinsults.com
Yahoo! Greetings http://greetings.yahoo.com

Banner Greetings
www.bannergreetings.com
Create your own personalized greetings by uploading your photo and choosing from their music or art library.

Brides and Grooms
http://BridesandGrooms.com/cards
Propose to your loved one with an intimate virtual proposal card.

Card Corp
www.cardcorp.co.uk
Need some business cards or invitations fast? Design them online for snappy delivery via email or on the paper of your choice. Naturally, the latter option costs.

Digital Voodoo
www.pinstruck.com
Curse thy neighbour.

Hotpaper.com
www.hotpaper.com
Fill in the blanks to create handy everyday documents like greetings cards, references, eviction notices and credit card disputes.

over 1,667,413 served

Invites
http://invites.yahoo.com
www.regards.com
www.egreetings.com
Throwing a slide night? Here's an easy way to create an instant email invitation and manage the thousands of RSVPs. For help planning:
www.theplunge.com

ManCards
www.queerzone.com/mancards
Come out of the closet with a ManCard.

Matoox
www.matoox.com
Tell your boss he's a male chauvinist pig, tell your neighbour he's got bad breath, tell that fox in history lectures your true intentions – but all under the cover of anonymity.

the directory

Virtual Beer Server
http://beer.trash.net
Say it with a brew.

Virtual Presents
http://www.virtualpresents.com
www.it3c.co.uk
Why waste money on real gifts when, after all, it's the thought that counts?

Web Greeting Cards
www.web-greeting-cards.com
If you're after something classier than the average e-card, this site offers high-quality images that can be extensively customized.

Health

While the Net's certainly an unrivalled medical library, it's also an unri-valled promulgator of the twenty-first-century equivalent of old wives' tales. So by all means research your ailment and pick up fitness tips online, but like the pill bottles say, check with your doctor before put-ting them to work. And while you're with your GP, ask if they use the Net for research and if so, which sites they recommend.

Don't expect to go online for first-aid advice. If it's an emergency, you won't have time. The Net is better for in-depth research and anec-dotal advice, none of which comes quickly. But once you've spent a few sessions online studying your complaint, you'll be fully prepared to state your case. To find a doctor, dentist or specialist, try:

NetDoctor www.netdoctor.co.uk.

Or for a phone, fax or email response that could save your life on the road, try:

WorldClinic www.worldclinic.com

It's hard to say where to start your research. Perhaps a directory: Yahoo et al have seriously stacked medical sections, or you could try one of the specialist health portals:

Achoo www.achoo.com
Hospitalweb UK www.hospitalweb.co.uk
MedExplorer www.medexplorer.com
Patient UK www.patient.co.uk
SearchBug www.searchbug.com/health

Or a government gateway:

Health on the Net www.hon.ch
NHS Direct (UK) www.nhsdirect.nhs.uk
US National Library of Medicine www.nlm.nih.gov
World Health Organization www.who.int/home-page

the directory

You'll find tons of excellent self-help megasites, though the presence of sponsors may raise ethical questions. Their features vary, but medical encyclopedias, personal health tests and Q&A services are fairly standard fare. Starting with the former US Surgeon General's site, try:

Dr Koop www.drkoop.com
HealthAtoZ.com www.healthatoz.com
HealthCentral www.healthcentral.com
HealthWorld www.healthy.net
Intelihealth www.intelihealth.com
Mayo Clinic www.mayoclinic.com
Netdoctor.co.uk www.netdoctor.co.uk
Surgery Door www.surgerydoor.co.uk
24Dr.com www.24dr.com
WebMD www.webmd.com
WebMD (Lycos) http://webmd.lycos.com
Yahoo! Health http://health.yahoo.com

But for serious research go straight to Medline, the US National Library of Medicine's database. It archives, references and abstracts thousands of medical journals and periodicals going back to 1966. You can get it free at PubMed, but the subscription services may have access to more material. These are aimed more at health pros and students:

BioMedNet www.bmn.com
Medline Plus www.nlm.nih.gov/medlineplus
Medscape www.medscape.com
Ovid www.ovid.com
PubMed www.ncbi.nlm.nih.gov/PubMed

Despite first appearances, Martindale's maintains an outstanding directory of medical science links:

Martindale's www.martindalecenter.com/HSGuide.html

If you know what you have and you want to contact other sufferers, use a search engine (**www.google.com**) or directory (**http://dmoz.org**) to find organizations and personal home pages. They should direct you to useful mailing lists and discussion groups. If not, try Google Groups (**http://groups.google.com**) to find the right newsgroups.

Acne Regimen
www.acne.org
Out, out damn spot.

Acupuncture.com
http://acupuncture.com
Probably the best and certainly the most comprehensive site dealing with Chinese medicine. As well as acupuncture, it covers Chinese herbal remedies, Qi Gong and Tui Na (massage) for patients, students and practitioners alike. For more information, try Oriental Medicine:
www.orientalmedicine.com

Alex Chiu's Eternal Life Device
http://www.alexchiu.com
Live forever or come back for your money.

All Nurses
http://www.allnurses.com
Springboard to chat groups, research data, professional bodies, jobs and other nursing resources.

Alternative Medicine
http://altmedicine.about.com
www.alternativemedicine.com
www.wholehealthmd.com
www.alternativedr.com
http://dmoz.org/Health/Alternative
Part of the Net's ongoing research function is the ability to contact people who've road-tested alternative remedies and can report on their efficacy. Start here and work your way to an answer.

the directory

Aromatherapy
www.aromaweb.com
Psuedoscience it might be (http://skepdic.com/aroma.html), but you'll be on the way to smelling better. And surely that can't be a bad thing.

Ask Dr Weil
www.drweil.com
Popdoctor Andrew Weil's eagerness to prescribe from a range of bewildering and often conflicting alternative therapies has seen him called a quack in some quarters, but not by Warner. *Time* put him on the front cover and gave him a job peddling advice beside vitamin ads. Whether or not you believe in food cures, his daily Q&As are always a good read.

Biopharm Leeches
www.biopharm-leeches.com
Cure your ailments the old-fashioned way.

Calorie Counter
www.caloriecounter.co.uk
Diet sensibly. For more dieting advice, check out the Open Directory's Weight Loss pages:
http://dmoz.org/Health/Weight_Loss

CancerHelp UK
www.cancerhelp.org.uk
Jargon-free guide to living with the disease, plus information on treatments, ongoing studies and trials.

Chirohelp.com
www.chirohelp.com
Don't get bent out of shape: this is a good introduction to chiropractic health care.

Color Vision Test
www.umist.ac.uk/UMIST_OVS/UES/COLOUR0.HTM
Do you dress in the dark or are you merely colour-blind?

ConsumerLab
www.consumerlab.com
An independent testing authority which publishes its studies online. It tests herbal remedies, vitamins, supplements, sports products and functional foods for effectiveness, purity, potency, consistency and bioavailability (ie whether the body can deal with the product properly).

Dr Squat
www.drsquat.com
www.weightsnet.com
Avoid getting sand kicked in your face through deep full squats.

Drugs
www.erowid.org
www.lycaeum.org
www.trashed.co.uk
www.perkel.com/politics/issues/pot.htm
www.neuropharmacology.com
www.druglibrary.org
Everything you ever wanted to know about the pleasure, pain and politics of psychoactive drugs and the cultures built around them. Even more at Drugs, Solvents and Intoxicants:
http://area51.upsu.plym.ac.uk/~harl

Embarrassing Problems
www.embarrassingproblems.com
Help with everything from anal itching to wind.

GYN101
www.gyn101.com
Swot up for your next gynaecological exam. But if you're after honours, go straight to:
www.obgyn.net

the directory

Gyro's Excellent Hernia Adventure
www.cryogenius.com/mesh
Holiday snaps from under the knife.

HandHeldMed
www.handheldmed.com
http://medicalpocketpc.com
www.pdamd.com
Arm your pocket computer with medical software and references.

Health Fitness Tips
www.health-fitness-tips.com
Ironically, the site itself is somewhat flabby, but hopefully the exercise tips, low-fat
recipes and motivational quotes will help you shed the inches.

Internet Health Library
www.internethealthlibrary.com
Information on complementary therapy from the University of Essex.

Lab Tests
www.labtestsonline.org
Get inside your sample.

Medicinal Herb Faq
http://ibiblio.org/herbmed/faqs/medi-cont.html
If it's in your garden and it doesn't kill you, it can only make you stronger. More
leafy cures and love drugs at:
www.algy.com/herb
www.botanical.com
www.herbal-ahp.org

Mental Health
www.mentalhealth.com
It's guaranteed that you'll come out of this site convinced there's something wrong
with you. Worry your way along to:
www.anxietynetwork.com

Museum of Questionable Medical Devices
www.mtn.org/quack
Gallery of health-enhancing products where even breaks weren't bundled free.

National Institute of Ayurvedic Medicine
http://niam.com/corp-web
A good, low BS guide to balancing your life energies with the ancient Indian
practice.

Violet Ray Generators

The device we are most often
asked about is the Violet Ray
Generator, sometimes called an
"ultra violet device." Tens of
thousands of these devices
were sold for home use
between about 1915 and 1950
under brand names such as
Masters, Elco and
Renulife. Literature
accompanying the devices claimed to cure just about
everything including heart disease, paralysis, wry neck and
writers cramp!

19th Century Medical Curios
www.zoraskingdom.freeserve.co.uk
The Elephant Man, bearded women and other strange Victoriana.

Nutritional Supplements
www.nutritionalsupplements.com
First-hand experiences with vitamins, bodybuilding supplements, and other dubious health-shop fodder. For the real deal, go to the British Nutrition Foundation:
www.nutrition.org.uk

Quackwatch
www.quackwatch.com
www.ncahf.org
www.hcrc.org
http://nccam.nih.gov
Separating the docs from the ducks. Don't buy into any alternative remedies until you've read these pages.

Reuters Health
www.reutershealth.com
Medical newswires, reviews, opinion and reference.

the directory

RxList
www.rxlist.com
Look up your medication to ensure you're not being poisoned.

Spas Directory
www.thespasdirectory.com
Locate a British spa or health resort.

Talk Surgery
www.talksurgery.com
Discuss your operation with people who appear interested.

ThinkNatural
www.thinknatural.com
Order homeopathic, herbal, Ayurvedic and Chinese remedies for next-day delivery,
plus advice on how to use them properly.

Travel Health
www.travelhealth.co.uk
Come back in one piece.

The Virtual Hospital
www.vh.org
Patient care and distance learning via online multimedia tools such as illustrated
surgical walkthroughs.

The Visible Human Project
www.nlm.nih.gov/research/visible
Whet your appetite by skimming through scans of a thinly filleted serial killer, and
then top it off with a fly-through virtual colonoscopy. For higher production values,
see the Virtual Body:
www.medtropolis.com

What Have I Got?
www.whathaveigot.net
Worry yourself sick through self-diagnosis.

Wing Hop Fung
www.winghopfung.com
Chinese cures by mail order.

Womens' Health
www.bbc.co.uk/health/womens
A refreshingly relatively unbranded site from the Beeb.

World Sexual Records
www.sexualrecords.com
Go for gold in slap and tickle.

World Wide Online Meditation Center
www.meditationcenter.com
Connect with your essence.

The Yoga Site
www.yogasite.com
A good, general site on the various asanas and vinyasas so you can stretch your-self back into shape. For even more karma try:
www.holisticonline.com/Yoga/hol_yoga_home.htm
www.yoganation.com

History

ArchNet
http://archnet.asu.edu
Digital directory to online archeology sites with a leaning towards the academic.
See also: Archaeological Resource Guide to Europe:
http://odur.let.rug.nl/arge

BBC Online – History
www.bbc.co.uk/history
As you'd expect, the Beeb's history pages are well designed and informative – if a bit too traditional and not as complete as you'd like.

Britannia
http://britannia.com/history
One of the best British history sites on the Web, with biographies of the "bravest knights of the fourteenth century", virtual tours of Sussex churches, a history of Welsh royalty and an electronic version of the *Anglo-Saxon Chronicle*.

the directory

Dead Media Project
www.deadmedia.org
Documenting the roadkill on the information superhighway.

History Buff
www.historybuff.com
A collection of press clippings through the ages.

History Channel
www.historychannel.com
This Web home of the American cable TV channel has perhaps too much of an American slant for most British users, but it does have some great features like an amazing archive of great speeches, both as text and as RealAudio documents.

History House
www.historyhouse.com
Dedicated to rescuing history from the historians, this excellent American site tells the stories of real people with very real human foibles who have had an impact on the world's major and not so major events. A necessary corrective to the "great man of history" myths.

History Ring
http://members.tripod.com/~PHILKON/ring.html
Homepage of the history ring, linking you to hundreds and hundreds of non-commercial history sites.

Internet History Sourcebooks Project
www.fordham.edu/halsall
Professor Paul Halsall's site is a fantastic resource for students of history, especially the marginalized variety. His directory of Internet articles has links to thousands of articles on women's history, Jewish history, Islamic history, African history, lesbian and gay history, medieval studies and the more standard ancient and modern cultures.

Journal for Multimedia History
www.albany.edu/jmmh
Academic history journal with hyperlinked bells and whistles.

1940s Sound Library
http://freespace.virgin.net/ian.bayley/sounds/sounds.htm
Ian Bayley's amazing sound archive of the 1940s, including Lord Haw Haw's broadcasts.

Regia Anglorum
www.regia.org
Relive the age of the vikings.

Hobbies

All Magic Guide
www.allmagicguide.com
Your passport to the world of illusion.

Balloon HQ
www.balloonhq.com
Become a part of pop culture.

The Contortion Home Page
http://www
.contortionhomepage.com
Hey, Stretch, how do you do that?

Experimental Aircraft
http://exp-aircraft.com
Online resource for lunatics interested in building their own planes.

Firewalking.com
www.firewalking.com
The official website of Tolly Burkan, the father of the fire-walking movement.

Home Sewing Association
www.sewing.org
Pick up hints from a bunch of sew and sews.

International String Figure Association
www.isfa.org
Perfect your cat's cradle technique.

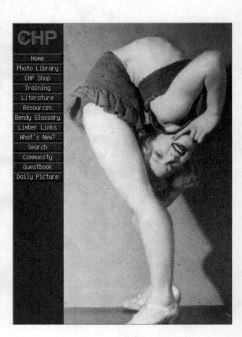

Joseph Wu's Origami Page

www.origami.vancouver.bc.ca
Gateway to the wide world of paper folding, including diagrams, galleries and links.
To make your folds fly, see:
www.paperairplanes.co.uk

Juggling Information Service

www.juggling.org
If you can't keep your balls up, this site has just about everything any sane human
could ever want to know about juggling. There's a collection of juggling software
so you can see how the pros do it, a history of juggling and other arcane stuff. For
the "best beanbag kit on the market" try the Juggling Store:
www.jugglingstore.com

Kitez

www.kitez.com
Go fly a kite at this dedicated search engine for kitesurfers.

Knots on the Web

www.earlham.edu/~peters/knotlink.htm
Why knot?

Model Mart

www.modelmart.co.uk
Model online community for modellers. There's more putty filler at Modelmasters
Online:
www.modelmasters-online.com

NMRA Directory of World Wide Rail Sites

www.ribbonrail.com/nmra
The National Model Railroad
Association's vast site of model rail-
way links across the world.

Potato Cannon Fun Page

www.geocities.com/
Yosemite/Rapids/1489
Charm and delight your parents for
years to come.

The Puppetry Homepage

www.sagecraft.com/puppetry
The ups and downs of puppetry,
from animatronics to ventriloquism.

the directory

Reenactors World
www.reenactorsworldplus.com
A Web directory of sites devoted to historical re-enactment and living history.

Rocketry.org
www.rocketry.org
Send your worst enemy to the Moon. To buy a "really big, potentially dangerous air-craft loaded with large amounts of propellant", try:
www.suborbital.com

TreasureNet
www.treasurenet.com
Exchange tall tales and learn about metal detection.

Home Improvement

Ask the Master Plumber
www.clickit.com/bizwiz/homepage/plumber.htm
Save a small fortune by unblocking your own toilet.

B&Q
www.diy.com
B&Q's site may look like a Sunday paper pull-out ad, but there's plenty here. Also see Homebase:
www.homebase.co.uk

BarPlans
www.barplans.com
Move the Queen Vic into your basement.

Buy.co.uk
www.buy.co.uk/Personal
Clinch the best deal on UK utilities and loans.

Cooksons
www.cooksons.com
The best place for power tools on the Net, with loads of special offers and free delivery if you spend more than £45.

Coping With Winter
www.ag.ndsu.nodak.edu/coping
Building a ski house in the Alps or moving to Irkutsk? Follow these building and DIY tips from North Dakota State University.

DIY Fix It

www.diyfixit.co.uk
Since most of the best DIY sites are American, this decent UK home improvement
encyclopedia is very useful for information regarding Brit-specific problems.

Fine Homebuilding

www.taunton.com/fh
American magazine for real DIY enthusiasts, with loads of information on frame
construction, garage doors, tools and safety.

Fix it now

www.fixitnow.com
Battling with a washing machine or microwave? Help is at hand from the Samurai
Appliance Repair Man. Also see:
www.repairclinic.com

HomeCentral

http://homecentral.sierrahome.com
Standard DIY site, but with a range of calculators and estimators that will tell you
the exact amount of paint and wallpaper you need for your job, or how much leaving the outside light on all night will cost.

Home Improvement Encyclopedia

www.bhglive.com/homeimp
Lots of step-by-step guides and illustrated how-tos from the American *Better
Homes and Gardens* magazine. Again the information is designed for Yanks, but
the language is simple, the illustrations clear and the animated guides are a very
clever idea.

Home Repair Stuff

www.factsfacts.com/MyHomeRepair
Design-free site answering questions like "Which caulk?" and "Squirrel in your bel-
fry?", plus beginner's guides and basic tool kits.

the directory

Home Tips
www.hometips.com
www.homestore.com
www.doityourself.com
www.naturalhandyman.com
Load your toolbox, roll up your sleeves and prepare to go in.

How to Clean Anything
www.howtocleananything.com
Just add elbow grease.

Improveline
www.improveline.com
www.homepro.com
Peruse the latest design ideas and find someone to do the job. You can even screen your local builders against public records and find the one least likely to quaff all your home brew and sell your nude holiday snaps to the *National Enquirer*.

ImproveNet
http://improvenet.com
Yankee DIY giant with more advice, calculators, shopping facilities and so on than

any sane person can handle. It even includes archives from *Popular Mechanics* and *Today's Homeowner* as well as energy conservation articles, project guides and personal project managers.

MFI

www.mfi.co.uk
Redo your kitchen with some modular cabinets. For more chi-chi options, try Kensington Kitchens, Magnet and PS4 Kitchens:
www.kensington-kitchens.co.uk
www.magnet.co.uk
www.ps4kitchens.co.uk

The Old House Web

www.oldhouseweb.net
An excellent resource for those restoring the old money pit. Again, the site is American so the product info may not be entirely appropriate, but there are good articles on choosing the right primer, selecting synthetic slates and quick fixes for wallpaper repair problems.

ThePlumber.com

www.theplumber.com
Includes tips and online repair handbooks plus the history of plumbing from Babylonia through the inventions of Thomas Crapper to waterworks in the White House. For more plumbing sites, try The Plumbing Web:
www.plumbingweb.com

Self Build

www.selfbuildanddesign.com
If you'd rather build your own house than visit an estate agent, click here. Also try:
www.ebuild.co.uk
www.self-build.co.uk
And if the banks laugh in your face when you ask them to help, visit:
http://a-mortgages-website.co.uk/self-build

Skills Register

www.skills-register.com
Thinking of hiring a plumber or handyman? Try this great service: a directory of British tradespeople who have passed site owner Will Stevens' stringent quality assurance tests. For a bigger database, try Improveline:
www.improveline.com

This to That

www.thistothat.com
So what would you like to glue today?

the directory

Wacky Uses
www.wackyuses.com
Using Coca-Cola to clean corrosion from batteries, pantyhose to polish furniture and other wacky household hints from Joey Green.

Horoscopes and Fortune-telling

800 Predict
www.800predict.com
Put your hands on your mouse for free psychic readings, love compatibility charts, daily lottery numbers, love casts and star gossip.

American Federation of Astrologers
www.astrologers.com
Impress your hairdresser by becoming a fully accredited seer by correspondence course.

Astro Advice

www.astroadvice.com

Aside from its treasure trove of arcane astrological systems (like Nine Star Ki) and slightly dodgy advice pages (astrological financial forecasts, for example), this site's best feature is its free, in-depth astrological charts.

Astrology.com

www.astrology.com

This sprawling site contains advice and predictions from just about every soothsaying system under the sun. There are horoscopes both free and charged, past-life reports, celebrity horoscopes, self-empowerment guides, karmic profiles, crystal balls, Chinese astrological readings and plenty more.

Astrology – Atlas and Time Zone Database

www.astro.com/cgi-bin/atlw3/aq.cgi?lang=e

Know exactly what was happening upstairs the second of your birth. Or if you prefer your cold readings:

www.skepdic.com/coldread.html

With a touch less pseudoscientific mumbo-jumbo, try:

http://astrology.about.com

www.astrocenter.com

Then see what old sensible shoes has to say:

www.skepdic.com/astrolgy.html

Biorhythm Generator

www.facade.com/attraction/biorhythm

Generate a cyclical report that can double as a sick note.

Dreamstop

www.dreamstop.com

Analyse your night visions and jot them into a journal to share with your friends.

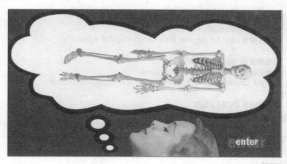

the directory

Metalog
www.astrologer.com
The home of the Astrological Association of Great Britain and the Centre for Psychological Astrology, this site "is devoted to promoting serious quality astrology; hopefully a place where many people will discover the richness of their own unique chart and learn that they are more than 'just' their sun-sign."

Oracle of Changes
www.iching.com
This excellent site enables you to virtually consult the I Ching, the ancient Chinese book of divination and soothsaying. The user casts coins into a pool six times which creates a hexagram that the oracle interprets according to the laws of ancient wisdom. See also:
www.facade.com/Occult/iching

Panchang
www.panchang.com
Get a personalized time-planner based on this ancient Indian astrological system.

Past Life Regression
www.pastlives.cc
All the information you need to send your worst enemy back to the Stone Age.

Psyche Tests
www.psychtests.com
www.keirsey.com
www.queendom.com/tests.html
www.emode.com
http://buster.cs.yale.edu/implicit
So, what breed of dog are you? Smug sceptics (www.skepdic.com/myersb.html) say you'll get closer to the truth here:
www.learner.org/exhibits/personality

RealAge
www.realage.com
Compare your biological and chronological ages.

Russell Grant Astrology
www.live-astro.com/horoscopes
Chirpy, cheerful advice from the chubby prognosticator.

Sarena's Tarot Page
www.talisman.net/tarot
Look no further if you need help with your chandelier, fan or seven triplet spreads. Also, for the expert only, a section on tarot spells. Also consult Tarot Magi:
www.tarot.com

Spirit Network

http://spiritnetwork.com

Portal for horoscopes, psychic readings, biorhythms, I Ching readings, paranormal activity and other New Age pursuits.

Stichomancy

www.facade.com/stichomancy

Type in your question and the computer will choose a book and a passage at random that miraculously will apply to your query. See also Bibliomancy, which chooses Bible passages at random to aid you in your quest for the answers: www.facade.com/bibliomancy

The Voice of the Woods

www.pixelations.com/ogham

Seek guidance from the Ogham, an ancient Celtic divination method.

What's in your name?

www.kabalarians.com

The Kabalarians claim names can be boiled down to a numerical stew and served back up as a character analysis. Look yourself up in here and see what a duff choice your parents made. Then blame them for everything that's gone wrong since.

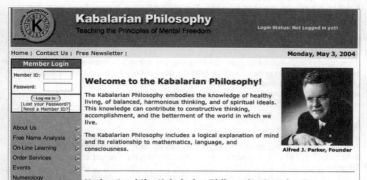

the directory

Kids and Teens

It's your choice whether to let them at it headlong or bridle their experience through rose-coloured filters. But if you need guidance or pointers towards the most kidtastic chowder, set sail into these realms:

American Libraries Assoc www.ala.org/ala/oif/foryoungpeople/childrenparents
Cybersmart Kids www.cybersmartkids.com.au
Internet Detectives www.madison.k12.wi.us/tnl/detectives
Kids Domain www.kidsdomain.com
NetMom www.netmom.com
Open Directory: Kids http://dmoz.org/Kids_and_Teens
Scholastic International www.scholastic.com
Surfing the Net with Kids www.surfnetkids.com
Yahooligans (Yahoo! for kids) www.yahooligans.com

The search engines Google and Altavista can also be set to filter out adult content. For encyclopedias and dictionaries, see p.263.

The Angry Beavers
http://members.tripod.com/~foab
A cool fan-site with loads of links etc. The official Beaver hangout can be found at:
www.nick.com

Barbie
www.barbie.com
It's a huge, Flash-intensive, slow-loading site, but there's a massive amount of stuff here to keep any girl entertained for hours – so just give in to the inevitable. Your Little Madam might also like to visit:
www.care-bears.com
www.mylittlepony.com

Beakman & Jax
www.bonus.com
Answers to typical kid questions from the likes of "why poo is brown" and "why farts smell" to "why your voice sounds different on a tape recorder" and "why the TV goes crazy while the mixer is on".

The Belch Page
www.goobo.com/belch
Gross out your parents and your little sister.

Bizarre Stuff

─────── Read this first ───────

Home made hurricane

This is a classic from the 1950's editions of the World Book Encyclopedia. I have fond memories of seeing one of these as a kid. It is a good, silly science project, and fairly safe for the kids. You need:

- 4 pieces plywood 3/4" x 4 1/2" x 16"
  (19mm x 114mm x 406mm)
- 4 pieces plywood 3/4" x 4 1/2" x 14 1/2"
  (19mm x 114 mm x 368mm)
- 2 pieces plywood 3/8" x 16" x 16"
  (9.5mm x 406mm x 406mm)
- 4 ceramic standard incandescent light bulb holders
- wiring for above
- 3 pieces glass 14" x 20" (355mm x 508mm)
- 1 piece masonite 14" x 20"
- quarter round, 21 feet (6.5m)
- four 2-foot (610 mm) sections of 1" (25mm) angle iron
- pie pan
- stove or vent pipe
- hot plate

Bigchalk
www.bigchalk.com
Study collections for all grades through to college.

Bizarre Things You Can Make In Your Kitchen
http://home.houston.rr.com/molerat
Rainy-day science projects and general mischief such as volcanoes, stink bombs, cosmic ray detectors, fake blood and hurricane machines.

Bullying Online
www.bullying.co.uk
Advice and support channels for bullied children and their parents. Perhaps a few sessions of self-defence might be a good place to start:
www.blackbeltmag.com/bbkids

the directory

The Bug Club
www.ex.ac.uk/bugclub
Creepy-crawly fan club with e-pal page, newsletters and pet care sheets on how to
keep your newly bottled tarantulas, cockroaches and stick insects alive.

CBeebies
www.bbc.co.uk/cbeebies
This is Auntie's portal for the little 'uns; there are loads of games, stories and things
to colour in – a great site. Everyone from *The Fimbles* to *Pingu* get a look in.

Censored Cartoons
www.toonzone.net/looney/ltcuts
Find out what was removed from your favourite classic cartoon.

Children's Literature Web Guide
www.ucalgary.ca/~dkbrown
Critical round-up of recent kids' books and links to texts.

Club Girl Tech
www.girltech.com
Encourages smart girls to get interested in technology without coming across all
geeky.

Cyberteens
www.cyberteens.com
Submit your music, art or writing to a public gallery. You might even win a prize.

Decoding Nazi Secrets
www.pbs.org/wgbh/nova/decoding
www.thunk.com
Use World War II weaponry to exchange secret messages with your clued-in pals.

Disney.com

www.disney.com

Guided catalogue of Disney's real-world movies, books, theme parks, records, interactive CD-ROMs and such, plus a squeaky-clean Net directory. For an unofficial Disney chaperone, see:

http://laughingplace.com

eHobbies

www.ehobbies.com

Separating junior hobbyists from their pocket money.

Funbrain

www.funbrain.com

Tons of mind-building quizzes, games and puzzles for all ages.

Funschool

www.funschool.com

Educational games for preschoolers.

Goofyface

www.goofyface.com

Gurning from the pros.

what's new at goofyface.com

Goofyface.com continues its journalistic tradition with this month's **Goofy Gazette**. At the **Goofy Gazette**, we provide formal documentation of our illustrious gooficolonimal achievements. The **Goofy Gazette** takes a unique and hard (and slightly twisted) nosed look at the events that make up our Goofy world. As the photograph attests, even world leaders are never too far away from a good goof.

the directory

Goosebumps
www.tcfhe.com:80/goosebumps/thrillold.html
Scary stories for your next sleepover.

The History Net
www.thehistorynet.com
www.historybuff.com
Bites of world history with an emphasis on the tough guys going in with guns.

Horse-Country.com
www.horse-country.com
A great site for horse-crazy kids, with a seemingly endless array of games and
quizzes designed to teach children about horses and how to care for them.

The Idea Box
www.theideabox.com
If your pre-schoolers are bored of *Teletubbies* already, try this site for activities to
keep them entertained.

Remember these... ?

Show your kids what you were glued to back in the day ... it's gotta be better
than the nonsense they watch now.

Bagpuss www.smallfilms.co.uk/bagpuss
Battle Of The Planets www.akdreamer.com/botp
The Clangers www.clangers.co.uk
The Flumps http://members.lycos.co.uk/theflumps
Hector's House http://freespace.virgin.net/dave.roberts2/hector/hectors.htm
Ivor The Engine www.smallfilms.co.uk/ivor
Jamie And The Magic Torch
          http://freespace.virgin.net/greg.taylor1/watched_it/jamie.htm
Noggin The Nog www.smallfilms.co.uk/noggin
Pinky & Perky www.pinkyandperky.com
Smurfs www.smurf.com

And for everything else, including *The Littlest Hobo*, *Hear Bear Bunch* and
even *Roger Ramjet*, see:

SausageNet www.sausagenet.com

the directory

I Used to Believe
http://iusedtobelieve.com
Confess your childhood phobias.

Kid's Domain
www.kidsdomain.com
Huge array of stuff here for kids and their parents: brain-builders, games (both online and downloadable), tips on safe surfing, Pokémon, crafts, desktop icons, etc.

Kids' Games
http://dmoz.org/Kids_and_Teens/Games
www.wicked4kids.com
www.kidsdomain.com/games
www.randomhouse.com/seussville/games
http://games.yahoo.com/games/yahooligans.html
Give the babysitter a break.

Kids' Jokes
www.kidsjokes.co.uk
www.users.bigpond.com/lander
Reams of clean jokes, riddles and knock-knocks.

Kids-Party
www.kids-party.com
Ideas to prevent your child from crying at their own birthday party.

Kids' Space
www.kids-space.org
Hideout for kids to swap art, music and stories with new friends across the world.

Liana's Paper Doll Boutique
http://www-personal.umich.edu/~lsharer/paperdolls
If you've got a printer you've now got a rather large paper doll collection, with costumes ranging from ballerina outfits to Scarlett O'Hara.

The Little Animals Activity Centre
www.bbc.co.uk/education/laac
The second the music starts and the critters start jiggling you know you're in for a treat. Let your youngest heir loose here after breakfast and expect no mercy until afternoon tea. As cute as it gets.

Magic Tricks
www.magictricks.com
www.trickshop.com
www.magicweek.co.uk
Never believe it's not so.

the directory

Neopets
www.neopets.com
Nurture a "virtual pet" until it dies.

Roper's Knots
www.realknots.com
It's not what you know; it's what knots you know.

Secret Languages
www.factmonster.com/ipka/A0769354.html
Learn Double Dutch, Pig Latin and Skimono Jive.

Seussville
www.seussville.com
The online home of the Cat in the Hat, Sam-I-Am, Horton, The Grinch and The Whos.

StarChild
http://starchild.gsfc.nasa.gov
NASA's educational funhouse for junior astronomers. See also:
www.earthsky.com
www.starport.com

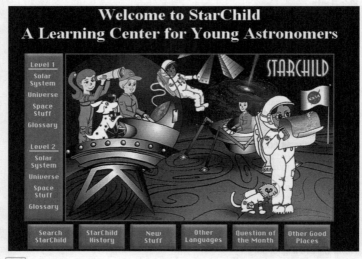

Star Wars Origami

www.happymagpie.com/Origami.html
Graduate from flapping birds onto Destroyer Droids and Tie Fighters. Prefer something that will actually fly? See:
www.aricraft.com.
For more paperfolding, try:
www.origami.com

Teen Advice

www.teenadvice.net
Part of the enormous Student Center Network, this site has loads of forums and experts for advice on anything from acne to (surprise, surprise) sex. For more advice on tricky subjects, try Embarrassing Problems:
www.embarrassingproblems.co.uk

Toy Stores

www.faoschwartz.com
www.imaginarium.com
www.toysrus.co.uk
It's just like Christmas all year round.

The Unnatural Museum

www.unmuseum.org
Lost worlds, dinosaurs, UFOs, pyramids and other mysterious exhibits from the outer bounds of space and time.

What is Happening to Me?

www.thehormonefactory.com
Find out what's throbbing in your glands.

the directory

The Yuckiest Site on the Internet
www.yucky.com
Fun science with a leaning towards the icky-sticky and the creepy-crawly. But if
you want to get thoroughly engrossed in the gross, slither right along to:
www.grossology.org

Law and Crime

For legal primers, lawyer directories, legislation and self-help:

Compact Law www.compactlaw.co.uk
Delia Venables www.venables.co.uk
FindLaw www.findlaw.com
InfoLaw www.infolaw.co.uk
UKLegal www.uklegal.com

For more on criminal activities, trends, arrests and law enforcement,
rustle through the following guides:

About Crime http://crime.about.com
Crime Spider www.crimespider.com
Open Directory http://dmoz.org/Society/Crime

A–Z Guide to British Employment Law
www.emplaw.co.uk
Get the upper hand on your boss.

The Absolute Worst Things to Say to a Police Officer
www.geocities.com/Heartland/Prairie/7559/copjokes.html
"Aren't you the guy from The Village People?"

APBnews.com
www.apbonline.com
Highly acclaimed network news service focusing on crime, justice and safety.

Brutal.com
www.brutal.com
Bad news from around the world, as it breaks.

Burglar.com
http://www.theburglar.com
Profit from stolen goods that somehow happened to be in your possession.

Copyright Myths
http://whatiscopyright.org
www.templetons.com/brad/copyright.html
Just because it's online doesn't make it yours.

The Court Service
www.courtservice.gov.uk
In amongst all the dull information and legalese is a collection of recent judgements
handed down by the country's Justices.

Crime Magazine
www.crimemagazine.com
Encyclopedic collection of outlaw tales.

the directory

Cybercrime
www.cybercrime.gov
www.cybersnitch.net
How to report online crooks.

Desktop Lawyer
www.desktoplawyer.net
Cut legal costs by doing it online.

Divorce Online
www.divorce-online.co.uk
DIY D.I.V.O.R.C.E. for residents of England and Wales.

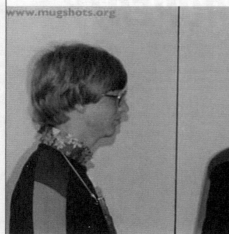

Bill Gates Mugshot
mugshots.org

Famous Mugshots
www.mugshots.org
Lifestyles of the rich and famous. As well as naughty Mr. Gates, you'll find the likes of Frank Sinatra, Charles Manson and Steve McQueen.

Dumb Crooks
www.dumbcrooks.com
Let the masters teach you how not to do it.

Dumb Laws
www.dumblaws.com
Foreign legislation with limited appeal.

ECLS
www.e-commercelawsource.com
Global monitor and directory of online business law.

The Evidence Store
www.evidencestore.com
"Need a hand for your day in court? How about a foot or a skull?... Accident reconstructions? The Evidence Store's experts will create all the visual exhibits you'll need to educate even the toughest jury."

FBI Files
http://foia.fbi.gov/alpha.htm
Download the FBI's reports, released by the Freedom of Information Act, on the Black Panthers, Al Capone, Pablo Picasso, Elvis and Winston Churchill.

Freelawyer
www.freelawyer.co.uk
Ask a legal question and get a jargon-free response from a qualified solicitor with a list of local specialists as well as no-obligation estimates.

Gang Land
www.ganglandnews.com
This amazing site from former New York *Daily News* reporter Jerry Capeci has just about everything you could want to know about Salvatore "Sammy Bull" Gravano, John Gotti, Wing Yeung Chan and their ilk.

Guide to Lock Picking
www.lysator.liu.se/mit-guide/mit-guide.html
Never climb in through the window again.

Legal Services Commission
www.legalservices.gov.uk
Information on Community Legal Service and Criminal Defence Service from the public body that oversees their administration.

the directory

Police Officer's Directory
www.officer.com
www.crimespider.com
Top of the pops cop directory with more than 1500 baddy-nabbing bureaux snuggled in with law libraries, wanted listings, investigative tools, hate groups, special ops branches and off-duty homepages. To see who's in Scotland Yard's bad books: www.met.police.uk

PursuitWatch
www.pursuitwatch.com
Get paged when there's a live police chase on TV.

Society of Will Writers
www.willwriters.com
Information on wills and bequests from the will writers' professional body.

Speedtrap.com
www.speedtrap.com
Ironically, this site is rather slow, but still a great resource for drivers who want to know, umm, where traffic flashpoints might occur. See also UK Speed Traps: www.ukspeedtraps.co.uk

Video Vigilante
www.videovigilante.com
If you lived in Oklahoma City, what else would you do but wander the city streets with a video camera looking for guys picking up prostitutes?

the directory

Money and Banking

money and banking

If your bank's on the ball it should offer an online facility to check your balances, pay your bills, transfer funds and export your transaction records into a bean-counting program such as Quicken or Money. If that sounds appealing and your bank isn't already on the case, start looking for a replacement. Go for one you can access via the Internet rather than by dialling direct. That way you can manage your cash through a Web browser whether you're at home, work or in the cyber-café on top of Pik Kommunisma. For help finding a true online bank:

Online Banking Report www.netbanker.com
Qualisteam www.qualisteam.com

If you can resist the urge to daytrade away your inheritance, the Net should give you greater control over your financial future. You can research firms, plot trends, check live quotes, join tip lists and stock forums, track your portfolio live, trade shares and access news. By all means investigate a subscription service or two – at least for the free trial period – but unless you need split-second data feeds or "expert" timing advice you should be able to get by without paying. Start here:

Yahoo! UK http://quote.yahoo.co.uk

Apart from housing the Net's most exhaustive finance directory, Yahoo! pillages data from a bunch of the top finance sources and presents it all in a seamless, friendly format. Enter a stock code, for example, and you'll get all the beef from the latest ticker price to a summary of insider trades. In some markets stocks have their own forums, which, let's face it, are only there to spread rumours. In other words, be very sceptical of anything you read or that's sent to you in unsolicited email. Yahoo! is by no means complete nor necessarily the best in every area, so try a few of these as well:

Bloomberg www.bloomberg.co.uk
CBS MarketWatch http://cbs.marketwatch.com
Digital Look www.digitallook.com

the directory

money and banking

UK Banks and Building Societies

Online banks

Cahoot www.cahoot.com
First Direct (HSBC) www.firstdirect.com
Intelligent Finance www.if.com
Smile (Co-Op) www.smile.co.uk
Virgin One Account www.oneaccount.com

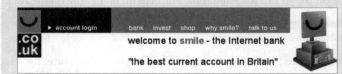

> ▶ account login   bank   invest   shop   why smile?   talk to us
> .co.uk
>
> welcome to smile - the Internet bank
>
> "the best current account in Britain"

Highstreet banks and building societies – online

Abbey www.abbey.com
Aliance & Leicester www.alliance-leicester.co.uk
Co-Operative Bank www.co-operativebank.co.uk
Halifax www.halifax.co.uk
HSBC www.hsbc.co.uk
Lloyds TSB www.lloydstsb.com
Nationwide www.nationwide.co.uk
Natwest www.nwolb.com
Barclays http://ibank.barclays.co.uk

And for a critical look at who's offering the best deals, see:

Find.co.uk www.find.co.uk/Top10/Online_Banks_Top_10

> **www.find.co.uk**   The leading internet directory for UK financial websites - since 1996   Home
>
> | home page | loans | credit cards | insurance | mortgages | investment | banking & savings | life & pensions | advice & information | business services |
>
> Credit Cards   Personal Loans   Car Insurance   Last Updated 28/04/04

198

Free Real Time Quotes www.freerealtime.com
Gay Financial Network www.gfn.com
Hemscott www.hemscott.net
Interactive Investor www.iii.co.uk
Microsoft MoneyCentral http://moneycentral.msn.com
Money Extra www.moneyextra.com
Raging Bull www.ragingbull.com
Sharepages www.sharepages.com
Thomson FN www.thomsonfn.com
Wall Street City www.wallstreetcity.com
Wall Street Research Net www.wsrn.com

You'll no doubt be after a broker next. As with banking, any broker or fund manager who's not setting up online probably doesn't deserve your business. In fact, many traders are dumping traditional brokers in favour of the exclusively online houses. **E★Trade** (www.etrade.co.uk), for example, offers discount brokerage in at least nine countries (click on "International" to find your local branch). But traditional brokers are catching on. Many have cut their commissions, and offer online services in line with the Internet competition, so it pays to shop around. You might find you prefer to research online and trade by phone. Compare brokers at

Gomez http://uk.gomez.com

For a British e-trading portal, try E-Trader UK:

Trader UK www.e-traderuk.com

A word of warning, though: some online brokers have experienced outages where they were unable to trade. So if the market crashes in a big way, it mightn't hurt to play safe and use the phone instead.

Advice Online
www.adviceonline.co.uk
Contact an independent financial advisor for help on everything from mortgages to PEP transfers.

the directory

Bank of England
www.bankofengland.co.uk
Keep tabs on financial policy decisions.

BigCharts
http://bigcharts.marketwatch.com
http://stockcharts.com
Whip up family-sized graphs of US stocks, mutual funds and market indices. Or if
you'd prefer them streaming at you live, proceed to:
www.livecharts.com
For UK charts, try:
www.advfn.com
www.citycomment.co.uk

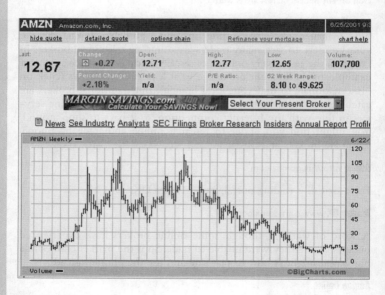

BillPay
www.billpayment.co.uk
Pay your electricity, gas and water bills over the Net with this new service from
Girobank.

200

the directory

Blay's Guides
www.blays.co.uk
Tracks and ranks finance rates across every UK market. Also links to hundreds of banking sites and investment products. For more rates, try:
www.buy.co.uk
www.moneygator.com
www.moneynet.co.uk

Bonehead Finance
http://ourworld.compuserve.com/homepages/Bonehead_Finance
No-nonsense financial basics for dummies.

British Bankers' Association
www.bankfacts.org.uk
Review the Banking Code, find a cash machine, convert currency and consult a glossary of banking terms.

Clearstation
http://clearstation.etrade.com
Run your stock picks through a succession of gruelling obstacle courses to weed out the weaklings, or simply copy someone else's portfolio.

Debt Advice
www.debtadvicecentre.co.uk
Get yourself out from the hole.

The Desktop Accountant
www.thedesktopaccountant.com
Advice and tips to help small businesses and freelancers navigate their way around the tax code.

Earnings Whispers
www.earningswhispers.com
When a stock price falls upon the release of higher-than-expected earnings, chances are that the expectations being "whispered" amongst traders prior to opening were higher than those circulated publicly. Here's where to find out what's being said behind your back.

Financial Planning Horizons
www.financial-planning.uk.com
Good, unbiased information on the full range of financial products available in the UK.

Financial Times
www.ft.com
Business news, commentary, delayed quotes and closing prices from London. It's free until you hit the archives.

the directory

Find
www.find.co.uk
The Financial Information Net Directory houses some 6000 links to UK financial sites, organized into categories like investment, insurance, information services, advice and dealing, bankings and savings, mortgages and loans, business services and life and pensions.

Foreign Exchange Rates
http://quote.yahoo.com/m3?u
www.xe.net/ucc
Round-the-clock rates, conversion calculators and intraday charts on pretty close to the full set of currencies. To chart further back, see:
http://pacific.commerce.ubc.ca/xr/plot.html

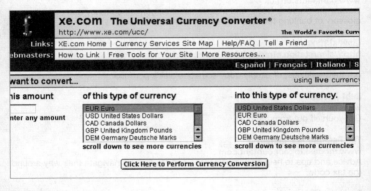

Frugal Corner
www.frugalcorner.com
Learn how to be thrifty from the experts.

FTSE
www.ftse.com
All the data and indices you could ever want.

HedgeWorld
www.hedgeworld.com
Allowing the average Joe a peek inside the secretive world of hedge funds.

Hoovers
www.hoovers.com
Research US, UK and European companies.

Tax Return

These days you can do your tax return online – it's easy. For more details and information on obtaining a logon ID, and to get tax information straight from the horse's mouth, go to:

Inland Revenue www.inlandrevenue.gov.uk

To find a qualified advisor, try:

The Chartered Institute of Taxation www.tax.org.uk

For a rough estimate of how much you'll have to pay, try:

UK Wage/Tax Calculator http://listen.to/taxman

For more help and advice with your tax return, as well as links to providers of tax calculating software, visit:

CAB Advice Guide www.adviceguide.org.uk/em/index/life/tax/tax_returns.htm
QCK www.tax-advice.qck.com
TaxBuddies www.taxbuddies.com

iCreditReport
www.icreditreport.com
Dig up any US citizen's credit ratings.

Investment FAQ
www.invest-faq.com
Learn the ropes from old hands.

InvestorWords
www.investorwords.com
Can't tell your hedge rate from your asking price? Brush up on your finance-speak here.

Island
www.island.com
See US equity orders queued up on dealers' screens.

MAXfunds
www.maxfunds.com
Great site that allows you to track the performance of mutual funds. You have to

the directory

register, but it's free. For more on managed funds and unit trusts, try Standard &
Poor's Find Services and TrustNet:
www.funds-sp.com
www.trustnet.com

Missing Money
www.missingmoney.com
www.findcash.com
Reclaim those US dollars you're owed.

MoneyChimp
www.moneychimp.com
Plain English primer in the mechanics of financial maths.

MoneyExtra
www.moneyworld.co.uk
Compare financial products and get the best deals.

Money Origami
http://members.cox.net/crandall11/money
It's not how much you earn – it's the way you fold it.

Motley Fool
www.fool.co.uk
Forums, tips, quotes and sound advice. More people telling you what to do with
your money at City Pigeon, Citywire and This Is Money:
www.citypigeon.co.uk
www.citywire.co.uk
www.thisismoney.com

Paypal
www.paypal.com
Arrange online payments through a third party. The payment method of choice for
many on Ebay.

Pension Sorter
www.pensionsorter.com
Protect yourself against the scandals of the 1980s with this site's impartial advice.
Also check out the Pension Advisory Service at:
www.opas.org.uk
For the Government's angle, try Pension Guide or the DWP's site:
www.pensionguide.gov.uk
www.dwp.gov.uk/lifeevent/penret

Screentrade
www.screentrade.co.uk
General insurance site, offering quotes from a range of insurers. Try also 1st Quote
and InsuranceWide:
www.1stquote.co.uk
www.insurancewide.co.uk

Tax & Accounting Sites Directory
www.taxsites.com
Links to everything you need to know about doling out your annual pound of flesh.

Technical Analysis Tutorials
www.e-analytics.com/techdir.htm
Beginner's guide to fortune-telling the markets using charts and indicators.

UK Insurance Guide
www.ukinsuranceguide.co.uk
Star ratings of nearly all of the UK's insurers.

Wall Street Journal Interactive
www.wsj.com
Not only is this online edition equal to the print one, its charts and data archives give it
an edge. That's why you shouldn't complain that it's not free. After all, if it's your type of
paper, you should be able to afford it, bigshot.

Museums and Galleries

Homepages of bricks-and-mortar museums

British Museum www.thebritishmuseum.ac.uk
Guggenheim www.guggenheim.org
The Hermitage www.hermitagemuseum.org
Louvre www.louvre.fr
Metropolitan Museum of Art www.metmuseum.org
Museo Del Prado http://museoprado.mcu.es
Museum of Modern Art www.moma.org
National Gallery www.nationalgallery.co.uk
National Portrait Gallery www.npg.org.uk
Natural History Museum www.nhm.ac.uk

the directory

Tate Gallery www.tate.org.uk
Uffizi Gallery www.uffizi.firenze.it
Victoria & Albert Museum www.vam.ac.uk

Artists

Leonardo da Vinci http://sunsite.dk/cgfa/vinci
Matisse www.ocaiw.com/matisse.htm
Michelangelo www.ibiblio.org/wm/paint/auth/michelangelo
Monet http://webpages.marshall.edu/~smith82/monet.html
Picasso www.tamu.edu/mocl/picasso
Rembrandt www.ibiblio.org/wm/paint/auth/rembrandt
Van Gogh www.vangoghgallery.com

ArtMuseum
www.artmuseum.net
Infrequent exhibitions of modern US classics.

Bitstreams
www.whitney.org/bitstreams
A fine exhibit of minimal digital art from New York's Whitney Museum, with downloadable art.

British Lawnmower Museum
www.lawnmowerworld.co.uk
SEE: the world's fastest lawnmower. SEE: Prince Charles's lawnmower. SEE: the water-cooled egg boiler lawnmower. SEE: Vanessa Feltz's lawnmower.

Dia Center for the Arts
www.diacenter.org
Web exclusives from "extraordinary" artists, plus the lowdown on the NY Dia Center's upcoming escapades.

The Exploratorium
www.exploratorium.edu
No substitute for visiting this great San Francisco museum in the flesh, but The Exploratorium's Website is filled with fun and educational sections on sports medicine, the solar system, the Hubble Telescope and the Panama Pacific Exposition.

Isometric Screenshots
http://whitelead.com/jrh/screenshots
An online exhibition by artist Jon Haddock in which he has rendered some of the

the directory

twentieth century's defining moments (the protests at Tiananmen Square, the beating of Rodney King, the assassination of Martin Luther King) in the visual style of video games.

Museum of Menstruation and Women's Health
www.mum.org
Its curator may be a man, but this is a rather weird and wonderful site that takes its subject pretty seriously.

Sulabh International Museum of Toilets
www.sulabhtoiletmuseum.org
There goes the neighbourhood.

24 Hour Museum
www.24hourmuseum.org.uk
Portal for British museums, with an excellent search feature which allows you to look for museums with food, baby changing facilities or that tie-in with national curriculum requirements. Also try MuseumNetwork or Museums Around the World:
www.museumnetwork.com
www.icom.org/vlmp/world.html
For galleries as well as museums see The Art Guide and The Gallery Channel:
www.artguide.org
www.thegallerychannel.com

Unusual Museums of the Internet
www.unusualmuseums.org
Homepage of the Unusual Museums Webring, your gateway to such exotic destinations as the Toilet Paper Museum, World of Crabs, Cigar Box Art and the Toilet Seat Art Museum.

Washington Banana Museum
www.geocities.com/NapaValley/1799
The world's greatest collection of banana ephemera. No plantains, please.

Web Gallery of Art
http://gallery.euroweb.hu
For fans of everything from Giotto frescoes to Rembrandt's *The Nightwatch*, this fantastic site houses digital reproductions of some eight thousand works from between 1150 and 1750.

Web Museum
www.southern.net/wm
Easily one of the best sites on the Web, the Web Museum hosts a fantasy collection of art – like having the Louvre, the Metropolitan Museum of Art, the Hermitage and the Prado all right around the corner. There is also an extensive glossary of terms, artist biographies and enlightening comment on each of the works displayed.

the directory

Music

If you're at all into music you've certainly come to the right place. Whether you want to hear it, read about it or watch it being performed you'll be swamped with options. If you're after a specific band, label or music genre, the Ultimate Band List on Artists Direct should be your first port of call:

Ultimate Band List www.ubl.com

Then try these directories:

About.com http://about.com/arts
Open Directory http://dmoz.org/Arts/Music
SonicNet www.sonicnet.com
Yahoo! http://launch.yahoo.com

As ever, if these fail to satisfy, try:

Google www.google.com

For an astoundingly complete music database spanning most popular genres, with bios, reviews, ratings, and keyword crosslinks to related sounds, sites, and online ordering, see:

All Music Guide www.allmusic.com

And don't overlook our own monthly album reviews and online guides to rock, classical and world music:

Rough Guides to Music www.roughguides.com/music

Much of the mainstream music press is already well established online. For the latest music news:

Artists Direct http://artistsdirect.com

You'll find thousands of archived reviews, charts, gig guides, band bios, selected features, shopping links, news, and various sound artefacts courtesy of these familiar beacons:

Billboard www.billboard.com
Blues and Soul www.bluesandsoul.co.uk
Dirty Linen www.dirtylinen.com
Folk Roots www.frootsmag.com
Mojo www.mojo4music.com
NME http://nme.com
Q www.q4music.com
Rolling Stone www.rollingstone.com
Spin www.spin.com
Vibe www.vibe.com

And if your concentration is up to it, MTV:

Europe www.mtveurope.com
UK www.mtv.co.uk

Don't buy a stereo component until you've consulted the world's biggest audio opinionbases:

AudioReview.com www.audioreview.com
AudioWeb www.audioweb.com
What Hi-Fi www.whathifi.com

Or if you wouldn't settle for less than a single-ended triode amp:

Audiophilia www.audiophilia.com
GlassWare www.glass-ware.com
Stereophile www.stereophile.com
Triode Guild www.meta-gizmo.com

Consult these directories for shops and other audio sites:

AudioWorld www.audioworld.com
Hifiheaven.com www.4music.net
UK Hi-Fi Dealers http://hifi.dealers.co.uk

African Music
www.africanmusic.org
World Music aficionados should make a beeline for this library, searchable by country or artist, and with an accompanying shopping area.

the directory

All About Jazz
www.allaboutjazz.com
Don't let the expensive corporate layout fool you, this American site doesn't just cover Kenny G. As its name suggests, it aims to deal with the entire spectrum of jazz from Anthony Braxton to John Scofield. That it succeeds is down to an easily navigable layout, a wealth of info and contributions from the biggest names in jazz journalism.

Ari's Simple List of Record Labels
http://recordlabels.nu/index.htm
Exactly what it says on the tin.

Art of the Mixed Tape
www.artofthemix.org
"If you have ever killed an afternoon making a mix, spent the evening making a cover, and then mailed a copy off to a friend after having made a copy for yourself, well, this is the site for you." Kind of says it all, really.

The Bad MIDI Museum
http://littleitaly.fortunecity.com/vatican/791/midi.htm
Not that even "good" MIDI doesn't suck.

Band Family Tree
www.bandfamilytree.com
Secure your place in pop music's genealogy

B-Boys.com
www.b-boys.com
Hip-hop portal with lots of multimedia content.

Boom Selection
http://boomselection.n3.net
The headquarters of the British bootleg mix scene.

The Breaks
www.the-breaks.com
Ever wondered what beat The Beastie Boys ripped off for "Shadrach" or who's sampled Isaac Hayes? This whistle-blowing website tears the lid off the record crates of hip-hop's most famous producers.

Classical Music on the Net
www.musdoc.com/classical
Gateway to the timeless.

Classical Net
www.classical.net
An excellent resource for the beginner, with guides to the basic repertoire and building a CD collection. More adventurous listeners may find it a bit wanting, however.

Corporate Anthems – IBM
www.digibarn.com/collections/songs/ibm-songs
What to whistle while you work. There are loads more of these little gems out there – if you find any, please let us know.

The Covers Project
http://covers.wiw.org
The musical version of Six Degrees of Kevin Bacon.

The Dance Music Resource
www.juno.co.uk
New and forthcoming dance releases for mail order, UK radio slots and a stacked directory.

Dancetech
www.dancetech.com
One-stop shop for techno toys and recording tips. For more on synths, try:
www.synthzone.com
www.sonicstate.com
For software downloads, guitar tabs and loads of other resources for musicians, try:
www.hitsquad.com

Dave D's Hip-Hop Corner
www.daveyd.com
Hip-hop portal, more at:
www.rapstation.com

the directory

Buying records online

Shopping for music is another area where the Net not only equals but out-shines its terrestrial counterparts. Apart from the convenience of not having to tramp across town, you can find almost anything on current issue, whether or not it's released locally, and in many cases preview album tracks in RealAudio. You might save money, too, depending on where you buy, whether you're hit with tax and how the freight costs stack up. Consider splitting your order if duty becomes an issue.

The biggest hitch you'll find is when stock is put on back order. Web operators can boast a huge catalogue simply because they order everything on the fly, putting you at the mercy of their distributors. The trouble is your entire order might be held up by one item. The better shops check their stock levels before confirming your order and follow its progress until delivery.

As far as where to shop goes, that depends on your taste, but, unless your tastes are very esoteric, you can't go too far wrong with most of the blockbusters:

Amazon www.amazon.co.uk
AudioStreet www.audiostreet.co.uk
BOL www.uk.bol.com
HMV www.hmv.com
101 CD www.101cd.com
Tower Records http://uk.towerrecords.com
Virgin Megastore www.virginmegastores.co.uk

Or, if you're after something more obscure, you'll find no shortage of options under the appropriate Yahoo categories or at: www.offitsface.com/links.html Like these, for example:

CDEmusic www.cdemusic.org
This American site carries not only electronic music from a time when it was made only by men in white labcoats but specialist books, music software and seriously sexy musical equipment like the Moog Moogerfooger processor.

CD Wow www.cd-wow.com
Cheap chart CDs (£9 at press time). See also:
www.play.com

CyberCD www.cybercd.de • www.musicexpress.com
German outfits with enormous catalogues, though not so cheap.

Descarga www.descarga.com
If you are a fan of Latin music, you must, must check out this site. ¡Sabroso!

Dusty Groove www.dustygroove.com
The website of this renowned Chicago record shop created the blueprint for
Internet-based record mail order services, and they're still doing it better than
anyone else. If you're interested in hip-hop, funk, soul, reggae, Latin or
obscure soundtracks, it's nearly impossible to leave the site empty-handed.

Forced Exposure www.forcedexposure.com
This Massachusetts distributor is the colossus of underground music, and its
informative, easy-to-use website is another jewel in its crown. Along with an
excellent search feature (which, unlike too many mail order sites, searches
the personnel lists as well as the main artist name), the reviews are opinionated and informative.

Global Electronic Music Market http://gemm.com
One-point access to over two million new and used records from almost two
thousand sources. See also:
www.secondspin.com

Hard to find records www.htfr.com
Record-finding agency that specializes in house, hip-hop, soul and disco vinyl.

Other Music www.othermusic.com
Since opening in 1996 opposite Tower Records, New York City's bastion of the
weird, wacky and just plain great has made a name for itself as one of
America's best record emporia. Divided into sections like "Out" (avant-garde
music from this world and others), "In" (1990s indie rock) and "Le Decadanse"
(sophisto pop), its site embodies the virtues that made it so good in the first
place: friendly, helpful and attitude-free.

Penny Black www.pennyblackmusic.com
Indie pop, punk and electronica.

Record Finder www.recordfinders.com
Deleted vinyl, including over 200,000 45s.

continued overleaf

---

the directory

music

Buying records online (continued)

Rough Trade www.roughtrade.com
The website of London's underground landmark is housed in a slick designer package. It would benefit from less time-consuming graphics, but the stock is excellent and the prices, while not the bargain level of the giants, ain't bad. Additional bonuses include an old t-shirt section, chat rooms and downloads – plus there's no tricky spiral staircase to navigate.

Sandbox Automatic www.sandboxautomatic.com
Without a doubt the best source for independent hip-hop on the Net. There are no bells and whistles, but what a choice.

Secondsounds www.secondsounds.com
Buying used CDs online may be even more risky than in an actual shop because you can't check out the merchandise, but if you're after a bargain this site is hard to beat.

Sterns African Records Centre www.sternsmusic.com
The UK's number-one retailer of world music does a fine job online as well.

For a listing of price comparison agents, see Shopping (p.291).

Cooking your own CD

Fancy whipping up your own custom CD but don't have the equipment? Simply run through the catalogue, preview what looks good, submit your track listing, and they'll burn it to disc:

CD Now www.cdnow.com
Emusic www.emusic.com

Detritus
www.detritus.net
An excellent website devoted to the fringes working on "recycled culture".

Dial-the-Truth Ministries
www.av1611.org
So why does Satan get all the good music?

Dictionaraoke
www.dictionaraoke.org
Hilarious MIDI/Talking Dictionary versions of all your favourite pop hits.

Digizine
www.digidesign.com/digizine
E-zone dedicated to Pro Tools, *the* music editing tool.

Disco-Disco.com
www.disco-disco.com/index.html
Where disco is more than just afro wigs and flares. More strobe-lit remembrances at:
www.discomusic.com/index.html

DJ University
http://dju.prodj.com
Become a wedding spinner.

Donna's Long and Short of It
www.metal-sludge.com/LongShort.htm
The most essential music resource on the Net: Donna and her gaggle of groupies give you the lowdown on the vitals of 150-plus heavy metal gods.

dotmusic
www.dotmusic.com
Top source of UK and global music news, weekly charts, and new releases in RealAudio. See also:
www.music3w.com

The Droplift Project
www.droplift.org
Join in some plunderphonic fun by smuggling some avant-garde sampladelic CDs onto the shelves of major chain retailers.

Electronic Musical Instruments
www.obsolete.com/120_years
From the ondes martenot to the sampler, this online museum is the liveliest, least techie source of information on the rapidly expanding world of music technology.

Everything Starts With an E
www.everythingstartswithe.co.uk
Sorted old skool rave site with vintage mixes from the early 1990s.

Evil Music
www.evilmusic.com
Don't know the difference between Black Metal and Doom Metal, or what constitutes Original Death Metal as opposed to Brutal Death Metal? Let Spinoza Ray Prozac be your guide to the dark world of the Metal underground.

the directory

Fat Lace
www.fat-lace.com

The Internet presence of the hilarious "Magazine for ageing B-boys" contains mostly copy from the print version which covers hip-hop with an irreverent slant only possible in the UK. An added bonus is the Random Old School Name Generator for all the Lord Disco Loves out there.

Freestyling
www.freestyling.com

Fancy yourself as the next Tupac or Jay-Z? Post your best rhyme here and wait to be discovered. For more traditional battling, try Ughh:
www.ughh.com

Funk45.com
www.funk45.com

A great entrée into the murky world of deep funk collecting. The site is chock-full of MP3s and RealAudio files of hopelessly obscure funk records. The only catch is that the files are only one minute long, with the aim being to introduce people to this arcane world rather than destroying its informal economy.

Funky Groovy Lexicon
www.funk.ch/funk-lexikon.htm

Over 322 pages (in PDF format), the FGL catalogues nearly everything that can be construed as funky, from 100 Proof Aged in Soul to Zzebra. There's also a gallery of suave cats in dashikis and killer Afros. Believe it or not, it's from Switzerland.

Garage Music
www.garagemusic.co.uk

If you don't live in the East End and want to keep up with what the pirates are playing, click here for the latest news, events and downloads. See also:
www.dubplate.net

Get Out There
www.getoutthere.bt.com

Expose your unsung talents or listen to other unsigned acts. More audition opportunities at:
www.aandronline.com
For tips on getting signed try:
www.getsigned.com

Gracenote
www.cddb.com
Automatically supplies track listings for the CDs playing in your PC drive.

Gramophone
www.gramophone.co.uk
There is no better site for serious classical music aficionados. The Web home of *Gramophone* magazine boasts access to its database of 25,000 CD reviews. Need more reasons to visit? How about audio clips, the option to buy from the site, links, listings, glossary, artist bios and feature articles?

Harmony Central
http://www.harmonycentral.com
Directory and headspace for musicians of all persuasions.

Hyperreal
www.hyperreal.org
Perhaps the godfather of all music sites, Hyperreal has been going since 1992. It's a one-stop window shop for all things rave and
Ambient. Erowid's Psychoactive Vaults host the raver's version of the *Physician's Desk Reference* – a library of info on mind-altering substances.

Independent Underground Music Archive
www.iuma.com
Full-length tracks and bios from thousands of unsigned and indie-label underground musicians.

Jazz
www.jazzreview.com
www.allaboutjazz.com
www.downbeat.com
Bottomless drawer of beard-stroking delights.

Kareoke.com
www.kareoke.com
Sing along in the privacy of your own home.

Kompaktkiste
www.kompaktkiste.de
The bluffer's guide to electronic music: an extensive list of CDs of electronic music organized by artist with track listings and running times. It makes no judgements, but if you're looking for that-hard-to-find Phthalocyanine remix, come here first.

the directory

Large Hot Pipe Organ
www.lhpo.org
Thrill to the throb of the world's first MIDI-controlled, propane-powered, explosion organ.

Launch.com
http://launch.yahoo.com
Thousands of music videos, audio channels, record reviews and chat forums.

Libretto List
http://php.indiana.edu/~lneff/libmlist.html
A fantastic resource for opera buffs, this site has links to just about every public domain libretto available on the Net.

London Musicians Collective
www.l-m-c.org.uk
The LMC has been promoting the cause of improvised music in the Big Smoke for over a quarter of a century. Their site features content from their journal, *Resonance*, streaming audio from their radio show and information on studio facilities. For more sonic experiments, see:
www.planktone.co.uk

planktone is your friend...

Lyrics Search Engine
http://lyrics.astraweb.com
Finding song lyrics on the Web is a science constantly fraught with difficulty due to
copyright laws, but for now this site reigns. See also:
www.thesonglyrics.com
www.lyricstime.com

The Manual
www.klf.de/online/books/bytheklf/manual.htm
Fancy trying pop superstardom? Have a glance at the essential guide to pop
superstardom, written by the ace pranksters in The KLF.

Metal Sudge
www.metal-sludge.com
Heavy metal portal that treats the genre with the dignity and respect it deserves.

MIDI Farm
www.midifarm.com
Synthesized debasements of pop tunes, TV themes and film scores. More cheesy
listening at MIDI World:
www.midi-world.net

Minidisc.org
www.minidisc.org
Keep in tune with Sony's troubled Minidisc format.

Mr Lucky
http://www.mrlucky.com
Get smooth with rhythm 'n' booze.

the directory

Niceup
www.niceup.com
Probably the most irie reggae site on the Net, Niceup contains discographies, articles on topics like "Studio One Riddims", a lyrics archive, histories, news and a patois dictionary.

Online Guitar Archive
www.olga.net
A truly awesome site for guitarists and bassists. No more scurrying through back issues of *Guitar Player* for tablature for Blue Öyster Cult's "Godzilla" – OLGA boasts some 40,000 tabs.

Opprobrium
www.info.net.nz/opprobrium
No longer printed on paper, the legendary *Opprobrium* has been strictly digital ever since editor Nick Cain moved to London. Nevertheless, its coverage of avant jazz, Japanoise, Improv and radical minimalism remains almost peerless.

Original Hip Hop Lyrics Archive
www.ohhla.com
Mind-blowingly complete archive of all of your favourite rhymes.

Perfect Sound Forever
www.furious.com/perfect
Calling itself "the online magazine with the warped attitudes", PSF is one of the best music sites on the Net. Although most of the articles are straight interview transcripts and don't take advantage of the Web format, the writing on left field heroes is passionate and informative.

Pitchfork Media
www.pitchforkmedia.com
Indie news, reviews and features and more.

Rap Dictionary
www.rapdict.org
Can't understand your teenage son anymore? Log on here, dun, and you'll get the 411.

Roadie.net
www.roadie.net
No backstage pass necessary.

Rocklist
www.rocklist.net
Quarter of a decade's worth of best-of-the-year lists from the top mags.

Scratch Simulator
www.turntables.de
Can't afford a pair of SL 1200s? Practise your reverse orbit scratches and beat juggling here, or at Infinite Wheel:
www.infinitewheel.com

Shareware Music Machine
www.hitsquad.com/smm
Tons of shareware music players, editors and composition tools, for every platform.

Sheet Music Archive
www.sheetmusicarchive.net
A great resource of copyright-free downloadable sheet music. You can only download two scores each day – but that shouldn't be a problem, unless you are a very fast learner.

Show and Tell Music
www.showandtellmusic.com
Albums much cooler than anything you own.

Bizarre Records

American Song Poem Archives www.aspma.com
Archive of the bizarre mid-century phenomenon where studio hacks set music to the lyrics of ordinary Joes – resulting in some of the weirdest records ever.

Frank's Vinyl Museum http://franklarosa.com/$spindb.query.new.vinyl
Exhibition of charity shop flotsam, including such timeless classics as *Ken Demko Live at the Lamplighter Inn* and an album of Beatles covers done by dogs.

The Internet Museum of Flexi/Cardboard/Oddities
www.wfmu.org/MACrec
Records made out of metal, souvenirs from the Empire State Building and other curios.

Songs in the Key of Z www.keyofz.com/keyofz
Irwin Chusid's fantastic introduction to the world of outsider music. More at www.incorrectmusic.com

the directory

Smithsonian Institution
www.si.edu
Although this site is as gigantic as the famous American museum itself, if you're interested in folk music (from both America and the rest of the world) it's an absolute paradise, with info on their Folkways record label, webcasts, galleries and articles (augmented with RealAudio files).

Songplayer
www.songplayer.com
Can't read music and still want to play guitar like Hendrix or keyboards like Keith Emerson? Try this music tuition site which has some four thousand songs in its files, and there are no cumbersome staves, bars or clefs to wrestle with.

Sonic Net
www.sonicnet.com
Big-name live cybercasts, streaming video channels, chats, news and reviews.

Sony
www.sony.com
Think about everything that Sony flogs. Now imagine it all squeezed under one roof.

Soul City
www.soulcity.ndo.co.uk
Listen to hundreds of 1960s and Northern Soul clips.

Soulman's World of Beats
www.worldofbeats.com/old_site
E-zine for all the crate diggers, with articles focusing on the samples from all of your favourite hip-hop records. More vinyl obsession at:
www.breakz4dayz.com
www.samplehead.com

Sounds Online
www.soundsonline.com
Preview loops and samples, free in RealAudio. Pay to download studio quality. If it's effects you're after, try:
www.sounddogs.com

Taxi
http://www.taxi.com
Online music A&R service. And guess what? You and your plastic kazoo are just what they're looking for.

Theremin Resources
www.thereminworld.com
All the history of those "Good Vibrations", and a whole lot more. To build your own, see:
http://home.att.net/~theremin1

This Day in Music
www.thisdayinmusic.com
Find out which member of the Bay City Rollers shares your birthday, and other essential music trivia.

Uncensored Celebrity Outtakes
www.fadetoblack.com/outtakes
Priceless recordings by William Shatner and the legendary tape of Linda McCartney singing "Hey Jude".

Urban Sounds
www.urbansounds.com
Excellent, well-planned and designed electronica site from the US. The Minimalism issue features hot names on the underground and is sexily intercut with Rem Koolhaas sketches and Donald Judd reproductions.

the directory

MP3s

Unlike every music delivery system since the development of 33⅓ and 45 rpm records, the MP3 format was not forced upon consumers by the record industry. Short for "MPEG-1 audio layer 3", MP3 is a file format that allows compression of recorded music without a significant degradation in sound quality, and it has become the standard way of storing music on the Internet. In order to make the most of MP3 you need a PC or Mac with at least 32MB of RAM, a 56K modem, lots of room on your hard drive and, if you have an older machine, you might have to install a sound card. You will also need some MP3 player software such as **Soundjam** for a Mac or **Winamp** or **RealJukebox** for PC, though you will probably find that your computer can already handle the files using built-in tools such as **Windows Media Player** or Apple's **iTunes** on a Mac. For more on software, see **MP3.com**, which as well as lots of music has links to all the downloadable MP3 players and lots of information for beginners:

MP3.com www.mp3.com

You shouldn't have any trouble finding MP3 music online, though not everything you'll find is legal. The legal side consists mainly of pay-to-download tracks and free previews authorised by the record label. These tend to be from acts that can't get radio airplay and are eager for exposure, but that's not necessarily the case. As for pay-to-download, you can usually preview pay tracks in a lo-fi format, such as RealAudio or streaming MP3, before purchasing. Try these sites for legal MP3s:

All of MP3 www.allofmp3.com
Artist Direct www.artistdirect.com
AudioGalaxy www.audiogalaxy.com
ClickMusic www.clickmusic.co.uk
Dmusic www.dmusic.com
eClassical www.eclassical.com
Epitonic www.epitonic.com
IUMA www.iuma.com
Launch.com www.launch.com
Liquid Audio www.liquid.com
Listen.com www.listen.com
Peoplesound www.peoplesound.com

There are also subscription services that provide a certain number of downloads (usually combined with lots of lo-fi streams) for a monthly fee. For example:

MusicNet www.musicnet.com
Pressplay www.pressplay.com
Rhapsody www.listen.com

So what about the illegal side? Basically, many programs allow computer users to "rip" music – convert a track on a CD into an MP3 file. Once that's done, they can distribute their files around the world – and download other people's – without any record company mediation. Now that millions of people are doing just this, almost any music can be found for free online by those willing to break the law.

Most illegal MP3s are exchanged not via the Web but via peer-to-peer file-sharing networks. These aren't illegal in themselves, but they are mostly used to illegally share music (plus software and film) without the copyright holder's consent. To connect to a network and search for files, a user simply needs an appropriate program for that network. The four biggest networks are accessible with:

Emule www.emule-project.net
KaZaA Lite www.kazaalite.com
WinMX www.winmx.com
XoloX www.xolox.nl

Other software allows users to share files via instant messaging software. For example, Madster takes advantage of AOL Instant Messenger:

Madster www.madster.com

Some file-sharers claim that their activities will ultimately benefit musicians by removing the corporate domination of an art form and allowing wider audiences to sample their works. Naturally, the record industry – led by the Record Industry Association of America – are unconvinced and have tried to put a stop to free file exchanges, so far with very little success. And it's not just pop stars and big business that are complaining. Independent musicians, too, are worried about their royalties. Read various points of view at:

continued overleaf

the directory

MP3s (continued)

Coalition for the Future of Music www.futureofmusic.org
Free Music Philosophy www.ram.org/ramblings/philosophy/fmp.html
RIAA www.riaa.com

To learn the news on the audio compression format destined to replace MP3, see:

Advanced Audio Coding www.aac-audio.com

The Apple Music Store

Finally, there's the Apple Music Store, a web-based music download site which can only be accessed by using Apple's iTunes software. Once you have the program installed you can register your payment details with the store and start browsing the music and eBooks on offer directly from the iTunes program. Though this was once strictly the domain of US Apple Mac users, and more often than not those that owned an iPod, the store is now available to both UK credit card holders and PC owners. For the full story, visit:

Apple.com www.apple.com/itunes/store

Alternatively, pick up a copy of *The Rough Guide to The iPod, iTunes and Music Online*.

WholeNote
www.wholenote.com
Guitar resources and chat boards. For live lessons, see:
www.riffinteractive.com

The Wire
www.thewire.co.uk
Subtitled "Adventures in Modern Music", the online home of the British avant-garde music magazine *The Wire* features in-depth articles from past issues on a pantheon of underground gods and goddesses, and a comprehensive set of links to set you exploring the labyrinthine demimonde of experimental music.

Nature

3D Insects
www.ento.vt.edu/~sharov/3d/3dinsect.html
Whizz around a selection of 3D bugs. They're not real insects but at least they don't have pins through their backs. For a bigger range of bug bios, see:
http://insects.org

African Wildlife Foundation
www.awf.org
Great site covering everything from the aardvark to the zebra.

Animal Diversity Web
http://animaldiversity.ummz.umich.edu
Database of animal history, classification, distribution and conservation from the University of Michigan. More at Natureserve:
www.natureserve.org

Aquatic Network
www.aquanet.com
A good site promoting sustainable aquaculture, with some great photography and solid information saving it from being too earnest.

ARKive
www.arkive.org
Electronic archive of the world's endangered species.

the directory

Birding
http://birding.about.com
www.camacdonald.com/birding
http://dmoz.org/Recreation/Birding
Birds are such regional critters that one site couldn't hope to cover them all. Use these to find the chirpiest one on your block.

Birds of Britain
www.birdsofbritain.co.uk
Webzine devoted to our fine feathered friends, with an illustrated guide of around a hundred species.

Cetacea.org
www.cetacea.org
Excellent encyclopedic source of information on whales, dolphins and porpoises.

Dinosaur Interplanetary Gazette
www.dinosaur.org
It may be as slow and cumbersome as a brontosaurus stuck in the LaBrea tar pits, but patience does pay off with a wealth of information and features.

The Electronic Zoo
http://netvet.wustl.edu/e-zoo.htm
Up and running since 1993, this virtual menagerie is the best collection of animal-related links on the Web.

EMBL Reptile Database
www.embl-heidelberg.de/~uetz/LivingReptiles.html
Slither through for info on everything from turtles to amphisbaenae.

eNature.com
www.enature.com
Vibrant field guides to North American flora and fauna.

Field Trips
www.field-guides.com/vft/index.htm
A neat idea, if not perfectly executed: visit this site and take virtual field trips involving deserts, oceans, hurricanes, sharks, fierce creatures, salt marshes, volcanoes and other natural wonders of the world.

Forces of Nature
http://library.thinkquest.org/C003603
Thinkquest's student-designed website devoted to avalanches, droughts, landslides, earthquakes and other natural disasters.

ForestWorld
www.forestworld.com
http://forests.org
Timber tales from both sides of the 'dozer.

Great Cats of the World
www.greatcatsoftheworld.com
The homepage of the Bridgeport Nature Center in Texas functions as a mini-ency-clopedia of lions, tigers, leopards and cougars.

Insects on the Web
www.insects.org
Definitely not one for your little girl, this excellent educational resource of creepy-crawlies features some rather too detailed photography of everyone's least favourite bugs.

Mr Winkle
www.mrwinkle.com
Okay, so how cute is Mr Winkle? But is he really real?

Nessie on the Net
www.lochness.co.uk
Watch the Loch Ness webcam, spot the monster and win £1000.

Predator Urines
www.predatorpee.com
Bewitch neighbouring Jack Russells with a dab of bobcat balm or true blue roo poo:
www.roopooco.com

Sea turtle migration-tracking
www.cccturtle.org/satwelc.htm
Adopt a bugged sea reptile and follow its trail.

World Wildlife Fund
http://www.worldwildlife.org.uk
Teach your kids that the WWF isn't all about pile drivers and steroid cases in skimpy shorts. More animal lovers at the World Society for the Protection of Animals and the Royal Society for the Protection of Animals:
www.wspa.org.uk
www.rspca.org.uk

News, Newspapers and Magazines

Now that almost every magazine and newspaper on the globe from *Ringing World* (www.ringingworld.co.uk) to the *Falkland Island News* (www.sartma.com) is discharging daily content onto the Net, it's beyond this guide to do much more than list a few of the notables and then point you in the right direction for more. The simplest way to find your favourite read would be to look for its address in a recent issue. Failing that, try entering its name into a subject guide or search engine. If you don't have a title name and would prefer to browse by subject or region, try:

Open Directory http://dmoz.org/News
Yahoo! http://dir.yahoo.com/News_and_Media

Some newspapers replicate themselves word for word online, but most provide enough for you to live without giving you the complete paper edition. Still, that's not bad considering they're generally free online before the paper even hits the stands. Apart from whatever proportion of their print they choose to put online, they also tend to delve deeper into their less newsy areas such as travel, IT, entertainment and culture. Plus they often bolster this with exclusive content such as breaking news, live sports coverage, online shopping, opinion polls and discussion groups. In most cases they'll also provide a way to search and retrieve archives, though this might incur a charge. There are also a few sites that index multiple news archives, again usually at a price. Such as:

Electric Library www.elibrary.com
FindArticles.com www.findarticles.com

NewsLibrary www.newslibrary.com
Northern Light www.nlsearch.com

A few of the more popular news bugles, to get you started:

Arab News www.arabnews.com
Christian Science Monitor www.csmonitor.com
Daily Mail www.dailymail.co.uk
Daily Mail & Guardian www.mg.co.za
Economist www.economist.com
Evening Standard www.thisislondon.co.uk
Express www.express.co.uk
Financial Times www.ft.com
Guardian www.guardian.co.uk
The Hindu www.hinduonline.com
Independent www.independent.co.uk
International Herald Tribune www.iht.com
Irish News www.irishnews.com
LA Times www.latimes.com
Mirror www.mirror.co.uk
Le Monde www.lemonde.fr
National Enquirer www.nationalenquirer.com
National Geographic News http://news.nationalgeographic.com
News of the World www.newsoftheworld.co.uk
Newsweek www.newsweek.com
NY Times www.nytimes.com
Observer www.observer.co.uk
El País www.elpais.es
Scotsman www.scotsman.com
South China Morning Post www.scmp.com
La Stampa www.lastampa.it
Sun www.thesun.co.uk
Tehelka www.tehelka.com
Telegraph www.telegraph.co.uk
Time Daily www.time.com
Times www.timesonline.co.uk
Times of India http://timesofindia.indiatimes.com
USA Today www.usatoday.com
Village Voice www.villagevoice.com

the directory

Washington Post www.washingtonpost.com
Weekly World News www.weeklyworldnews.com

Like much you do online, reading news is addictive. You'll know you're hooked when you find yourself checking into newswires throughout the day to monitor moving stories. Try these for breaking news:

Ananova www.ananova.com
Associated Press http://wire.ap.org
BBC http://news.bbc.co.uk
CNN www.cnn.com
ITN www.itn.co.uk
NBC www.msnbc.com
Reuters www.reuters.com
Sky www.sky.com
Wired News www.wired.com

REUTERS
NEWS AND FINANCIAL INTELLIGENCE FROM THE WORLD LEADER

HOME   FINANCE   NEWS   Symbol ◆ _____   QUOTE   News ◆

REUTERS.COM
Finance
News

REUTERS RawVideo

Regulators to Examine U.S. Market Structure

Thu June 5, 11:39 PM ET

By Deepa Babington

NEW YORK (Reuters) - The head of the top U.S. markets regulator said on Thursday his agency would review the system of self-regulation that some have blamed for not preventing the brokerage and accounting scandals of the last year. **More...**

Or perhaps best of all, use a free news aggregator, which taps into several sources simultaneously. These ones are good for UK content:

Google News UK http://news.google.co.uk
NewsNow www.newsnow.co.uk

News tickers

News tickers place a thin ticker-tape-like strip along the top or bottom of the Desktop or sometimes a floating panel, which, depending on the ticker you have, displays a continuous trickle of headlines, share prices, weather reports, etc. More often than not they are downloadable from, and updated by, one particular site, such as the BBC's, but there are also news aggregating tickers available which draw from multiple news sources. They work best with an always-on connection, but, the best thing about these little utilities is that they are free.

BBC Newsline www.bbc.co.uk/newsline
CoolTick (stock ticker) www.cooltick.com
Desktop News www.desktopnews.com
Weather tickers http://weather.about.com/cs/weathertools
WorldFlash www.worldflash.com

Yahoo News UK http://uk.news.yahoo.com

But there's plenty more at:

Arts & Letters Daily www.aldaily.com
Asia Observer www.asiaobserver.com
FastAsia (Asia) www.fastasia.com
NewsHub www.newshub.com
Russian Story www.russianstory.com
TotalNews www.totalnews.com

If you want to search news blogs (see p.236), probably the best way is to use:

DayPop www.daypop.com

To find more specialist publications, you may want to try a directory

the directory

of newspapers and news organizations on the Web, which will help you track down everything from Bulgarian National Radio to Zambian broadsheets.

The Paper Boy www.thepaperboy.com
NewsLink http://newslink.org
Editor & Publisher www.mediainfo.com
Metagrid www.metagrid.com
NewsDirectory www.newsdirectory.com
Online Newspapers www.onlinenewspapers.com
Publist www.publist.com

As for magazines, most maintain a site but they're typically more of an adjunct to the print than a substitute. Still, some are worth checking out, especially if they archive features and reviews or break news between issues. Again, check a recent issue for an address, or a directory such as:

The Magazine Boy www.themagazineboy.com

If you'd rather subscribe to the paper edition, try:

iSUBSCRIBE www.isubscribe.co.uk

Naturally, there's no shortage of tech news online:

NewsLinx www.newslinx.com
SiliconValley www.siliconvalley.com
Tech News www.news.com
TechWeb www.techweb.com
ZD Network News www.zdnet.com

Or for For e-business news:

InternetNews www.internetnews.com

AlterNet
www.alternet.org
Roundup of almost all of America's alternative weekly papers.

American Newspeak
www.scn.org/news/newspeak
Celebrating the arts of doublethink, spin, media coaching and other ways to mangle meaning.

Crayon
www.crayon.net
Most of the major portals such as Excite, Yahoo! and MSN also allow you to create a custom news page that draws from several sources – though none does it quite so thoroughly as Crayon. Infobeat does similar things but delivers by email:
www.infobeat.com

Electric Library
www.elibrary.com
A great resource that allows you to view full text versions of some seven million articles, books, pictures, TV and radio transcripts. Unfortunately you have to pay $59.95 a year for the privilege.

Inside
www.inside.com
Media news with a heavy US slant.

A Journalist's Guide to the Internet
http://reporter.umd.edu
No design whatsoever, but a useful set of links to resources for journalists. More for hacks at:
www.journaliststoolbox.com
www.cyberjournalist.net
http://mediapoint.press.net

A Journalist's Guide to the Internet
By Christopher Callahan - University of Maryland - College of Journalism

Maps Sources Directories | Courts & The Law | Federal Govt. | Profnet & E-Mail

Records & FOIA | Business & Non-Profits | State Govt. | Listservs

Online Newspapers | Politics | Search Tools | Newsgroups

the directory

E-zines

"E-zines" are magazines that only exist online or are delivered by email. But because almost any regularly updated webpage or blog fits this description, the term has lost much of its currency. Although most e-zines burn out as quickly as they appear, a few of the pioneers are still kicking on.

For more, try browsing a directory at:

http://dmoz.org/News/Magazines_and_E-zines
www.ezine-dir.com
http://zinos.com

ABC All 'Bout Computers http://personal-computer-tutor.com/abc
Loads of handy PC tips, tricks and advice.

Drudge Report www.drudgereport.com
The shock bulletin that set off the Lewinsky avalanche. A one-hit wonder perhaps, but still a bona fide tourist attraction on the info goat track.

Future File http://futurefile.com
Thought-provoking e-zine portal from technocrat Todd Maffin, featuring ideas and trends to look for in the next decade.

Gurl.com www.gurl.com
Zine dedicated to hip young things pitched somewhere between the original *Sassy* and *Jane*.

IGN www.ign.com/affiliates/index.html
IGN (Internet Gaming Network) treads similar – though generally tamer – ground to UGO, partnering mostly with high-quality gaming, sci-fi, wrestling and comic sites.

MediaLens
www.medialens.org
Suspicious of our "free" press? You will be once you've visited this site.

Moreover
www.moreover.com/news
The best free service for searching current or recent stories across hundreds of international news sources. Also try News Index and What the Papers Say:
www.newsindex.com
www.whatthepaperssay.co.uk

The Music Box www.musicbox-online.com
A great music ezine, with a definite slant toward rock, indie and alt-country.

NTK www.ntk.net
Sarcastic high-tech media magazine. For geeky Popbitch (see Gossip) fans.

The Register www.theregister.com
The best source for daily tech news straight to your inbox.

Salon www.salon.com
The real e-zine success story. It spans the arts, business, politics, lifestyle and technology in a style that's both smart and breezy.

Slate http://slate.msn.com
Microsoft's long-suffering Slate marks similar territory to Salon, but succeeds more in being terribly dull.

Spiked www.spiked-online.com
Caustic, political e-zine from former *Living Marxism* supremo Mick Hume.

Suck www.suck.com
Arguably the only e-zine that ever mattered, Suck sat in a smug class all by itself. Its archives are still worth reading, if not for its cocked eye on all that's wired and painfully modern then at least for Terry Colon's cartoons.

Underground Online www.ugo.com
Big men's magazine-style network devoted to music, wrestling, film, TV, books, technology and so on.

Like someone to monitor the Web and assorted newswires for mention of your product or misdeeds? Try:
www.webclipping.com

MyVillage
www.myvillage.com
Online community with a heavy emphasis on local news. Best in and around London, but slowly increasing their profile across the country.

the directory

news, newspapers and magazines

The Onion
www.theonion.com
News the way it was meant to be.

This Is True
www.thisistrue.com
Randy Cassingham's weekly column of preposterous-but-true news stories and
headlines, collated from the major wire services.

Wireless Flash News Service
www.flashnews.com
News service specializing in pop culture stories, featuring some of the least news-
worthy headlines in history.

World Press Review
www.worldpress.org
Keeping tabs on the people who keep tabs on us. Also keep an eye on News Watch:
www.newswatch.org

Outdoor Pursuits

Birdlinks
www.birdlinks.co.uk
Gateway to the world of birdwatching. More to look at on:
http://birding.about.com
www.camacdonald.com/birding
http://dmoz.org/Recreation/Birding
www.birdsofbritain.co.uk

The Butterfly Website
www.butterflywebsite.com
The Monarch of butterfly sites, with galleries, lists of gardens and butterfly gardens and loads of information on biology, conservation and behaviour.

Camp Sites
www.camp-sites.co.uk
www.campinguk.com
Find a place to pitch your tent in the UK.

Go Fishing
www.go-fishing.co.uk
Your complete angling resource. Other sites that would make Isaak Walton proud:
Angler's Net www.anglersnet.co.uk
Angling News www.angling-news.co.uk
Sea Angler http://sea-angler.org

Great Outdoor Recreation Pages
www.gorp.com
Ignore all the multivitamin and SUV adverts and the American bias because this is the best outdoors site on the Web. The superlative how-to pages alone make it

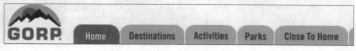

the directory

worth navigating the pop-up ads, plus there are good articles, trail finders, destination guides, discussion groups and photo galleries, and you can book holidays and buy gear from the site.

Ramblers' Association
www.ramblers.org.uk
All the latest news on walking and other pedestrian pursuits. For more info, take your browser on a stroll over to Walking World or Walking Britain:
www.walkingworld.com
www.walkingbritain.co.uk

Rock Climbing in the UK
www.ukcrags.com
Great resource for British rock climbers, with news, articles, webcams, events listings, routes and crag descriptions. More handholds can be found at Climb Guide:
www.climb-guide.com
And for all things bouldering related, check out this US site's links page:
www.bouldering.com

Pets

About Veterinary Medicine
http://vetmedicine.about.com
About's vet pages are an excellent resource for pet owners worried about their moggie or pet lizard and are filled with advice, news, disease indexes and forums.

The Aviary
www.theaviary.com/ci.shtml
Everything you'd ever want to know about companion birds – and then some.

Barbara's Canine Café
www.k9treat.com
Only In America part 346: If your mutt's got a food allergy or you just want to get your hound a "celebration gift basket" made from all-natural ingredients, look no further.

Cat Tips
www.networkstudios.com/cattips
"Understanding kitty psychology", "Litterbox blues" and other feline facts.

Chazhound
www.chazhound.com
Resources for dog lovers as well as screensavers, games and doggie greeting cards.

the directory

The Dogpatch
www.dogpatch.org
Advice on training your pooch, plus the best canine links on the Web.

Dogs
www.dogs.co.uk
Pages for British dog owners, including loads of links to dog-friendly accommodation.

Equine World
www.equine-world.co.uk
Great site covering all things equestrian. See also Equiworld:
www.equiworld.net

FishDoc
www.fishdoc.co.uk
All the information you need if your goldfish is looking a bit green around the gills.
For aquarium links go to Fish Link Central:
www.fishlinkcentral.com

House Rabbit Society
www.rabbit.org
Online community and resource for rabbit owners. Also try the Rabbit Welfare
Association:
www.rabbitwelfare.co.uk/index.htm

Kingsnake.com
www.kingsnake.com
A mind-bogglingly enormous portal for reptile and amphibian enthusiasts.

Moggies
www.moggies.co.uk
In addition to the usual information and advice, this feline resource allows you to
create a virtual cat and even offers horoscopes for Tiddles. Also, visit Frank the
cat at:
www.cathospital.co.uk

Museum of Non-Primate Art
www.monpa.com
Online home of the people behind the "Why cats paint" caper, with special exhibitions devoted to dancing with cats and "bird art".

New Pet.com
www.newpet.com
Friendly and informative site for new or soon-to-be owners of a cat or dog.

Pet Mad

www.petmad.com

Despite first appearances, this Irish site is probably the best (and cheapest) online pet shop for UK surfers. For organic food and alternative remedies try Blue Pet: www.bluepet.co.uk

Pet Planet

www.petplanet.co.uk

Not to be confused with the American site listed below, this site houses one of the UK's best online pet shops, with special features like a lost pet service and rehoming facilities.

The Pet Project

www.thepetproject.com

There's a whiff of New Age aromatherapy here ("the special bond between human and animal") and the focus is firmly on the US, but this is surely the most comprehensive pet resource on the Web, with all manner of advice on everything from canine nutrition to interpreting the sounds your chinchilla makes. Other good resources are Acme Pet and Pet Planet: http://acmepet.petsmart.com www.petplanet.com

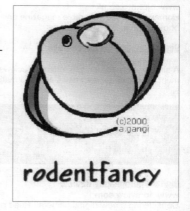

(c)2000
a.gangi

rodentfancy

Rodent Fancy

www.rodentfancy.com

With information on everything from African rock rats to Mongolian gerbils, rodent fanciers shouldn't look anywhere else.

RSPCA Online

www.rspca.org.uk

The RSPCA's homepage offers advice, allows the kids to adopt a cyber-pet before getting the real thing and features news and information on campaigns for animal welfare.

Tubcat

www.tubcat.com

Fat cats.

the directory

Photography

American Museum of Photography
www.photographymuseum.com
Exhibitions from back when cameras were a novelty.

Black & White World
www.photogs.com/bwworld
A celebration of black-and-white photography.

British Journal of Photography
www.bjphoto.co.uk
Homepage of the venerable magazine and a valuable resource for the professional photographer.

Digital Camera Resource Page
www.dcresource.com
A simple, easy-to-use site, offering reviews of loads of digital cameras and equipment as well as product news and information on issues like Mac OS X compatibility.

Digital Photography Review
www.dpreview.com
Considering a new digital camera? Read on.

Digital Truth: Photo Resource
www.digitaltruth.com
Perhaps the best photographic resource for the advanced photographer, with loads of tips, downloadable f-stop calculation software and "the world's largest" film development chart.

Exposure
www.88.com/exposure
A beginner's guide to photography, whose neatest feature is the simulated camera which mimics the effects of adjustments in shutter speed and aperture on pictures.

Invisible Light
www.atsf.co.uk/ilight/photos/index.html
Your complete guide to infrared photography.

Life
www.lifemag.com
View *Life* magazine's Picture of the Day then link through to some of the world's
most arresting photographs. There's even more over at *Time*'s Picture Collection
and Australia's Newsphotos:
www.thepicturecollection.com
www.newsphotos.com.au

the directory

Online Photo Albums

Got some snaps you'd like to show the world – or just your friends (through selective password access)? Upload them here:

Album Pictures www.albumpictures.com
Club Photo www.clubphoto.com
MSN Photos http://photos.msn.com/home.aspx
Photobox www.photobox.co.uk
PhotoLoft www.photoloft.com
Picture Trail www.picturetrail.com
Web Shots www.webshots.com
Yahoo! Photos http://photos.yahoo.com

Masters of Photography
www.masters-of-photography.com
An excellent collection of the works of some of history's greatest snappers, from Berenice Abbott to Garry Winogrand. In addition to the images, there are links to articles and other websites with biographical and technical information.

Photodisc
http://creative.gettyimages.com/photodisc
Plunder these photos free, or pay for the hi-res versions.

PhotoWave
www.photowave.com
Portal for professional photographers. Amateurs should try:
www.photo.net
www.photolinks.net
www.stilljournal.com
http://photography.about.com

PhotoZone
www.photozone.de
This site offers comparative analysis of cameras and lenses, and loads of technical information on all sorts of equipment.

Pinhole Visions
www.pinhole.com
A great site devoted to the art of pinhole photography, a primitive form of picture-taking that creates a dreamlike effect unattainable with conventional photography. There are two gallery spaces, discussion groups, news and links to other resources.

Shutterbug
www.shutterbug.net
The online home of the American *Shutterbug* magazine includes a massive archive of past articles, product reviews, news, hints, galleries, competitions and more. Digital photographers should focus on eDigital Photo:
www.edigitalphoto.com

Take Better Photos
http://betterphotos.cjb.net
No-nonsense site offering tricks and tips on correcting common photographic errors, picking the best viewpoint, compensating for parallax, computer enhancement, etc, etc. For more serious (really serious) tuition at a cost, try Photo Seminars:
www.photo-seminars.com
For an online database of British photography courses click:
www.photocollege.net

Year in the Life of Photojournalism
www.digitalstoryteller.com/YITL
Tag along with pros and see what they do day to day.

24 Hours in Cyberspace
www.cyber24.com
One thousand photographers save the day.

Politics and Government

Most governmental departments, politicians, political aspirants and causes maintain websites to spread the word and further their various interests. To find your local rep or candidate, start at their party's homepage. These typically lie dormant unless there's a campaign in progress, but can still be a good source of contacts to badger. Government departments, on the other hand, tirelessly belch out all sorts of trivia right down to transcripts of ministerial radio interviews. So if you'd like to know about impending legislation, tax rulings, budget details and so forth, skip the party pages and go straight to the department. If you can't find its address through what's listed below, try:

Yahoo! http://dir.yahoo.com/Government
Open Directory http://dmoz.org/Society/Government

the directory

For the latest election night counts, check the breaking news sites (p.230). Below is a selection of the most useful starting points.

British Politics Links www.ukpol.co.uk
Government Portal www.ukonline.gov.uk
Green Party www.greenparty.org.uk
Labour www.labour.org.uk
Liberal Democrats www.libdems.org.uk
National Assembly for Wales www.wales.gov.uk
Natural Law www.natural-law-party.org.uk
Northern Ireland Assembly www.ni-assembly.gov.uk
Plaid Cymru www.plaidcymru.org
Prime Minister www.pm.gov.uk
Scottish National Party www.snp.org
Scottish Parliament www.scottish.parliament.uk
Sinn Féin www.sinnfein.ie
Social Democratic and Labour Party www.sdlp.ie
Socialist Party www.socialistparty.org.uk
Socialist Workers Party www.swp.org.uk
Tories www.conservatives.com
Ulster Unionist Party www.uup.org

Adopt-A-Minefield
www.adoptaminefield.com
Help clear war-torn communities of deadly explosives.

Amnesty International
www.amnesty.org
Join the battle against brutal regimes and injustice.

Antiwar
www.antiwar.com
www.iacenter.org
Challenges US intervention in foreign affairs, especially the Balkans and Middle East.

The Big Breach
www.thebigbreach.com
Download a free copy of the British MI6 spy-and-tell book.

Bilderberg Group
www.bilderberg.org
Read about the people who really rule the world.

the directory

politics and government

The British Monarchy
www.royal.gov.uk
Tune into the world's best-loved soap opera.

British Politics Pages
www.ukpolitics.org.uk
News and history for politicos, with a great links page.

Center for the Moral Defense of Capitalism
www.moraldefense.com
www.aynrand.org
Is greed still good in the Y2Ks? Maybe not good but legal, says Microsoft's last
bastion of sympathy.

Central Intelligence Agency
www.cia.gov
Want the inside on political assassinations, arms deals, Colombian drug trades,
spy satellites, phone tapping, covert operations, government-sponsored alien sex
cults and the X-files? Well, guess what? Never mind, you won't go home without
a prize – see:
www.copvcia.com

Communist Internet List
www.cominternet.org
www.yclusa.org
Angry intellectuals and workers unite.

The Complete Bushisms
http://slate.msn.com/default.aspx?id=76886
The subliminal wit and wisdom of George Dubya.

249

the directory

Conspiracies
www.mt.net/~watcher
www.conspire.com
Certain people are up to something and, what's worse, they're probably all in it together. Click here for the biggest cover-ups of all time.

Council for Aboriginal Reconciliation
www.reconciliation.org.au
Unfinished business in the Lucky (for some) Country.

Disinformation
www.disinfo.com
The dark side of politics, religious fervour, new science, along with current affairs you won't find in the papers.

Doonesbury
www.doonesbury.com
Over thirty years of Gary Trudeau's legendary political cartoon.

Electronic Frontier Foundation
www.eff.org
Protecting freedom of expression on the Internet.

ePolitix
www.epolitix.com
British politics portal.

Fax Your MP
www.faxyourmp.com
Pester your local member through an Internet-to-fax gateway.

FBI FOIA Reading Room
http://foia.fbi.gov
FBI documents released as part of the Freedom of Information Act. Includes a few files on such celebrities as John Wayne, Elvis, Marilyn and the British Royals. Check out who's most wanted now at: www.fbi.gov

Political blogs

As you might expect, some of the best blogs to be found online are politically charged. Browse the eTalking directory to find your political allies:

eTalkinghead http://directory/etalkinghead.com

Some of the most interesting political blogs are those by MPs and councillors:
Richard Allan http://richardallan.org.uk (Lib Dem)
Paul Cumming www.paulcumming.blogspot.com (Conservative)
Austin Mitchell www.austinmitchell.org (Labour)
Tom Watson www.tom-watson.co.uk (Labour)

For further commentry and insight, try:
Paul Anderson http://libsoc.blogspot.com
Bloggerheads www.bloggerheads.com/polititians.asp
British Politics http://britishspin.blogspot.com

Federation of American Scientists
www.fas.org
Heavyweight analysis of science, technology and public policy including national security, nuclear weapons, arms sales, biological hazards, secrecy and space policy.

Foreign Report
www.foreignreport.com
Compact subscription newsletter with a track record of predicting international flashpoints well before the dailies.

Free Tibet
www.freetibet.org
Favourite website of the Beastie Boys and Richard Gere.

Freedom Forum
www.freedomforum.org
Organization dedicated to free-speech issues, newsroom diversity and freedom of the press.

the directory

The Gallup Organization
www.gallup.com
Keep track of opinion trends and ratings.

Gates Foundation
www.gatesfoundation.org
See where the world's second richest man is spreading it around.

Gay & Lesbian Alliance against Defamation
www.glaad.org
Stand up against media stereotyping and discrimination against those deviating
from the heterosexual norm. For more news, advice and dispatches from the
activist front, try:
www.gmhc.org
www.stonewall.org.uk
www.actupny.org

Gendercide
www.gendercide.org
Investigates mass killings where a single gender is singled out.

German Propaganda Archives
www.calvin.edu/cas/gpa
Who did you think you were kidding, Mr Hitler?

Grassroots.com
www.grassroots.com
Tracks (US) political action and election policies across the board, aided by *TV
Nation* champ Michael Moore, whose homepage is:
www.michaelmoore.com
Not everyone likes Mr. Moore:
www.moorewatch.com

Greenpeace International
www.greenpeace.org
Rebels with many a good cause.

GW Bush Art
http://gwbushart.port5.com
Distort the American president to your heart's content.

Hindu Holocaust Museum
www.mantra.com/holocaust
Contends that the massacre of Hindus during Muslim rule in India was of a scale
unparalleled in history, yet it has largely gone undocumented.

# the directory

InfoWar
www.infowar.com
Warfare issues from prank hacking to industrial espionage and military propaganda.

Jane's IntelWeb
http://intelweb.janes.com
Brief updates on political disturbances, terrorism, intelligence agencies and sub-terfuge worldwide. For a full directory of covert operations, see:
www.virtualfreesites.com/covert.html

Liberty
www.liberty-human-rights.org.uk
Championing human and civil rights in England and Wales. For a more global per-spective, see Human Rights Watch:
www.hrw.org

National Charities Information Bureau
www.ncib.org
www.charity-commission.gov.uk
Investigate before you donate. Once you're convinced, give at:
www.charitiesdirect.com

National Forum on People's Differences
www.yforum.com
Toss around touchy topics such as race, religion, and sexuality with a sincerity that is normally tabooed by political politeness.

One World
www.oneworld.net
Collates news from over 350 global justice organizations.

Open Secrets
www.opensecrets.org
Track whose money is oiling the wheels of US politics.
More keeping 'em honest at:
www.commoncause.org

opensecrets.org

Oxfam
www.oxfam.org
Pitch in to fight poverty and inequality.

the directory

Political Arena
www.planetquake.com/politicalarena/c2k.htm
Stage American elections on Quake.

The Political Graveyard
www.politicalgraveyard.com
Find out where over 81,000 politicians, diplomats and judges are buried.

Political Leanings of Selected Cartoon Characters
www.unknown.nu/cartoon
Uncover the ideologies of those seemingly innocent Saturday morning fixtures.

Political Wire
http://politicalwire.com
In-depth political news aggregator that is US-heavy but which does cover international politics as well.

Politics Online
www.PoliticsOnline.com
It may be subtitled "Fundraising and Internet tools for politics", but this is actually a good general political site, with an emphasis on how connectivity is changing the face of the game.

The Progressive Review
www.prorev.com
Washington dirt dug up from all sides of the fence. For darker soil, try:
www.realchange.org

Protest.net – A Calendar of Protest Worldwide
http://protest.net
Find a nearby riot you can call your own.

Public Education Network
www.penpress.org
Frightening statistics about global inequality and political madness.

Spin On
www.spinon.co.uk
Play games such as "Stay to the Right of Jack Straw", "Egg Prescott" and the "Hague Goes Trucking Simulator".

Spunk Press
www.spunk.org
www.infoshop.org
All the anarchy you'll ever need, organized neatly and with reassuring authority.

This Modern World
www.thismodernworld.com
Archive of Tom Tomorrow's scathing political cartoon.

Tolerance.org
www.tolerance.org
Shining the public flashlight on hate groups and political forces that threaten to undermine democracy and diversity. See also:
www.publiceye.org
www.splcenter.org

Trinity Atomic Web Site
www.fas.org/nuke/trinity
See what went on, and what went off, fifty-odd years ago, then file into the archives of high-energy weapons testing and see who else has been sharpening the tools of world peace.

UK Census
www.statistics.gov.uk
More statistics on the UK and its citizens than you'd care to know.

UK Online
www.ukonline.gov.uk
Not to be confused with the ISP, this UK Online aims to be the place where people interact with the government. Like most governmental policies, it seems pretty hazy and to get anywhere you have to dig far too hard.

US Presidential Candidates and their Evil Genes
www.nenavadno.com/usaelections2000.html
Biocybernetic criminals from the 33rd dimension take America.

YouGov
www.yougov.com
A good attempt at using the Internet to make government more accountable. There are columns and comment from John Humphrys, Fay Weldon and Ian Hargreaves, plus constantly updated political news. The best features, though, are the People's Parliament, which allows users to vote on the same issues as parliament, a service to create e-petitions and GovDoctor, which identifies MPs, councillors and service managers.

ZNet
www.zmag.org
Fresh stuff from dissident writers around the world, including big names such as Chomsky.

the directory

Property

The Web is a great way to look for property to rent or buy. You can see hundreds of offerings in half an hour without even leaving your front room. Try the following sites as well as those of your local estate agents:

Accommodation Directory www.accommodation.com
Assertahome www.assertahome.com
Easier www.easier.co.uk
Find A Property www.findaproperty.com
Home Sale www.home-sale.co.uk
Homefile www.homefileuk.co.uk
Homepages www.homepages.co.uk
HouseWeb www.houseweb.co.uk
HouseNet www.housenet.co.uk
Let's Direct www.letsdirect.co.uk
LondonHomeNet www.londonhomenet.com
Pavilions of Splendour www.heritage.co.uk
Property Finder www.propertyfinder.co.uk
Property Live www.propertylive.co.uk
Property Watch www.propwatch.com
Property World www.propertyworld.com
Vebra www.vebra.com

For commercial property, try:

Comproperty www.comproperty.com

For help with getting the best mortgage see our Money and Banking section (p.197), or see what's recommended here:

Find www.find.co.uk
MoneySupermarket www.moneysupermarket.com/mortgages
UKMortgagesOnline www.ukmortgagesonline.com

British Association of Removers
www.barmovers.com
Search for a mover who meets the BAR's standards of service.

FinanCenter
www.financenter.com
Figure out your monthly payments or what you can't afford.

Help I Am Moving
www.helpiammoving.com
Tries to remove the hassle from moving. Also try The Move Channel and Really
Moving:
www.themovechannel.com
www.reallymoving.com

Home Check
www.homecheck.co.uk
An excellent service for prospective home buyers: type in your future postcode and it
will tell you if you need to worry about subsidence, pollution, air quality, flood risk or if
the Triads are likely to firebomb the flat below.

Homewatch & Neighbourhood Watch Directory
www.localhomewatch.co.uk
Join with your neighbours to keep property values high.

ihavemoved.com
www.ihavemoved.com
Bulk-notify UK companies of your new address.

International Real Estate Digest
www.ired.com
Locate real estate listings, guides, and property-related services world wide.

the directory

Islands for Sale
www.islandsforsale.com
Get away from it all. For more opportunities for isolation, try Tropical Islands or World of Private Islands:
www.tropical-islands.com
www.vladi-private-islands.de

NACOSS
www.nacoss.org
Homepage of the National Approval Council for Security Systems: keep tabs on the guys installing your alarm. To make sure your lock doesn't get picked, check out: www.locksmiths.co.uk

Property Broker
www.propertybroker.co.uk
If you live within the M25 you can avoid the middleman and advertise your property here for a flat fee of £78.

UpMyStreet
www.upmystreet.com
Astounding wealth of house prices, health, crime, schools, tax and other statistics on UK neighbourhoods. Mighty useful if you're shifting base.

Radio and Webcasts

Not only do almost all radio stations have a website, most now pipe their transmissions online. However, as of press time the state of Internet radio was in perilous shape due to the American CARP (Copyright Arbitration Royalty Panel) substantially increasing the royalty rates that Internet broadcasters have to pay. The stations that are still online broadcast (webcast) in RealAudio and/or Windows Media Format, so grab the latest copies of both before setting out. Both players come with in-built station directories along with Web-based event guides which are fine for starting out, but nowhere near complete.

RealGuide http://realguide.real.com
Windows Media Guide http://windowsmedia.com

Not enough? Then buy the Rough Guide to Internet Radio or try one of the specialist radio directories, which list physical radio stations with websites along with full-time stations that only exist online, normally lumped together by country or genre. If they don't provide a direct link to the live feed, visit the station's site and look for a button or link that says "live" or "listen".

BRS Web Radio www.web-radio.fm
ComFM www.comfm.fr/live/radio
Live Radio www.live-radio.net
Radio Crow www.radiocrow.com
Radio Jump www.radiojump.com
Radio Locator www.radio-locator.com
RadioNow www.radio-now.co.uk
Shoutcast www.shoutcast.com
Sunset Radio http://sunsetradio.com
Virtual Tuner www.virtualtuner.com

Apart from the traditional single-stream broadcasters, dozens of sites host multiple feeds. These might be live, on demand, on rotation, archived or one-off events. They tend to work more like inflight entertainment than radio.

the directory

Air Bubble www.airbubble.com
Anime Hardcore http://animehardcore.net
Betalounge www.betalounge.com
CD Now www.cdnow.com/radio
Groovetech www.groovetech.com
House of Blues www.hob.com
Interface http://interface.pirate-radio.co.uk
Live 365 www.live365.com
Online Classics www.onlineclassics.net
Spinner www.spinner.com
Yahoo! Radio http://radio.yahoo.com

There are thousands upon thousands of webcasters sending their signals into the ether. These are some of the more familiar names and some of the oddest:

BBC Radio
www.bbc.co.uk/radio1
www.bbc.co.uk/radio2
www.bbc.co.uk/radio3
www.bbc.co.uk/radio4
Auntie online, with something for everyone.

BitBop Turner
www.audiomill.com
Stupid name, but a great tool: download the software and it monitors online radio stations most likely to play your favourite songs, then records them for playback at your leisure.

De Concertzender
www.concertzender.nl
A real boon for lovers of "highbrow" music: jazz, classical and New Music from this Dutch terrestrial station.

Dance Portal
www.danceportal.co.uk
Can't get out on Friday night? Put on your dancing shoes and point your browser here for webcasts from, as Pete Tong would probably say, "the most upfront clubs" in the UK. Also check out CNSoho:
www.cnsoholive.co.uk

Gaialive
www.gaialive.co.uk
Trance, House, Techno and Hard House 24/7.

MTV
www.mtv.com
It may not be radio, but it does have hundreds of video streams available.

On the Wire
http://onthewire.hypermart.net
The best reggae on the Web from BBC Lancashire's Steve Barker, with an extra-special 24-hour dub loop for echo fanatics. Try also Black Ark:
www.blackark.com

Solid Steel
www.ninjatune.net/solidsteel
Coldcut have been airing their essential mixes since 1988 on various terrestrial stations; you can listen to almost all of them (with playlists) here.

Swank Radio
www.swankradio.com
Spaceage bachelor pad muzak for cocktail enthusiasts and Tiki lovers everywhere.

Van Halen Radio Network
www.vhradio.com
Yup, all Van Halen, all the time.

WFMU
www.wfmu.org
Lucky residents of the New York metropolitan area have been able to call this treasure theirs for thirty-odd years. Now you can listen to the best freeform radio station on earth no matter where you live.

the directory

WNUR
www.wnur.org
Another great American station (from Chicago) covering experimental and local music better than nearly anyone else.

Xfm
www.xfm.co.uk
Catch London's indie station live online, all the time.

If you fancy setting up your own station or listening to the online equivalent of pirate radio, try:

Icecast.org www.icecast.org
Live365 www.live365.com
Shoutcast www.shoutcast.com

To promote your own station or search for a song or artist currently playing across thousands of others:

RadioSpy www.radiospy.com

Crystal Radio
www.midnightscience.com
Build a simple wireless that needs no battery.

Interface Pirate Radio
www.pirate-radio.co.uk
Attempting to bring the aural ambience of east London to the Net.

Phil's Old Radios
www.antiqueradio.org
If you've ever drifted to sleep bathed in the soft glow of a crackling Bakelite wireless, Phil's collection of vacuum-era portables may instantly flood you with childhood memories.

Pirate Radio
http://pirateradio.about.com
Stake your claim on the airwaves. More piracy info at How to Be a Radio Pirate: www.irational.org/sic/radio

Police Scanner
www.policescanner.com
www.apbnews.com/scanner
www.javaradio.com
Live emergency scanner feeds piped into RealAudio. Eavesdrop on busts in
progress. More on scanners at:
www.strongsignals.net

Reference

With the Net threatening the very foundations of the encyclopedia
industry, it should come as no surprise to find most of the household
names well entrenched online. While they're not all entirely free,
they're certainly cheaper and more up-to-date than their bulky paper
equivalents.

Britannica www.eb.com
Columbia www.bartleby.com/65
Encarta www.encarta.com
Macquarie www.macnet.mq.edu.au

Acronym Finder
www.acronymfinder.com
www.ucc.ie/info/net/acronyms/acro.html
Before you follow IBM, TNT and HMV into initializing your company's name, make
sure it doesn't mean something blue.

All Experts
www.allexperts.com
www.askme.com
www.abuzz.com
Ask any question and let unpaid experts
do the thinking.

Alternative Dictionary
www.notam.uio.no/~hcholm/altlang
Bucket your foreign chums in their
mother tongue.

263

the directory

reference

American ASL Dictionary
www.handspeak.com
Learn sign language through simple animations.

Anagram Genius
www.anagramgenius.com
Recycle used letters.

Aphorisms Galore
www.ag.wastholm.net
Sound clever by repeating someone else's lines.

Babelfish Translator
http://babelfish.altavista.com/translate.dyn
Translate text, including webpages, in seconds. Though run some text back and forth a few times and you'll end up with something that wouldn't look out of place on a Japanese T-shirt. If you can't identify a language, try: www.dougb.com/ident.html

Bartleby Reference
www.bartleby.com/reference
Free access to several contemporary and classic reference works such as the American *Heritage* dictionaries, *Columbia Encyclopedia*, Fowler's *King's English*, Emily Post's *Etiquette*, the *Cambridge History of English and American Literature* and Gray's *Anatomy*.

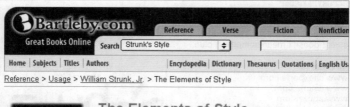

Reference > Usage > William Strunk, Jr. > The Elements of Style

The Elements of Style

William Strunk, Jr.

Make definite assertions. Avoid tame,

Asserting that one must first know the rules to break them, this classic reference book is a must-have for any student and conscientious writer. Intended for use in which the practice of composition is combined with th study of literature, it gives in brief space the principal requirements of pla English style and concentrates attention on the rules of usage and princi of composition most commonly violated.

Biography
www.biography.com
Recounting more than 25,000 lives.

Calculators Online
www.math.com
Awesome collection of online tools.

Cliché Finder
www.westegg.com/cliche
Submit a word or phrase to find out how not to use it.

Earthstation1
www.earthstation1.com
The twentieth century captured in sound and vision.

Encyclopedia Mythica
www.pantheon.org
Hefty album of mythology, folklore and legend.

Encyclopedia
Mythica™

An encyclopedia on mythology, folklore, and legend.

▸ **Explore**
Browse through the encyclopedia.

▸ **Search**
Search for articles.

▸ **What's New?**
Recent changes and additions.

▸ **About...**
Information about this project.

the directory

Famous Quotations Network
www.famous-quotations.com
Perk up essays and letters with a witticism from Oscar Wilde or a Senegalese proverb. For more quotes, try:
www.quotationspage.com
www.sillyquotes.com
www.motivational-quotes.com

Find Articles
www.findarticles.com
No fuss, no muss search engine of more than three hundred magazines and journals. The results are all printable and free.

GuruNet
www.gurunet.com
A powerful reference tool: type in a term and you'll immediately get definitions, pronunciation, explanations and more. Unfortunately, anything more than two weeks' use will cost you.

How Stuff Works
www.howstuffworks.com
Learn the secrets behind fake tans, animal camouflage and cable modems.

InfoPlease
www.infoplease.com
Handy, all-purpose almanac for stats and trivia.

Librarian's Index
www.lii.org
Naturally there are oodles of reference portals brimming with helpful reference tools. These are some of the best:

Learn a language

Arabic http://i-cias.com/babel/arabic
The French Tutorial www.frenchlesson.com
German For Travellers www.germanfortravellers.com
The Japanese Tutor www.japanese-online.com
StudySpanish.com www.studyspanish.com

Also useful:
BBC www.bbc.co.uk/languages
Word Reference www.wordreference.com

www.libraryspot.com
http://dmoz.org/Reference
www.refdesk.com
http://dir.yahoo.com/reference

Megaconverter 2
www.megaconverter.com/mega2
Calculate everything from your height in angstroms to the pellets of lead per ounce of buckshot needed to bring down an overcharging consultant.

Nonsensicon
www.nonsensicon.com
Non-existent words and their meanings.

Nupedia
www.nupedia.com
Nupedia is a new open content encyclopedia project collated by volunteers. You're invited to contribute.

Oxford Reference
www.oxfordreference.com
Mind-blowing reference library of some one hundred titles now online.
Unfortunately, you have to subscribe.

Questia
www.questia.com
A contender for the title of world's biggest library, this site has the full contents of nearly half a million books and journals.

Rap Dictionary
www.rapdict.org
Hip-hop to English. Parental guidance recommended.

RhymeZone
www.rhymezone.com
Get a hoof up in putting together a classy love poem.

the directory

Roget's Thesaurus
www.thesaurus.com
New format; useless as ever.

Skeptic's Dictionary
www.skepdic.com
Punch holes in mass-media funk and pseudosciences such as homeopathy, astrology and iridology.

The Straight Dope
www.straightdope.com
Cecil Adams's answers to hard questions. Find out how to renounce your US citizenship, what "Kemosabe" means and the difference between a warm smell of colitas and colitis.

Streetmap.co.uk
www.streetmap.co.uk
Find a location anywhere in the UK with a postcode, phone number, street name or latitude and longitude. If you're planning a US road trip, try Mapquest:
www.mapquest.com

Strunk's Elements of Style
www.bartleby.com/141
The complete classic of English usage in a nutshell, though unfortunately not the latest edition. For more on grammar and style:

Slang dictionaries

Playground Slang
www.odps.cyberscriber.com
Bridge the generation gap.

A Prisoner's Dictionary
http://dictionary.prisonwall.org
Shhh, a 5-0 is coming.

Pseudo Dictionary
www.pseudodictionary.com
Slang and more to help you talk the talk.

Twists, Slugs and Roscoes: A Glossary of Hardboiled Slang
www.miskatonic.org/slang.html
And you thought soup was something to eat.

www.edunet.com/english/grammar
www.garbl.com
www.canada.com/montreal/montrealgazette/specials/styleguide

Symbols
www.symbols.com
Ever woken up with a strange sign tattooed on your buttocks? Here's where to find what it means without calling in Agent Mulder.

What is?
www.whatis.com
www.webopedia.com
Unravel cumbersome computer and Internet jargon without having even more thrown at you.

Whoohoo
www.whoohoo.co.uk
If you come from Berwick and find yourself in the East End unable to understand a word anyone says, this site may be of help.

The Why Files
http://whyfiles.org
The science behind the headlines.

Wikipedia
www.wikipedia.org
The encyclopedia you can be a part of. As with all "wikis", the entries of this amazing resource (quarter of a million and growing) are user-editable, so if you see a mistake or a misplaced semi-colon, you can simply change it. This collaborative approach has created a surprisingly comprehensive and accurate multi-language encyclopedia, which, due to the "open-content" arrangement, will be freely available to the public until the end of time.

World Atlas
www.worldatlas.com
Maps, flags, latitude and longitude finder, population growth and so on – though you might prefer the maps on paper. For more maps, geography and GPS resources, try:
http://geography.about.com
www.nationalgeographic.com/mapmachine
http://dmoz.org/Reference/Maps

the directory

World Factbook
www.odci.gov/cia/publications/factbook
Information for spies from the CIA.

Xrefer
www.xrefer.com
Consult this site to query a broad selection of prominent reference works from Oxford University Press, Houghton Mifflin, Penguin, Macmillan, Bloomsbury and Market House Books.

Yellow Pages
www.yell.com
If you're too lazy to flip through the book.

YourDictionary.com
www.yourdictionary.com
For one-point access to over a thousand dictionaries across almost every language. Try also Dictionary.com and One Look:
www.dictionary.com
www.onelook.com

Relationships, Dating and Friendship

The Internet is the biggest singles bar humankind has ever created: with millions and millions of users from around the world, even the most lovelorn are bound to find someone worth cyber-flirting with. However, it's worth bearing in mind that the World Wide Web is no different from the real world and there are plenty of scam artists, hustlers, leeches and other unsavoury characters lurking in unsuspected corners. By all means enjoy dropping virtual handkerchiefs to perspective suitors, but keep your wits about you. Before engaging in any social intercourse on the Net, go to Wildx Angel (www.wildxangel.com) for advice on the safest way to go on the pull online.

To help you on your way, here are some of the Web's biggest dating agencies:

Dateline www.dateline.co.uk
Dating Direct www.datingdirect.com
Elite Dating www.elite-dating.co.uk

Friendfinder www.friendfinder.com
Lavalife www.lavalife.com
Lovefinder www.lovefinder.co.uk
Match.com www.match.com
SocialNet www.relationships.com
UDate www.udate.com
UK Singles www.uksingles.co.uk
Where's My Date? www.wheresmydate.com

To find a chat room, try a chat portal like:

The Chat Room Directory www.webarrow.net/chatindex
Chatseek http://chatseek.com
Chat Shack Network http://chatshack.net
The Ultimate Chatlist www.chatlist.com

For more, try the Open Directory's chat portal list:

Open Directory http://dmoz.org/Computers/Internet/Chat

Coincidence Design
www.coincidencedesign.com
For a mere $78,000, the "professionals" at this site will engineer a meeting with the
girl/boy of your dreams.

Cyberspace Inmates
www.cyberspace-inmates.com
Strike up an email romance with a prison inmate – maybe even one on Death Row.

Everything you say or do

Cyberspace Inmates

Rehabilitation Through Correspondence

the directory

relationships, dating and friendship

Dating
http://dating.about.com
About's dating advice page hosts a motherload of sensible information on dating both on- and offline.

Dating Directories
www.singlesites.com
www.100hot.com/directory/lifestyles/dating.html
Come aboard, they're expecting you.

The Divorce Support Page
www.divorcesupport.com
Lots of friendly ears and shoulders to cry on.

Friends Reunited
www.friendsreunited.co.uk
You haven't forgotten. Now track them down one by one. More people who teased you in the common room are at:
www.classmates.com
If you were behind bars rather than in school, try:
www.convictsreunited.com

Gentle, Romantic Woman Seeks Agnostic or Atheist for Strong Attraction, Friendship, Eventual Marriage and Deepest Love
http://hometown.aol.com/mary1777/index.htm
Middle-aged divorcée lays down the law.

Hot or Not?
www.hotornot.com
www.ratemyface.com
Submit a flattering photo and have it rated by passing chumps.

The Hugging Site
http://members.tripod.com/~hugging
The history of embracing, hugging stories and tips to improve your cuddling technique.

Javina's Prostitution FAQ
www.javina.com/JJ3/faq.html
Learn the truth behind the *Pretty Woman* fantasy.

Love Calculator
www.lovecalculator.com
Enter your respective names to see if you're compatible.

The Hugging Site (Halia suomeksi)

Most of us have some type of difficulties in expressing ourselves or we just don't share our feelings enough with the people next to us. Often it's all because our western culture has this peculiar way to emphasize solidness and individualism in our behaviour. One way to enrich communication, and at the side the best and sometimes even the worst parts of our lives, is hugging.

Meg's Boyfriend of the Week
www.drizzle.com/~knuckles
In which Meg rates TV stars by their proximity to that paragon of perfection:
MacGyver.

Pen Pal Directory
http://dir.yahoo.com/Social_Science/Communications/Writing/Correspondence/
Pen_Pals
Exchange email with strangers.

PlanetOut
www.planetout.com
www.rainbownetwork.com
www.qrd.org
www.datalounge.com
www.queertheory.com
Directories to all that's that way inclined.

the directory

The Rejection Line
www.lazystudent.co.uk/rejectline.html
Let the professionals break it to that not so special someone.

Romance 101
www.rom101.com
Chat-up lines, compatibility tests and advice from men to women like "Never buy a 'new' brand of beer because 'it was on sale'."

Secret Admirer
www.secretadmirer.com
www.ecrush.com
Find out whether your most secret crushed one digs you back.

So There
www.sothere.com
A place to post your parting shots.

Swoon
www.swoon.com
Dating, mating, and relating. Courtesy of Condé Nast's *Details*, *GQ*, *Glamour*, and *Mademoiselle*. For dessert, try:
http://dating.about.com

Things My Girlfriend and I Have Argued About
http://homepage.ntlworld.com/mil.millington/things.html
Add this page to that list.

Tips for Dating Emotional Cripples
www.grrl.com/bipolar.html
The site all women must visit.

Vampire Exchange
www.vein-europe.demon.co.uk
www.sanguinarius.org
Give blood as an act of love.

Social Networks

Touted by many as the next big Internet revolution, social networks are designed to cultivate every type of relationship, from friendship and romance to business partnerships. They're based on the idea of "degrees of separation". You set up a list of your friends or colleagues and invite them to join and do the same. Soon a network is established where you can make contact with people you may not know directly, but you know are "friends of friends", "friends of friends of friends", and so on. Most networks also include sub-networks combining people of similar interests, occupations and the like.

Many such networks are still pretty IT and new media focused, but more are appearing all the time.

Here are a few of the bigger networking sites worth visiting:

Orkut www.orkut.com
Tribe www.tribe.net
Ecademy www.ecademy.com

Way Too Personal
www.waytoopersonal.com
Wild and woolly adventures in Internet dating.

Weddings in the Real World
www.theknot.com
www.hitched.co.uk
Prepare to jump the broom – or untie the knot:
www.divorcesource.com
www.absolutedivorce.com
www.hell2u.com/divorce.htm

Religion

If you haven't yet signed up with a religious sect or are unhappy with the one passed down by your folks, here's your opportunity to survey the field at your own pace. Most are open to newcomers, though certain rules and conditions may apply. For a reasonably complete and unbiased breakdown of faith dealerships, try:

the directory

BeliefNet www.beliefnet.com
Comparative Religion www.academicinfo.net/religindex.html
Religious Tolerance www.religioustolerance.org

But don't expect such an easy ride from those demanding proof:

Atheism http://atheism.miningco.com
Christian Burner www.christianburner.com
The Secular Web www.infidels.org

Adherents.com
www.adherents.com
Statistical ranking of the world's religions from the Aaronic Order to Zurvanism.

Anglicans Online
http://anglicansonline.org
A gentle catapult into the Church of England worldwide.

Avatar Search
www.AvatarSearch.com
Search the occult Net for spiritual guidance and lottery tips.

The Bible Gateway
http://bible.gospelcom.net
Set your table with the Good Book.

The Brick Testament
www.thereverend.com/brick_testament
And on the eighth day God created Lego...

A Brief History of the Apocalypse
www.abhota.info
It takes a lickin' and keeps on tickin'.

The British Druid Order
www.druidorder.demon.co.uk
Dance around Stonehenge, make potions and meet fellow wizards.

BuddhaNet
www.buddhanet.net
Take a ride on the wheel of dharma and download the Diamond Sutra.

Catholic Church – God's One and Only Church
www.truecatholic.org
More troops armed with the truth.

Catholic Online
www.catholic.org
Saints, angels, shopping, discussion and a portal to the online territory occupied by Catholics.

Celebrity Atheist List
www.celebatheists.com
Big names you won't spot in Heaven.

Cheesy Jesus
www.cheesyjesus.com
www.ship-of-fools.com/Gadgets
Buy gadgets to bring you closer to God.

Chick
http://chick.com
Hardcore Christian pornography.

Christian Answers
http://christiananswers.net
Movies and computer games reviewed and hard questions answered, by Christians who know what's good for you and your family.

Christian Naturists
http://home.vistapnt.com/markm
Frolic with other Christian funseekers, the way God intended.

the directory

Christians vs. Muslims
http://debate.org.uk
www.rim.org/muslim/islam.htm
http://members.aol.com/AllahIslam
www.answering-islam.org
www.muslim-answers.org
www.biblicalchristianity.freeserve.co.uk
Put your faith on the line.

Church of England
www.cofe.anglican.org
The home of Anglicanism online. Presbyterians should head north of the border at
Church of Scotland
www.churchofscotland.org.uk

Church of the Subgenius
www.subgenius.com
Find the truth through slackness.

CrossSearch
www.crosssearch.com
Set sail through safe waters to find Christian groups of all denominations.

Crosswalk
www.crosswalk.com
Catch up with the latest on Jesus.

Demon Possession Handbook
http://diskbooks.org/hs.html
Train for a job with the Watcher's Council.

Exorcism
www.logoschristian.org/exorcism.html
Don't try this at home.

Free Deliverance
www.demonbuster.com
Use Jesus's teachings to cast out demons, wage spiritual warfare and overcome
bipolar disorder, depression, addiction, obesity and other modern ailments.

The Hindu Universe
www.hindunet.org
Hindu dharma – the philosophy, culture and customs.

The Holy See
www.vatican.va
Official hideout of the pope and his posse.

Islamic Gateway
www.ummah.net
www.musalman.com
www.fatwa-online.com
Get down with Muhammed (*sallallahu `alaihi wa sallam*).

Jah Rastafari
www.webcom.com/nattyreb/rastafari/everlasting.html
A packed site devoted to worshipping Haile Selassie as the living God.

Jesus, a Historical Reconstruction
www.concentric.net/~Mullerb
Getting to the truth about the man from Nazareth.

Jesus of the Week
www.jesusoftheweek.com
The original Mr Nice Guy in 52 coy poses per year. Catch him winking at:
www.winkingjesus.com

Latter Day Designs Vinyl Figures
www.lehi.com/vin1.html
Action figures from The Book of Mormon.

The Mark of the Beast
www.greaterthings.com/essays/666mark.htm
Did you know that "Holy Bible" is "666" in ASCII code?

Miracles Page
www.mcn.org/1/miracles
Spooky signs that point towards a cosmic conspiracy.

The 93 Current
www.93current.de
The magick of Aleister Crowley. Do more of what thou wilt at An Introduction to

the directory

Crowley Studies and The Works of Aleister Crowley:
www.maroney.org/Crowley Intro
www.netropic.org/crowley

Not Proud
www.notproud.com
Confess your most entertaining sins.

OrishaNet
www.orishanet.org
Learn about the Cuban religion of Santeria and consult with Oshun, Ifá and Elegba.

OrishaNet

Dedicated to being an accurate source of information on La Regla Lucumi for those learning the religion and other interested parties.

The 16 Mandates of Ifá (new article)

Orishanet en Español

The Pagan Library
www.paganlibrary.com
Pagan and Wiccan texts and other information on the mysteries of the Craft.

Peyote Way Church of God
www.peyoteway.org
Unless you're Native American or live in select southern US states, you stand to be locked up for finding God through the psychedelic cactus. Otherwise, feel free to fry your brain; just don't drive home from church.

Prophecy and Current Events
www.aplus-software.com/thglory
www.prophezine.com
You'll never guess who's coming to dinner. Don't bother cooking, though; he's supposed to be a real whizz with food.

Religious Frauds
http://religiousfrauds.50megs.com
Esteemed reptile slayer David Icke sniffs out Christian cons.

Roy Taylor Ministries
www.roytaylorministries.com
"American Pie" is God's song and other examples of questionable hermeneutics.

Satanism 101
www.satanism101.com
Enter this address and go straight to Hell:
www.what-the-hell-is-hell.com
www.virtualhell.net

Scientology
www.scientology.org.uk
The favoured religion of Hollywood stars.

Shamanism
http://deoxy.org/shaman.htm
Entheogens, plant sacraments and other ecstatic vehicles.

Ship of Fools: the Magazine of Christian Unrest
http://ship-of-fools.com
The lighter side of Christianity.

Sikh Museum
www.sikhmuseum.org
The teachings and history of the main religion of the Punjab region of India.

Skeptics Annotated Bible
www.skepticsannotatedbible.com
Contends that the Good Book is a misnomer.

Stories of the Dreaming
www.dreamtime.net.au
Selection of enchanting bedtime stories in text, video and audio that explain cre-

ation from an Aboriginal perspective. Don't believe in creation? Go tell it to the jury:
www.talkorigins.org

Totally Jewish
www.totallyjewish.com
www.maven.co.il
Spiritual guidance and community portals for the chosen people
(www.chosen-people.com) and curious goyim. More good mozel at JewishNet:
www.jewishnet.co.uk

24 Hour Church of Elvis
www.churchofelvis.com
No spiritual advice here, just the gift shop.

Universal Life Church
http://ulc.org
Become a self-ordained minister.

The Vodou Page
http://members.aol.com/racine125
Learn how to convene with the loas.

The Witches' Voice
www.witchvox.com
Expresses a burning desire to correct misinformation about witchcraft, a legally
recognized religion in the US since 1985.

Zen
www.do-not-zzz.com
Take a five-minute course in meditation.

Science

To keep abreast of science news and developments stop by Scitech,
which aggregates stories from the leading scientific media:

Scitech Daily Review www.scitechdaily.com

Or go straight to one of the numerous science journals, many of which
let you sign up for daily, weekly or monthly news emails:
Archeology www.archaeology.org
British Medical Journal www.bmj.com

the directory

Bulletin of Atomic Scientists www.bullatomsci.org
Discover www.discover.com
Discovery Channel www.discovery.com
Edge www.edge.org
Highwire Press http://highwire.stanford.edu
The Lancet www.thelancet.com
National Geographic www.nationalgeographic.com
New Scientist www.newscientist.com
Popular Mechanics www.popularmechanics.com
Popular Science www.popsci.com
Science à GoGo www.scienceagogo.com
Science Magazine www.sciencemag.org
Science News www.sciencenews.org
Scientific American www.scientificamerican.com
The Scientist www.the-scientist.com
Skeptical Inquirer www.csicop.org/si
Technology Review www.techreview.com

Looking for a something specific or a range of sites within a strand?
Try browsing or searching a directory:

Hypography www.hypography.com
Open Directory http://dmoz.org/Science
SciSeek www.sciseek.com
Treasure Troves of Science www.treasure-troves.com

the directory

Yahoo http://dir.yahoo.com/science

Albert Einstein Online
www.westegg.com/einstein
In essence an Albert Einstein portal, with links to biographies, quotes, articles and essays, photos and other pages related to *Time* magazine's Man of the Century.

Amusement Park Physics
www.learner.org/exhibits/parkphysics
If your kid has absolutely no interest in potential and kinetic energy, send them to this fantastic site for the coolest science lesson on the Web, and give them the chance to design their own rollercoaster.

AnthroNet

www.anthro.net
Gateway to the world of anthropology, archeology and other social sciences.

Battlebots
www.battlebots.com
Robots kick ass.

Biology
http://biology.about.com
Vast array of life science links and articles.

Bizarre Stuff You Can Make in Your Kitchen
http://freeweb.pdq.net/headstrong
A really fun archive of classic home science experiments from the 1930s to the 1960s. Brings out the Magnus Pike in everyone.

The Braintainment Center
www.brain.com
www.mensa.org
www.iqtest.com
www.mind-gear.com
www.mindmedia.com
Start with a test that says you're not so bright, then prove it by buying loads of self-improvement gear. Short on brains? Try:
www.brains4zombies.com

Bunny Survival Tests
www.pcola.gulf.net/~irving/bunnies
Determining whether marshmallow bunnies can survive lasers, flames, hot tubs, coyotes, radiation and oxygen deprivation. For more rabbit "science", go to The Bunnies Strike Back:
http://marks.networktel.net

Chemistry.org.uk
www.liv.ac.uk/Chemistry/Links/link.html
The chemistry section of the WWW Virtual Library has some 8500 links to chemistry sites. Advanced chemists should check out ChemWeb (www.chemweb.com) and its Available Chemical Directory of 278,000 compounds (you need to subscribe to gain access).

The Constants and Equations Pages
http://tcaep.co.uk
A great reference resource for students of maths and sciences: trigonometric identities, Avogadro's Number, SI units and other memorization headaches.

Cool Robot of the Week
http://ranier.hq.nasa.gov/telerobotics_page/coolrobots.html
Clever ways to get machines to do our dirty work. For a directory of simulators, combat comps, clubs and DIY bots, direct your agent to:
www.robotcafe.com

Dangerous Laboratories
www.dangerouslaboratories.org
Definitely don't try this at home.

the directory

Flat Earth Society
www.flat-earth.org
Proving five hundred years of science wrong.

Genewatch
www.genewatch.org
Dusting crops for genetic fingerprints.

Gray's Anatomy Online
www.bartleby.com/107
The complete edition of the essential anatomical text.

History of Mathematics
http://www-groups.dcs.st-andrews.ac.uk/~history
The life and times of various bright sparks with numbers.

HotAir – Annals of Improbable Research
www.improbable.com
Science gone too far, or around the bend. Includes the Ig Nobel awards for
achievements that cannot, or should not, be reproduced.

How Does a Thing Like That Work?
www.pitt.edu/~dwilley/hdatltwmenu.html
Entertaining physics demonstration experiments.

How Stuff Works
www.howstuffworks.com
Unravel the mysterious machinations behind all sorts of stuff from Christmas to
cruise missiles.

Institute of Physics
www.iop.org
Fast, well-designed physics portal. For articles like "The Industrial Physicist Who
Has it All", check out PhysicsWeb (http://physicsweb.org); for the history of the
second superstring revolution, try Physics.org (www.physics.org).

Interactive Frog Dissection
http://teach.virginia.edu/go/frog
Pin down a frog, grab your scalpel and follow the pictures.

The Lab
www.abc.net.au/science
ABC science news and program info with Q&As from Aussie pop-science superstar,
Dr Karl Kruszelnicki.

MadSciNet: 24-hour Exploding Laboratory
www.madsci.org
Collective of more than a hundred scientific smarty-pantses set up specifically to answer your dumb questions. More geniuses for hire at:
www.ducksbreath.com
www.wsu.edu/DrUniverse
www.sciam.com/askexpert
www.sciencenet.org.uk

MIT Media Labs
www.media.mit.edu
If you've read *Being Digital* or any of Nicholas Negroponte's *Wired* columns, you'll know he has some pretty tall ideas about our electronic future. Here's where he gets them.

National Inventors Hall of Fame
www.invent.org
Homepage of a museum based in Akron, Ohio, dedicated to the world's most important inventors. Includes short biographies and pictures of luminaries like Thomas Edison, Enrico Fermi and Louis Pasteur. For more modern inventions, go to Inventions And Technologies:
www.inventions-tech.com/epanel.htm
And for questionable inventions see Patently Absurd!:
www.patent.freeserve.co.uk

Netsurfer Science
www.netsurf.com/nss
Subscribe to receive weekly bulletins on science and technology sites.

Nobel e-Museum
www.nobel.se
Read all about Nobel Prize winners.

Rocketry Online
www.rocketryonline.com
Take on NASA at its own game.

Skeptics Society
www.skeptic.com
www.csicop.org
Don't try to pull a swift one on this crowd.

The Soundry
http://library.thinkquest.org/19537
A fun introduction to the science of acoustics.

the directory

Time Travel
http://freespace.virgin.net/steve.preston
"We discuss many of the common objections to time travel and we show that these objections are without foundation."

USGS National Earthquake Info Center
http://gldss7.cr.usgs.gov
www.gps.caltech.edu/~polet/recofd.html
Stats and maps of the most recent quakes worldwide.

Virtual Autopsy 2
www.le.ac.uk/pathology/teach/va/welcome.html
Definitely not for the squeamish, this site gives you the opportunity to fish around the insides of eight cadavers and try to determine the cause of death from their case histories.

Volcano World
http://volcano.und.nodak.edu
Monitor the latest eruptions, see photos of every major volcano in the world, and virtually tour a Hawaiian smoky without choking on sulphur fumes.

VoltNet
www.voltnet.com
Celebrate the power of electricity by blowing things up.

WebElements
www.webelements.com
www.chemsoc.org/viselements
Click on an element in the periodic table and suss it out in depth. Now cross-check its comic book reference:
www.uky.edu/Projects/Chemcomics

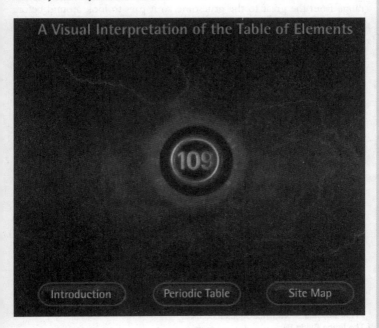

Weird Science and Mad Scientists
www.eskimo.com/~billb/weird.html
Free energy, Tesla, anti-gravity, aura, cold fusion, parapsychology and other strange scientific projects and theories.

the directory

Shopping

If you can't buy it on the Web, it probably doesn't exist, but shopping sites range from the great to the gruesome, so it pays to look around before tapping in your credit card details. For obscure things, you'll probably need to locate a specialist online store. To do this, you could either try a carefully phrased Google or Dmoz search (see p.6) – adding "price" or "buy" helps bring up the retail sites – or consult one of the online shopping directories, such as:

Buyers' Guide www.buyersguide.to
My Taxi www.mytaxi.co.uk
Shop Finger www.shopfinger.com
ShopSmart http://uk.shopsmart.com
UK Shopping www.ukshopping.com
UK Shop Search www.ukshopsearch.com

For more common items, you may want to try a shopping bot: enter a product name or keyword and it'll return a listing of prices and availability across a range of retailers. Of course, a bargain-finder is only as good as its sources, so it often pays to try more than one. Major UK bots include:

Checkaprice www.checkaprice.com
Dealtime www.dealtime.com
Easy Value www.easyvalue.com
Kelkoo http://uk.kelkoo.com
Price Checker www.PriceChecker.co.uk
The Price Guide UK www.price-guide.co.uk
ShopSmart http://uk.shopsmart.com

For price and service comparisons of mobile phone, credit card, electricity, water and gas suppliers, try:

Buy.co.uk www.buy.co.uk
UK Energy www.ukenergy.co.uk
U Switch www.uswitch.com
Or to compare the price of landline phone bills, go to:
PhoneBills.org.uk www.phonebills.org.uk

Of course, before you buy anything big, you'll probably want to do some research into the product itself, and the Net is one of the best places to look. Either try Usenet (see p.19) or one of the many websites that offer buying guides, customer opinions, ratings and links to external reviews. Perhaps the most thorough collection is:

Productopia www.productopia.com

But there's plenty more advice at:

Amazon www.amazon.co.uk
Consumer Review www.consumerreview.com
Dooyoo www.dooyoo.com
Epinions www.epinions.com
eSmarts www.esmarts.com
Google Groups http://groups.google.com
Rateitall.com www.rateitall.com

And there's always Which? for trustworthy consumer advice:

Which? www.which.net

the directory

BizRate
www.bizrate.com
Shopping sites rated and reviewed.

Catalogue City
http://uk.uk.catalogcity.com
If you're unconvinced by online shopping and would prefer it on paper, drive your postie crazy by ordering every catalogue in the world. For even more junk mail, try Buyers' Index, Catalink and Catalog Site:
www.buyersindex.com
www.catalink.co.uk
http://catalogsite.catalogcity.com

Consumer World
www.consumerworld.org
Not all of the information here may be appropriate because it's an American site, but this should be an automatic bookmark for anyone intending to do any shopping either on- or offline. Aside from the comparison engines, bargain listings and product reviews, it has alerts on the latest scams and annoying marketing practices.

How to Complain
www.howtocomplain.com
Let the professionals do it for you.

LetsBuyIt.com
www.letsbuyit.com
This site uses collaborative buying power to clinch lower prices for its members across Europe.

MyGeek
www.mygeek.com
Type in your shopping request here and they will approach several different merchants looking for the best price.

PriceWatch
www.pricewatch.com
If you're after computer products, this shopping bot is one of the best comparison engines on the Web. Also try Shopper.com:
www.shopper.com

Recall Announcements
www.recallannouncements.co.uk
Stay up-to-date on the consumer safety front.

Silver Surfers

ARP/050
www.arp.org.uk
News, information and forums from the Association of Retired and Persons Over 50.

BBC Health: Health at 50
www.bbc.co.uk/health/50plus
Easily among the best of the BBC sites, largely because – unlike most of the Beeb's pages – it's not dependent on Auntie's programming. The advice is honest

and trustworthy and there are no bells or whistles.

Better Government For Older People
www.bettergovernmentforolderpeople.gov.uk
Unfortunately, this governmental site is as dull, tedious and cumbersome as its domain name.

FiftyOn
www.fiftyon.co.uk
A portal for 50-pluses, with its best and most laudable feature being the advice and vacancies database it maintains for older jobseekers.

Hell's Geriatrics
www.hellsgeriatrics.co.uk
Grow old disgracefully.

I Don't Feel 50
www.idf50.co.uk
A fun, irreverent site run by Graham Andrews, with topics like "Is Age Concern too Old?" and "Mind the Generation Gap".

National U3A UK
www.u3a.org.uk
Continuing adult education from the Third Age Trust and the University of the Third Age.

Retirement Matters
www.retirement-matters.co.uk
Online magazine specializing in news, reviews and information for over-50s.

Saga Magazine
www.saga.co.uk/magazine
Homepage of the magazine for over 50s, with content from the current issue, although there is no archive of past articles.

See How They Grow
www.seehowtheygrow.com
A guide to grandparenting, with chat boards, advice and plenty of stories about little monsters.

Senior Site
www.seniorsite.com
American online community for grown-ups, with Pat Boone as the entertainment correspondent and an excellent section on protecting yourself against "senior scams".

Seniority.co.uk
www.seniority.co.uk
Like all online communities, this one for senior citizens is only as good as its contributors. While some of Seniority is hit-and-miss, it does have an impressive community spirit.

SeniorsSearch
www.seniorssearch.com
Search engine dedicated to resources for silver surfers.

Third Age
www.thirdage.com
This American online magazine for older women may look like some terrible advert for feminine hygiene products, but underneath the terrible design is an informative, friendly e-zine.

Write a Senior Citizen
www.writeseniors.com
Penpals for seniors.

Space

If you have more than a passing interest in space, skip the popular science mags (p.282) and newswires (p.230), and go straight to the source:

British National Space Centre www.bnsc.gov.uk
European Space Agency www.esrin.esa.it
NASA www.nasa.gov
Royal Greenwich Observatory www.rog.nmm.ac.uk

Or try any of these specialist space ports:

About Space http://space.about.com
Amateur Astronomy Magazine www.amateurastronomy.com
Astronomy.com www.astronomy.com
Astronomy Now www.astronomynow.com
Human Spaceflight http://spaceflight.nasa.gov
Jet Propulsion Lab www.jpl.nasa.gov
Planetary Society http://planetary.org

the directory

Alien Scalpel
www.alienscalpel.com
Protect yourself against abduction.

Artemis Project
www.asi.org
Join a queue to go to the moon.

AstroCapella
www.astrocappella.com
Learn astronomy through great tunes such as "Doppler Shifting" and "Habitable Zone".

Astronomy Picture of the Day
http://antwrp.gsfc.nasa.gov/apod/astropix.html
Enjoy a daily helping of outer space served up by a gourmet astrochef.

Auroral Activity
www.sec.noaa.gov/pmap
Instantly see the current extent and position of the auroral oval above each pole.

Auroras: Paintings in the Sky
www.exploratorium.edu/learning_studio/auroras
www.alaskascience.com/aurora.htm
If you're ever lucky enough to see the Aurora during a solar storm, you'll never take the night sky for granted again. The Exploratorium does a commendable job in explaining a polar phenomenon that very few people understand. Except maybe these champs:
www.haarp.alaska.edu

Bad Astronomy
www.badastronomy.com
Ditch your lifetime's supply of space misconceptions and clichés.

Chandra X-Ray
www.chandra.harvard.edu
Telescope's-eye view of black holes and supernovas.

Clickworkers
http://clickworkers.arc.nasa.gov
Wangle a NASA job onto your résumé by counting craters on Mars.

Comets & Meteor Showers
http://comets.amsmeteors.org
Be on the lookout for falling rocks.

Darksky
www.darksky.org
Join the campaign against
wanton street lighting. You'll
see why in the gallery.

Deep Cold
www.deepcold.com
Artistic mockups of chic
space racers that never left
the hangar.

Earth Viewer
www.fourmilab.ch/earthview
View the Earth in space and
time.

Eclipse Cam
http://eclipse.span.ch/liveshow.htm
You don't even need a special box designed by your science teacher to view this site.

Galactic Information Service
http://home.c2i.net/galactic/torealf
"Here you will find information about the technology of the spacepeople. UFO pictures. Space language and pictures from other dimensions/planets."

Geocentricity
www.biblicalastronomer.org
Dedicated to proving the Sun revolves around the Earth.

297

the directory

Heavens Above
www.heavens-above.com
Correctly identify nearby satellites and space stations.

Hubblesite
http://hubble.stsci.edu
Intergalactic snapshots fresh from the Hubble telescope.

Hypothetical Planets
http://seds.lpl.arizona.edu/nineplanets/nineplanets/hypo.html
Paul Schylter's history of planets that have vanished or perhaps existed only in the minds of pre-Hubble scientists.

Inconstant Moon
http://www.inconstantmoon.com
http://www.spacescience.co.uk
Click on a date and see what's showing on the Moon.

Intelligent Life on Mars
http://go.to/intelligentlifeonmars
The little green men know quantum physics.

International Star Registry
www.starregistry.co.uk
Raise your flag in outer space.

Mars Home Page
http://mpfwww.jpl.nasa.gov
Get a bit more red dirt live from NASA's space safari before you stake out your

first plot at:
www.marsshop.com
For the latest news, see:
www.marsnews.com

Mars Society UK
www.marssociety.org.uk
British chapter of an organization dedicated to getting humans to visit Mars.

The Martian Archives
www.infocom.com/~thomil/welcome.htm
Prepare yourself for the coming global superstorm.

MrEclipse
www.mreclipse.com
Dabble in the occultations.

Net Telescopes
http://denali.physics.uiowa.edu
Probe deep space by sending requests to remote telescopes.

The Nine Planets
www.ex.ac.uk/Mirrors/nineplanets
Bill Arnett's impressive multimedia tour of our solar system.

Planet Search
http://exoplanets.org
Info on planets in and outside our solar system.

Retro Aerospace
www.retro.com
Recycling simpler, sturdier rockets to make space travel more accessible to the
common man.

the directory

Rocket Guy
www.rocketguy.com
The homepage of Brian Walker who plans to shoot himself thirty miles into the
atmosphere. Wish him luck.

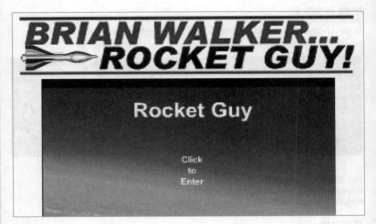

Scope Reviews
www.scopereviews.com
Read first, buy later – or maybe build your own:
www.atmjournal.com

Seti@home
http://setiathome.ssl.berkeley.edu
http://setifaq.org
Donate your processing resources to the non-lunatic end of the search for extraterrestrial intelligence by downloading a screensaver that analyses data from the
Arecibo Radio Telescope. Progress reports at:
www.seti.org
http://planetary.org
http://seti.uws.edu.au

Solar System Simulator
http://space.jpl.nasa.gov
Shift camp around the solar system until you find the best view.

Space Adventures
www.spaceadventures.com
If you've got $20 million lying around you could become the next Dennis Tito. For the more modest of means, this site offers zero gravity flights and personalized spacesuits just in case.

Space Calendar
www.jpl.nasa.gov/calendar
Guide to upcoming anniversaries, rocket launches, meteor showers, eclipses, asteroid and planet viewings and other happenings in the intergalactic calendar.

Space Weather
www.spaceweather.com
www.windows.ucar.edu/spaceweather
Monitor the influence of solar activity on the Earth's magnetic field.

Star Stuff
www.starstuff.com
Beginner's guides to astronomy for kids.

Sport

For live calls, scores, tables, draws, teams, injuries and corruption enquiries across major sports, try the newspaper sites (p.230), breaking news services (p.232) or sporting specialists like:

Eurosport www.eurosport.com
SkySports www.skysports.com
Sportal (INT) www.sportal.com
Sporting Life www.sporting-life.com
Sports.com (Euro) http://sports.com

But if your interest even slightly borders on obsession you'll find far more satisfaction on the pages of something more one-eyed. For clubs and fan sites, drill down through Yahoo! and the Open Directory. They won't carry everything, but what you'll find will lead you to the right forces:

Open Directory http://dmoz.org/Sports
Yahoo Sports http://dir.yahoo.com/recreation/sports

the directory

If you can't get to the telly or are looking for webcasts of that crucial Ryman's League derby, check Sport On Air (www.sportonair.com) for listings of streaming audio coverage of sport on the Web.

For the darker side of sport, check out Hofstetter's Sports Jerk of the Week (http://jerkoftheweek.com) which keeps tabs on all the stories clubs would prefer stayed buried.

American Football

NFL
www.nfl.com
www.nfluth.com
www.nfleurope.com
Media schedules, chats, news, player profiles, stats and streaming highlight videos from the National Football League's past and current seasons.

Athletics

The Athletics Site
www.athletix.org
Almost everything you could want to know about athletics – other than how to run as fast as Maurice Greene.

Aussie Rules

Australian Football League
www.afl.com.au
Men in tight shorts playing aerial ping-pong.

Baseball

Major League Baseball
www.mlb.com
Home of the second most boring sport on Earth.

The Baseball Archive
www.baseball1.com
The most outrageous complete statistical analysis of sport anywhere. For more lunatic scholarship, see Big Bad Baseball:
www.bigbadbaseball.com

Basketball

NBA.com
www.nba.com
Pro basketball news, picks, player profiles, analyses, results, schedules and high-light videos.

Boxing

Seconds Out
www.secondsout.com
With its merger with Boxing News, this site is effectively a pugilism portal, linking up to just about everything related to the sweet science.

Cricket

CricInfo
www.cricinfo.com
Perhaps a bit like cricket itself this site is a bit creaky and not exactly flashy, but it has all the news and information anyone who hasn't memorized *Wisden* could ever need – from Test level down to local leagues.

334 Not Out
www.334notout.com
The "Bodyline Series", the exploits of Donald Bradman and the rest of the history of the Ashes are enshrined at this fun site, along with current news.

Wisden
www.wisden.com
The bible of the cricket establishment has finally embraced the potential of the Net, but you have to pay (£37.50 a year) to get the most out of it.

the directory

Cycling

Cycling News
www.cyclingnews.com
Tour de force coverage of the Tour de France.

Cycle Source
www.cyclesource.co.uk
Portal for British cycling enthusiasts.

MTB Britain
www.mtbbritain.co.uk
Pretty much everything a mountain biker of any skill level could want from a site: movies, news, training tips, articles and product reviews.

Darts

Toe the Oche
www.toetheoche.co.uk
Complete coverage of the professional darts scene, plus a campaign to bring *Bullseye* back to British TV screens.

Extreme Sports

Adventure Sports Directory
www.adventuredirectory.com
http://dmoz.org/Sports/Extreme_Sports
For all that falls under the banner of "extreme sports" – from taking your pushbike off road to the sort of sheer recklessness that would get you cut from a will. For something more flashy, check out:
www.pie.com
http://expn.go.com

Goals – Global Online Adventure Learning Site
www.goals.com
Chase adventurous lunatics like Mick Bird, who's circling the globe in a canoe.

Fishing

Anglers Net
www.anglersnet.co.uk
The best British fishing portal on the Web.

Fishing Directories
www.thefishfinder.com
http://fishsearch.com
Trade tips and generally exaggerate about aquatic bloodsports.

Fitness

Abdominal Training
www.timbomb.net/ab
Build "abs ripped liked ravioli".

Fitness Online
www.fitnessonline.com
Log your training and nutrition regime online.

Football

Football Ground Guide
www.footballgroundguide.co.uk
Comprehensive guide to the homes of all 92 league clubs.

Football365
www.football365.com
Everything you need to know about the Premiership and beyond. Not enough news? Try:
www.fa-premier.com
www.football.nationwide.co.uk
www.onefootball.com
www.planetfootball.com

the directory

www.rivals.net
www.soccerassociation.com
www.soccernet.com
www.wsc.co.uk

Soccerbase
www.soccerbase.com
For game, club and player stats.

Team Talk
www.teamtalk.com
The latest news from every club in Britain constantly updated.

Golf

GolfWeb
www.golfweb.com
Unbeatable coverage of the American PGA. For European golf, try Europeantour.com
(www.europeantour.com). For women's golf, your clubhouse of choice should be the
LPGA site (www.lpga.com).

OnlineGolf
www.onlinegolf.co.uk
Very good all-round shopping site for clubs, shoes, fleeces and balls, plus tips for
beginners and experts alike.

Gymnastics

International Gymnast
www.intlgymnast.com
Peerless news and views from the competitive gymnastics world. For training tips
and advice on routines, try:
www.gym-routines.com

Hockey

Fieldhockey.com
www.fieldhockey.com
Sticks and stuff.

Ice Hockey

The A to Z Encyclopedia of Ice Hockey
www.azhockey.com
Complete coverage of ice hockey throughout the world. For results and stats from the best league in the world, go to NHL.com (www.nhl.com). For the real reason people watch ice hockey, check out:
http://zeroreality.com/fights
www.BroadStreetBully.com
www.ChicagoFighters.com

Ice Skating

SkateWeb
www.frogsonice.com/skateweb
News, pics and bios of your favourite stars on ice.

Martial Arts

Martial Arts Network
www.martial-arts-network.com
All you need to become the next Chuck Norris or Jet Li.

Motorsport

Atlas F1
www.atlasf1.com
Extensive coverage of F1.

Indy Car Racing
www.indyracingleague.com
All the news from the Brickyard.

Monster Truck Racing
www.monstertrucks.net
Put a pinch of chewing tobacco between your cheek and gum and watch Grave Digger and cohorts squash some bugs.

the directory

Motograndprix.com
www.motograndprix.com
Just about every motorcycle event in the world is covered here.

NASCAR
www.nascar.com
Dixie's favourite stock cars.

World Motorsport Index
www.worldmotorsport.com
Start here for your gasoline-induced pleasure. More revs at Auto Sport
(www.autosport.com). For more specific pleasures, try:

World Rallying

The World Rally Championship Infosystem

www.worldrally.net
Small cars sliding into trees and skidding in the mud.

Rugby

Planet Rugby
www.planet-rugby.com
www.rleague.com
www.ozleague.com
www.scrum.com
www.rugbyheaven.com
Up-to-the-minute coverage of hard men trotting in and out of the blood bin, plus
columnists, a historical archive, rules and a shop.

Sailing

Sailing Index
www.smartguide.com
www.madforsailing.com
Everything seaworthy: from swapping yachts to choosing a GPS.

Skiing

SkiCentral
www.skicentral.com
www.skiclub.co.uk
Indexes thousands of ski-related sites covering such things as snow reports, resort cams, snowboard gear, accommodation and coming events in resorts across the world. For snowboarding, see:
www.twsnow.com
www.board-it.com

Snooker

110 Snooker
www.110sport.com/snooker
All the news from the baize.

Surfing

Surf Link
www.surflink.com
Articles, numerous webcams, tips and surfing forecasts for the entire world – alerting you when a killer wave is headed to your local break. For British surfing, news, links and forcasts, try:
www.britsurf.co.uk
www.eyeball-surfcheck.co.uk
And for more localized forecasts, links and info, try:
www.sharkbait.co.uk (Brighton)
www.bournemouth-surfing.co.uk (Bournemouth)
www.troggs.com (Ireland)
www.a1surf.com/surfcheck-western.html (Devon and Cornwall)

the directory

www.westcoastsurf.co.uk/surfreport.htm (Wales)
www.croyde-surf-cam.com (Croyde)
www.northdevonuk.co.uk/NDUKSurf.html (North Devon)
And for surf reports straight to your mobile, sign up with:
www.6ftoffshore.com

World Surfing
www.goan.com/surflink.html
Every day's like Big Wednesday. For daily breaks and Aussie seaboard cams, see:
www.coastalwatch.com

Swimming

Swimmersworld.com
www.swimmersworld.com
Coverage of the competitive swimming scene.

WebSwim
www.webswim.com
The FAQ of the rec.sport.swimming newsgroup, with information on training, suits, etc.

Tennis

Tennis.com
www.tennis.com
All the news from the pros, plus instructional sections, racquet and shoe reviews, pro endorsements and fitness tips.

Wrestling

For the official line, go to WWF (www.wwf.com), but for the unofficial line and the bottom line, try:

The DDT Digest
www.ddtdigest.com
Great wrestling zine, with the history of blading, the downfall of the WCW in pictures, vintage programmes and other crucial tidbits of wrestling ephemera.

the directory

You call that a sport?

British Minigolf Association http://members.aol.com/MiniGolf98
You won't be laughing when you find out that tournament prize money can reach $100,000.

Canadian Amateur Tug of War Association www.tugofwar.ca
You're just pulling my leg.

Disc Golf World www.discgolfworld.com
The latest news from the frisbee golf scene, plus all the "drivers" and "putters" you'll ever need.

Beltsander Drag Racing Association www.beltsander-races.com
All the news and highlights from the fast-paced, laugh-in-the-face-of-death world of beltsander drag racing.

PaintBall.com www.paintball.com
All the information you need to make life hell for the groom-to-be.

Wife Carrying www.wifecarrying.com
The prize is your other half's weight in beer.

Wheelbarrow Freestyle www.wheelbarrowfreestyle.com
The one-wheel extreme sport.

World Elephant Polo Association http://elephantpolo.com
How is it that a team from Iceland is the best in the world?

1Wrestling.com
www.1wrestling.com
For coverage of the grappling world beyond the WWF and for the most influential coverage of the big boys, this should be your first wrestling bookmark.

Solie's Vintage Wrestling
www.solie.org
Do you remember grappling before Vince McMahon's delusions of grandeur or do you have no idea who Kerry Von Erich, Magnum TA or Bruno Sammartino are? Either way you need to visit this shrine to the squared circle's old school.

Telecoms

Campaign for Unmetered Telecommunications
www.telecom.eu.org
Rail against the call-charging system that's making Europe an Internet backwater.

Directory Enquiries
www.2bt.com/edq_resnamesearch
BT's directory enquiries site. For other British phone searches, try:
www.192.com
www.infospace.com
www.newdirectoryenquiries.com
www.118080.co.uk
www.yell.com

Efax
www.efax.com
www.j2.com
Free up a phone line by receiving your faxes by email.

Free Fax Services
www.tpc.int
Transmit faxes via the Internet free.

MobileWorld
www.mobileworld.org
Assorted info on mobile phones and cellular networks.

Oftel
www.oftel.gov.uk
Keep a watch on the telephone watchdog.

The Payphone Project
www.payphone-project.com
An utterly bizarre site devoted to that near-extinct dinosaur of twentieth-century technology, the payphone. Includes payphone news, history of the payphone, photos and numbers. For more payphone numbers, try the Pay Phone Directory:
www.payphone-directory.org

Reverse Phone Directory
www.reversephonedirectory.com
Key in a US phone number to find its owner. To find a UK location see:
www.warwick.ac.uk/cgi-bin-Phones/nng

SMS Text Messages
http://sms.lycos.co.uk/mobile
Send free text messages to mobile phones worldwide.

Splash Mobile
www.SplashMobile.com
Ring tones, logos, games and other essential accessories for your mobile. The site pays fees to the MCPS, so you can rest assured that the composer of the *Knight Rider* theme will get his just royalties. Other ring tone sites:

Jippii! www.jippii.co.uk
Mobile Tones www.mobiletones.com
Monstermob www.monstermob.com
Phoneringsong www.phoneringsong.com
Phunky Phones www.phunkyphones.com
Ringtones Online www.ringtones.co.uk
Your Mobile www.yourmobile.com

The Telegraph Office
http://fohnix.metronet.com/~nmcewen/tel_off.html
www.navyrelics.com/tribute/bellsys
Trip through the history of wired communications from Morse telegraphy to the Bell System.

WAP Sites

If you've got a WAP phone or just like to pretend that you do (get a WAP emulator which enables your PC to read WML encoded script at http://updev.phone.com), these are some of the best sites:

Ananova www.ananova.com
Get breaking news sent as customized WAP pages to your phone.

Ents24 www.ents24.co.uk
What's-on listings for the entire country.

Genie www.genie.co.uk
Get up-to-the-minute sports results.

Mail2Wap www.mail2wap.com
Collect your POP3 mail on a WAP phone.

Mobile WAP www.mobilewap.com
The largest WAP search engine.

Pocket Doctor www.pocketdoctor.co.uk/wap
Never forget to take your medicine, or get symptom descriptions sent to your mobile.

Railtrack http://railtrack.kizoom.co.uk
Why talk to an operator at the National Rail Enquiries line when you can have the info zapped to your phone instead? To check out how long your delay on the Tube will be, go to:
www.tflwap.gov.uk

Retrotopia Wireless Intellivison
www.intellivisionlives.com/retrotopia/wireless.shtml
Play 1980s classics like Astrosmash and Night Stalker on your mobile phone.

WAP Translator http://langues.ifrance.com/langues/index.wml
Translate to and from English, French, Italian, Spanish, German and Dutch with your phone.

UK STD Codes
www.brainstorm.co.uk/utils/std-codes.html
Keep up to date with the labrynthine complexities of the UK's phone exchanges.

UK Telecom FAQ
www.gbnet.net/net/uk-telecom
Satisfy your curiosity about the British phone network.

UK Telecom Tariff Comparisons
www.magsys.co.uk/telecom
www.phonebills.org.uk
Compare the prices of leading landline phone service providers for free, but if you want business-rate comparisons or to view the results in spreadsheet format you've got to subscribe. For mobile phone rates, try uSwitch:
www.uswitch.com/Mobiles

What Does Your Phone Number Spell?
www.phonespell.org
Enter your phone number to see what it spells. The reverse lookup might help you choose a number.

What does your phone number spell?

World Time & Dialing Codes
www.whitepages.com.au/wp/search/time.html
International dialling info from anywhere to anywhere, including current times and area codes.

Television

Most TV stations maintain excellent sites with all kinds of extras such as live sports coverage and documentary follow-ups. We won't need to give you their addresses because they'll be flashing them at you at every

the directory

opportunity. In any case, you'll find them all at:

tvshow.com www.tvshow.com

For personalized listings, perhaps delivered by email, try your local Yahoo! or:

Ananova www.ananova.com/tv
OnTheBox.com www.onthebox.com

The best of these, however, might be: **Digiguide** (www.digiguide.co.uk) which is a customizable listings database that covers terrestrial, cable, digital and satellite. You download the site's free software, tell the program which region you live in or whether you have cable or digital and then download the next two week's worth of listings.

asSeenonScreen
www.asseenonscreen.com
Buy stuff you've seen on TV or in movies.

Bigglethwaite.com
www.bigglethwaite.com
With its comprehensive links page to UK TV websites, this is a good place to start any search.

Digi Reels
www.digireels.co.uk
If you can't get enough of them on TV, then point your browser here immediately and search a mindblowing database of over 100,000 adverts. Also check out UK Television Adverts:
www.westwood.u-net.com/ads

Drew's Script-O-Rama
www.script-o-rama.com/snazzy/tvscript.html
A huge set of links to an astonishing array of predominantly American television scripts and episode transcripts. Also try Simply Scripts:
www.simplyscripts.com

Epguides
http://epguides.com
If you're serious about TV – really, really serious – this site is your holy grail. Containing complete episode guides for over 1700 shows (mostly American) which are linked to the Internet Movie Database for cross-referencing, this is an amazing research tool for academics, journalists, enthusiasts and general freaks. For similar

coverage of Britcoms, try TV Comedy Resources Hu's Episode Guides and
Television Without Pity:
www.phill.co.uk
www.episodeguides.com
www.televisionwithoutpity.com

Independent TeleWeb
www.itw.org.uk
The history of independent commercial television in the UK.

Jump The Shark
www.jumptheshark.com
Named after that episode in *Happy Days* when Fonzie ski-jumped over a shark,
starting the show's inexorable downward spiral, this brilliant site is dedicated to
documenting the moment when your favourite programe goes south. Signals of
impending doom include same-character-different-actor, puberty, "A very special..."
and the presence of Ted McGinley (aka Jefferson on *Married With Children*).

Like Television
www.liketelevision.com
The broadband-enabled can watch episodes of classic TV like *I Dream Of Jeannie*,
The Three Stooges and *Bugs Bunny*.

Live TV
www.comfm.fr/live/tv
Tune into live video feeds from hundreds of real world television stations. To record
US cable shows and play them back in Real Video (court case pending) see:
www.snapstream.com

Sausagenet
www.sausagenet.co.uk
Tribute to cult and vintage television shows that babysat for Generation X. It has a
reviews section (covering video and DVD releases of old programs) and downloadable sound files, but is most useful as a portal for retro TV enthusiasts.

Sitcoms Online
www.sitcomsonline.com
Very US-focused, but if you're looking for any information on a Yankee comedy,
this is the first place to look. There are also games, discussions and polls that are
fun for any comedy enthusiast regardless of nationality.

the directory

Soap City
www.soapcity.com
http://members.tripod.com/~TheSoapBox
Keep up with who's doing what to whom, who they told and who shouldn't find out in the surreal world of soap fiction.

Test Card Circle
www.testcardcircle.org.uk
The homepage of Test Card Circle, an organization of enthusiasts of the music that accompanied the test card sequences that reigned over British TV in the dark days before cable.

The 30 Second Candidate
www.pbs.org/30secondcandidate
A fascinating history of the political TV spot from PBS, America's answer to the BBC.

Transdiffusion
www.transdiffusion.org
A truly fantastic resource for anyone interested in the history of British broadcasting, this site hosts the archives of the Transdiffusion Organization, which is dedicated to preserving the history of radio and TV in the UK. Included are screen grabs from TV coverage of historical moments, jingles, theme tunes, in-depth articles on various aspects of broadcasting history and course notes for students and teachers.

TV Ark
www.tv-ark.co.uk
With its focus on arcana and minutiae, this online museum of British television is one for true believers. Mostly downloadable sound and video files of station identifications and theme tunes at the moment, but videos and information are promised in the future.

TV Eyes
www.tveyes.com
Informs you when your search term is mentioned on TV.

TV Go Home
www.tvgohome.com
Onion-style parodies of *The Radio Times*.

TV Party
www.tvparty.com
Irreverent, hilarious and more fun than a barrel of Keith Chegwins, this American site is the hall of fame that the medium truly deserves. Included are an amazing archive of uncensored out-takes, frighteningly in-depth articles about all manner of televisual ephemera and pull-no-punches features on programmes.

TV Show
www.tvshow.com
Everything TV – from schedules of every station worldwide and links to just about every show ever made to the technical aspects of production and broadcasting. Start all your TV-related searches here.

Regional TV archives

With big media companies like Carlton and Granada dominating ITV, the halcyon days of regional broadcasting are almost gone. However, since television breeds lunacy like no other medium, there are a number of enthusiasts throughout the country dedicated to preserving the memory of low production values, terrible clothes and hopeless segues.

Border Television Area www.bordertvarea.co.uk
Comprehensive archive of ITV in the North.

Harlech House of Graphics www.hhg.org.uk
Thirty years of ITV in the West and Wales.

ITV Southern England http://members.tripod.co.uk/Southern_TV
Independent telly from the South since 1958.

Television Southwest www.televisionsouthwest.com
Dedicated to ITV in the West Country.

Tyne Tees Logo Page www.ttlp.org.uk
A wry look at the Northeast's independent station.

the directory

TV Tickets
www.tvtickets.com
Secure your chance to clap on cue.

VCR Repair Instructions
www.fixer.com
How to take a VCR apart and then get all the little bits back in so it fits easier into the bin.

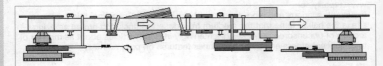

VCR Repair Instruction
"The Self Service Website"

Virtue TV
www.virtuetv.com
If you're one of the lucky few with broadband access, this virtual channel features independent short films, an archive of music concerts and sports footage, and classic movies like Roger Corman's *Little Shop of Horrors* and Buster Keaton's *Steamboat Bill Jr*.

Who Would You Kill?
www.whowouldyoukill.com
So who would you toss into *Dawson's Creek*?

WWITV
http://wwitv.com
Watch TV stations from around the world, mostly obscure.

Yahoo Platinum
www.platinum.yahoo.com
With this Yahoo! site you can watch local US stations to your heart's delight.

the directory

TV Programmes

The Web would be nothing without people who have obsessions that transcend rational thought, and television is particularly well-served by fanaticism. Here are some of the best sites devoted to a single show.

Angelic Slayer www.angelicslayer.com
Run by a teenage fan from Arizona, this rather amazing site devoted to *Buffy The Vampire Slayer* and *Angel* has attracted over two million hits.

Cookd And Bombd www.cookdandbombd.co.uk
Site devoted to the warped comedy and media terrorism of Chris Morris. More at www.koekie.org.uk/funnel

Corrie Net www.corrie.net
This *Coronation Street* archive has everything everyone could ever want to know about Ken Barlow and Hilda Ogden.

ER www.nbc.com/ER
Romance, blood and lots of helicopter crashes – what more could you want from a medical drama. If you aren't a fan of the show, you might enjoy: www.digiserve.com/er

Erinsborough.com www.erinsborough.com
Catch up with all the gossip from Ramsay Street.

Fisher And Sons www.sixfeetunderfan.com
Everything you need to know about undertaking, *Six Feet Under* style.

Frank Butcher's Philosophical Car Lot
http://geocities.com/SunsetStrip/Stadium/1123/page1.html
RealAudio clips of *EastEnders'* philosopher-king.

Friends Place www.friendsplace.com
Every script of every episode ever. But if you have that much spare time it might make you wish you had some of your own.

Sex And The City www.hbo.com/city
It may not be on the box any more, but there's enough trivia and nonsense here to keep devoted fans happy.

Time

Calendarzone
www.calendarzone.com
Calendar links and, believe it or not, calzone recipes.

DateReminder
www.datereminder.co.uk
Remind yourself by email.

The Death Clock
www.deathclock.com
Get ready to book your final taxi.

Horology – The Index
www.horology.com
This text-heavy portal to all things pertaining to the science of timekeeping includes
information on collecting timepieces, email addresses of "cyber-horologists" and
links to horological organizations.

International Earth Rotation Service
http://hpiers.obspm.fr
Ever felt like your bed's spinning? The truth is even scarier.

iPing (US)
www.iping.com
Arrange free telephone reminders for one or many.

Martian Time
http://pweb.jps.net/~tgangale/mars/index4.htm
Learn exactly when the little green men will be coming.

Metric Time
www.billcollins.com.au/bc/mt
Decimalized excuses for being late.

Online Planners
www.supercalendar.com
www.calendars.net
Maintain your planner online. Excite, Yahoo, MSN, and Netscape offer similar things.

Time and Date
www.timeanddate.com
Instantly tell the time in your choice of cities. Keep your PC clock aligned with a time synchronizer:
www.ntp.org

Time Cave
www.timecave.com
Schedule an email to be sent at a specific time in the future.

Time Cube
www.timecube.com
Disprove God through the simultaneous four-day Time Cube.

US National Debt Clock
http://brillig.com/debt_clock
Watch your children's future slip away.

USNO Master Clock Time
http://tycho.usno.navy.mil/what.html
Compute the local apparent sidereal time in your part of the world or listen to a live broadcast of the USNO Master Clock announcer. Get your computer's clock set by modem at:
http://tycho.usno.navy.mil/modem_time.html

the directory

trains

Trains

End of the Line
www.wigancrdc.co.uk
Site devoted to the faded (and rusting) glory of withdrawn locomotives lying on the scrap heap.

Rail Britain
www.railbritain.com
A big site aimed at both the traveller and the enthusiast, including news, chat rooms, timetables, maps, rolling stock guides and fleet information.

Steam Locomotive
www.steamlocomotive.com
A storehouse of information on steam trains geared towards the serious, tech-minded enthusiast. Includes detailed information on wheel arrangements, horse-power and hundreds of locomotives from the golden age of rail travel.

Track Bed
www.trackbed.com
An impressive site aiming to become the online authority on British rail history. The database includes comprehensive histories of the UK's main rail companies, routes, maps, an in-depth (100K) glossary and photos.

Train Orders
www.trainorders.com
Railway hobby site hosting lots of discussion groups, rail cams covering two Californian main lines, quizzes and an archive of over a thousand loco photos.

Steamy Affairs

Railway preservation may not have the hippest image in the world, but steam engines are enjoying a renaissance throughout the world. The UK currently boasts around 430 miles of track (more than the London Underground) used by the country's 1200 steam engines. Here are a few sites devoted to historical railways both in Britain and abroad.

Richard Leonard's Steam Locomotive Archive
http://members.aol.com/rlsteam
Nostalgia-sodden photos of North American railroads in the 1950s.

Mainline Steam Tours Index
www.uksteam.info
Listings of steam locomotive journeys in the UK.

Steam Central
www.steamcentral.com
Steam locomotion from an American perspective.

Steam Dreams
www.steamdreams.co.uk
The Cathedrals Express.

UK Heritage Railways
http://ukhrail.uel.ac.uk
Guide to the UK's heritage railway scene.

Vintage Trains
www.vintagetrains.co.uk
A collection of steam engines preserved by the
Birmingham Railway Museum Trust.

Train Web
www.trainweb.org
This portal is a trainspotter's paradise. In addition to a site catalogue cleverly organized as both white and yellow pages, Train Web hosts chat rooms, forums, photo collections, the Rail Search search engine and the ever-popular Railcams.com so you can catch the *Flying Scotsman* without ever leaving your armchair. More Internet junctions at:
www.railserve.com
http://communities.prodigy.net/trains

travel

Travel

Whether you're seeking inspiration, planning an itinerary, shopping for a ticket or already mobile, there'll be a tool online worth throwing in your box. You can book flights, reserve hotel rooms, research your destination, monitor the weather, convert currencies, learn the lingo, locate an ATM, scan local newspapers, collect your mail from abroad, find a restaurant that suits your fussy tastes and plenty more. For detailed listings, buy a copy of the *Rough Guide to Travel Online*. If you'd like to find first-hand experiences or travelling companions, hit the Usenet discussion archives at Google (http://groups.google.com) and join the appropriate newsgroup under the rec.travel or soc.culture hierarchies. As with all newsgroups, before you post a question, skim through the FAQs first:

Rec.Travel Library www.travel-library.com

You could also try consulting a volunteer "expert".

Abuzz www.abuzz.com/category/travel
All Experts www.allexperts.com/travel

Then see what the major guidebook publishers have to offer:

Fodors www.fodors.com
Frommer's www.frommers.com
Insiders www.insiders.com
Let's Go www.letsgo.com
Lonely Planet www.lonelyplanet.com
Michelin www.michelin-travel.com
Moon Travel www.moon.com
Robert Young Pelton www.comebackalive.com
Rough Guides www.roughguides.com
Rough Guides Directions www.directionsguides.com
Routard www.club-internet.fr/routard

Alternatively, check out online guides such as:

Beachtowel www.beachtowel.co.uk
CityVox www.cityvox.com
IExplore www.iexplore.com
World Travel Guide www.wtg-online.com

While it might seem like commercial suicide for the Rough Guides to give away the full text of its guides to more than ten thousand destinations, the reality is that books are still more convenient, especially on the road when you need them most. If you'd like to order a guide or map online you'll also find plenty of opportunities either from the above publishers, the online bookshops (p.70), or from travel bookshops such as:

Adventurous Traveler http://shop.gorp.com/atbook
Literate Traveller www.literatetraveller.com/index.html
Stanfords www.stanfords.co.uk

Many online travel agents also provide destination guides, which might include exclusive editorial peppered with chunks licensed from guide-

the directory

books linked out to further material on the Web. For example:

Away.com http://away.com
Escaperoutes www.reddirect.co.uk/travel.asp

The biggest problem with browsing the Web for regional information and travel tools is not in finding the sites, but wading through them. Take the following directories for example:

About Travel http://travel.about.com
Budget Travel www.budgettravel.com
Excite Travel http://travel.excite.com
Lycos Travel http://travel.lycos.com
Open Directory http://dmoz.org/Recreation/Travel
My Travel Guide www.mytravelguide.com
Traveller Online www.travelleronline.com
Trip Advisor (US) www.tripadvisor.com
Virtual Tourist www.vtourist.com
World Travel Guide www.travel-guide.com
World Travel Net www.world-travel-net.com
Yahoo Directory www.yahoo.com/Recreation/Travel
Yahoo! Travel http://travel.yahoo.com

These are perfect if you want to browse through regions looking for ideas, or find a range of sites on one topic – health, for example. But if you're after something very specific, you might find it more efficient to use a search engine such as **Google** (see p.12). Keep adding search terms until you restrict the number of results to something manageable. If you'd like your vacation to coincide with a festival or event, go straight to:

What's on When www.whatsonwhen.com
What's Going On www.whatsgoingon.com

Or for entertainment, eating, and cultural events, a city guide:

Citysearch www.citysearch.com
Time Out www.timeout.co.uk
Wcities.com www.wcities.com
Yahoo! Local http://local.yahoo.com

Zagat (Dining) www.zagat.com

If you're flexible, you might find a last-minute special. These Net exclusives are normally offered directly from the airline, hotel, and travel operator sites, which you'll find through Yahoo! There are also a few Web operators that specialize in late-notice and special Internet deals on flights, hotels, events, and so forth, such as:

Bargain Holidays www.bargainholidays.com
Best Fares www.bestfares.com
Lastminute.com www.lastminute.com
Lastminutetravel.com www.lastminutetravel.com
Opodo www.opodo.co.uk
Smarter Living www.smarterliving.com
Travel Zoo www.travelzoo.com

Then there are the reverse-auction sites like Priceline.com where you bid on a destination and wait. You might strike up a good deal if you bid shrewdly and don't mind the somewhat draconian restrictions (see: www.angelfire.com/nt/priceline). Hotwire offers similar discounts on undisclosed airlines but names the price up front. If you're super-flexible, you could try Airhitch or a courier company:

Air Courier Assoc. www.aircourier.org
Airhitch www.airhitch.org
Hotwire www.hotwire.com
IAATC Air Courier www.courier.org
Priceline.com www.priceline.com

Booking a flight through one of the online ticketing systems isn't too hard, but bargains are few. Unless you're spending someone else's money you'll want to sidestep the full fares offered on these major services:

Expedia www.expedia.co.uk
Travelocity www.travelocity.co.uk
Travel Select www.travelselect.co.uk

Although they list hundreds of airlines and millions of fares, the general consensus is that they're usually better for research, accommodation and travel tips than cheap fares and customer service. So if you think it's worth the effort, drop in and check which carriers haul your route, offer the best deals and still have seats available. You can then use their rates as a benchmark. Compare them with the fares on the airline sites and discount specialists such as:

Bargain Holidays www.bargainholidays.com
Cheap Flights www.cheapflights.com
Deckchair www.deckchair.com
EasyJet www.easyjet.com
Ebookers.com www.ebookers.com
Flight Centre www.flightcentre.com
OneTravel.com www.onetravel.com
Ryan Air www.ryanair.com

Or compare the prices across several agencies simultaneously using these sites:

Farechase www.farechase.com
Hotwire www.hotwire.com
QIXO www.qixo.com
Sidestep www.sidestep.com

Finally, see if your travel agent can better the price. If the difference is only marginal, favour your agent. Then at least you'll have a human contact if something goes wrong.

A2Btravel.com (UK)
www.a2btravel.com
www.ferrybooker.com
www.webweekends.co.uk
Resources for getting into, around, and out of the UK, such as car-rental comparison, airport guides, train timetables and ferry booking.

Africam
www.africam.com
Sneak a peek at wild beasts going about their business.

The Africa Guide
www.africaguide.com
Good, general guides of a region that nearly all the major guide books and travel services ignore. Try also Africa Net (www.africanet.com).

Maps and Atlases

You can generate road and airport maps for most cities worldwide, driving directions for North America and Europe, US traffic reports, world maps and more at:

Expedia http://maps.expedia.com
MapBlast www.mapblast.com
MapQuestUK www.mapquest.co.uk
Easymap www.easymap.co.uk
Mappy www.mappy.co.uk
Multimap www.multimap.com
Ordnance Survey www.ordsvy.gov.uk
Shell Geo Star Route Planner www.shellgeostar.com

To create UK street and road maps from postcodes or addresses, see:

Streetmap (UK) www.streetmap.co.uk

If you require highly detailed US topographic maps, try:

TopoZone www.topozone.com

For more maps, geographical and GPS resources see:

About http://geography.about.com
Open Directory http://dmoz.org/Reference/Maps

the directory

Art of Travel
www.artoftravel.com
How to see the world on $25 a day.

ATM Locators
www.visa.com/atms
www.mastercard.com/cardholderservices/atm
Locate a bowser willing to replenish your wallet.

Backpacker.com
www.backpacker.com
Excellent site for wilderness trekkers, including destination guides, tips on keeping
your boots in shape and the real dope on DEET-free insect repellents.

The Bathroom Diaries
www.thebathroomdiaries.com
One of the most essential sites on the Web: You're in Bamako, Mali when nature calls
and you're after a good, clean Western-style toilet, click here to find out the nearest
one. A wireless version is promised soon, so you'll have to hang on until then.

Bed & Breakfast.com
www.bedandbreakfast.com
www.bedandbreakfast-directory.co.uk
www.babs.com.au
www.innsite.com
Secure your night's sleep worldwide.

BizTraveler.org
www.biztraveler.org
Looking after commercial travellers.

British Waterways
www.britishwaterways.co.uk
All you ever wanted to know about canal barging.

Bugbog
www.bugbog.co.uk
Nice, compact, easy-to-navigate mini-guides for people wanting to go somewhere

a bit out of the ordinary. Good features include the best beaches in the world by month, and a destination finder giving you options like colourful culture, festivals and weather.

Caravan Sitefinder
http://caravan-sitefinder.co.uk
Where to hitch your rusting hulk of steel without looking like hippy scum. For places to pitch your tent, try Camp Sites:
www.camp-sites.co.uk

CIA World Factbook
www.cia.gov/cia/publications/factbook
Vital stats on every country. For the score on living standards:
www.undp.org

Concierge.com
www.concierge.com
Get packing with advice from *Traveler* magazine.

Danger Finder
www.comebackalive.com/df
Adventure holidays that could last a lifetime.

Days Out
www.virgin.net/daysout
You might not want to use their trains to get you there, but Virgin does at least provide an excellent service with this site, which is crammed with ideas for successful day trips. For more ideas, try About Britain and DaysOutUK:
www.aboutbritain.com
www.daysoutuk.com

Electronic Embassy
www.embassy.org
Directory of foreign embassies in DC plus Web links where available. Search Yahoo for representation in other cities.

Eurotrip
www.eurotrip.com
www.ricksteves.com
Look out Europe, here you come.

Family Travel Files
www.thefamilytravelfiles.com
Look here for help on what to do when the little monsters start asking, "Are we there yet?" For more UK-specific destinations, try PlanIt4Kids:
www.planit4kids.com

the directory

For holidays with toddlers, try:
www.babygoes2.com

Flight Arrivals & Departures
www.flightarrivals.com
Stay on top of takeoffs and touchdowns across North America.

FrequentFlier.com
http://frequentflier.com
The information here is definitely more useful for Americans, but it's nevertheless a great resource for frequent travellers after the best deal for their miles. See also Web Flyer:
www.webflyer.com

Gap Year
www.gapyear.com
Excellent site dedicated to students about to take a year out, with loads of travel tips and stories.

Global Freeloaders
www.globalfreeloaders.com
Take in a globetrotting dosser in exchange for some return hospitality.

Hotel Discount
www.hoteldiscount.com
www.hotelnet.co.uk
www.hotelwiz.com
Book hotels around the world. For backpacker rates, try:
www.hostels.com

How far is it?
www.indo.com/distance
Calculate the distance between any two cities.

IgoUgo
www.igougo.com
Packed full of travellers' photos and journals, this roughguides.com partner site offers candid first-hand information.

Incredible Adventures
www.incredible-adventures.com
Convert your cash into adrenaline.

Infiltration
www.infiltration.org
Confessions of a serial trespasser.

International Home Exchange Network
www.homexchange.com
www.sunswap.com
www.homebase-hols.com
Trade your dreary digs for a palatial beach house.

International Student Travel Confederation
www.istc.org
Save money with an authentic international student card.

Journeywoman
www.journeywoman.com
Reporting in from the sister beaten track.

Mail2Web
www.mail2web.com
Collect and send your POP3 mail instantly from any web browser. Faster than
Hotmail. If you can't get it to work, try another, such as:
www.pandamail.net

The Man in Seat 61
www.seat61.com
A superb resource – how to get from London to anywhere in the world by train (and
the occasional boat).

the directory

My Travel Rights
http://mytravelrights.com
Disgruntled? Maybe you'll be reimbursed. More at:
www.passengerrights.com

No Shitting in the Toilet
www.noshit.com.au
Delighting in the oddities of low-budget travel.

OAG
www.oag.com
Largest database of flight schedules on the Net, which can be downloaded to your Palm or mobile.

The Original Tipping Page
www.tipping.org
Make fast friends with the bell-hop.

Railtrack
www.railtrack.co.uk
Depress yourself at the state of the country's railways by looking at corporate reports or the timetable details. To book tickets online try The Train Line or Q Jump:
www.thetrainline.com
www.qjump.co.uk
And for general public transport information try Public Transport Info:
www.pti.org.uk

Resorts Online
www.resortsonline.com
Your way through three thousand resorts throughout the world categorized by beach, golf, spa, ski, etc.

Roadside America
www.roadsideamerica.com
Strange attractions that loom between squished animals on US highways.

Sahara Overland
www.sahara-overland.com
Leave the city in a cloud of dust.

Satellite and Aerial Imaging
www.terraserver.com
http://terra.nasa.gov
www.crworld.co.uk
www.photolib.noaa.gov
www.globexplorer.com
www.multimap.com
See why nine out of ten Martian honeymooners prefer your planet.

Subway Navigator
www.subwaynavigator.com
www.manhattanaddress.com
Estimate the travelling times between city stations worldwide, or find the right stop in NY.

Taken on the Road: American Mile Markers
www.kodak.com/US/en/corp/features/onTheRoad/home/index.shtml
Photographer Matt Frondorf travelled across the USA from New York to San Francisco and took a photo every mile; all 3304 are here.

Theme Parks of England
http://themeparksofengland.com
Reviews and info on all the major high G-force thrills to be had without leaving the country.

Tips4Trips
www.tips4trips.com
More than a thousand tips for the traveller, from packing to navigating customs on your way back home.

TNT Live!
www.tntmagazine.com
Survive London and venture onward with aid from expat streetmags, *TNT* and *Southern Cross*.

Tourism Offices Worldwide
www.towd.com
Write to the local tourist office. They might send you a brochure. For even more propaganda, try Official Travel Info:
www.officialtravelinfo.com

Traffic and Road Conditions
www.accutraffic.com
www.rac.co.uk/check_traffic/?view=Standard&nav
Live traffic and weather updates.

the directory

travel

Traffic Signs of the World
www.elve.net/rcoulst.htm
Next time you're in Kyrgyzstan, you'll know when to look out for the men at work.

Travel and Health Warnings
www.fco.gov.uk
www.dfat.gov.au
http://travel.state.gov
Don't ignore these bulletins if you're planning to visit a potential hot-spot or health risk, but seek a second opinion before postponing your adventure. If you're off on business, try a professional advisory such as Kroll:
www.krollworldwide.com

Travel Doctor
www.tmvc.com.au
www.cdc.gov/travel
www.masta.org
www.travelhealth.co.uk
www.who.int
Brace yourself against the bugs eagerly awaiting your arrival. For a list of travel medicine clinics worldwide, see Travel Health Online:
www.tripprep.com
And for more travel health information and a WAP service, try Medicine Planet:
www.medicineplanet.com

Travelmag
www.travelmag.co.uk
Several intimate travel reflections monthly.

Travel News Organization
www.travel-news.org
Independent travel news, holiday ideas and bargains for British travellers. For more, point your browser to eTravel:
www.etravel.org

Travel Paperwork
www.travelpaperwork.com
Sort out the red tape before you hit the border.

Travlang
www.travlang.com
Add another language to your repertoire.

Unclaimed Baggage
www.unclaimedbaggage.com
You lose it; they sell it.

UK Passport Agency
www.ukpa.gov.uk
Speed up your passport application at this streamlined site.

Underbelly
www.underbelly.com
Short, sharp, shocked guides to the places tourists rarely ever see.

Universal Currency Converter
www.xe.com/ucc
Convert Finnish Markkas into Central African Francs on the fly. More at Oanda:
www.oanda.com

Vindigo
www.vindigo.com
Is Vindigo the future of travel guides? Download its Palm Pilot or AvantGo city guides and decide for yourself.

Virtual Tourist
www.virtualtourist.com
Big database of travel reviews written by ordinary people, not travel journalists on press junkets. The reviews are hooked up to maps and links to other sites.

the directory

Visit Britain
www.visitbritain.com
www.uktravel.com
Understand the British way of doing things.

Walkabout
www.walkabout.com.au
Get the lowdown on the land down under.

WebFlyer
www.webflyer.com
Keep tabs on frequent flier schemes.

What's on When?
www.whatsonwhen.com
www.whatsgoingon.com
Annoyed you've missed *Thaipusam* or the *Turning of the Bones* yet again? Get your dates right here.

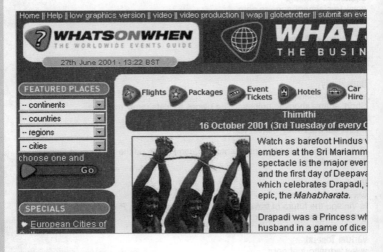

World Heritage Listing
www.unesco.org/whc
Plan your itinerary around international treasures.

Weather

Most news sites report the weather, but it's rarely up to the minute. For that you need to go directly to your local weather bureau or a specialist weather reporting service, or check the resources listed in the *Rough Guide to Weather*. For five-day forecasts, charts, storm warnings, allergy reports and satellite photos for thousands of cities worldwide, try:

Accuweather www.accuweather.com
CNN Weather www.cnn.com/WEATHER
Intellicast www.intellicast.com
Online Weather www.onlineweather.com
Weather Channel www.weather.com
Weather Organizer www.weather.org
Yahoo! Weather http://weather.yahoo.com

For more intricate and timely detail, particularly outside the USA, drop by:

The Met Office www.metoffice.gov.uk

Or for amateur observations and the fanatical extremes of weather watching, scan these specialist portals:

About Weather http://weather.about.com
Daniel's Weather Radar Page http://danielwxradar.tripod.com
European Centre for Medium Range Weather Forecasts www.ecmwf.int
Open Directory http://dmoz.org/News/Weather
The Very Useful UK Weather Page www.maalla.co.uk/uk-weather
The Weather Resource www.nxdc.com/weather
UM Weather http://cirrus.sprl.umich.edu/wxnet
WMO Members www.wmo.ch/web-en/member.html

Aviation Digital Data Service
http://adds.aviationweather.noaa.gov
If you're flying to the US, this pilot-orientated site will tell you if you need to pack extra sickbags.

the directory

Climate Ark
www.climateark.org
Fret about coming changes in the weather.

Everything Weather
www.everythingweather.com
The ultimate rainspotter's portal.

Hurricane Hunters
www.hurricanehunters.com
The homepage of the 53rd Weather Reconnaissance Squadron features photographs taken from the eye of the storm.

National Environmental Satellite and Data Information Service
www.nesdis.noaa.gov
Based in the US, this is the global headquarters of the world's weather trainspotters.

Ocean Weather
www.oceanweather.com
www.ssec.wisc.edu/data/sst.html
Chart the swells and temperatures across the seven seas.

Paul's Weather Satellite and Waffle Page
http://homepage.ntlworld.com/phqfh1
Learn how to build your own weather satellite and meet other climate fanatics.

Snoweye
www.snoweye.com
www.snow-forecast.com
Spy on thousands of ski resorts worldwide through strategically hidden cameras – or simply have the forecasts beamed directly to your WAP phone.

Space Weather
www.spaceweather.com
Monitor the effect of solar activity on the earth's atmosphere.

Tornado and Storm Research Organization
www.torro.org.uk
If you're into twisters, this site will spin you right round, baby, right round.

Weather Images
www.weatherimages.org
Depress yourself with images from Bondi Beach, and then cheer yourself up with the page of weather humour.

Focused Forecasts

Tired of imprecise regional forecasts? Do you need to know exactly what time of day it will be safe to mow your lawn? Try these sites (most of which have been set up by enthusiasts) offering weather reports right down to your postcode:

Bablake Weather Station
http://bws.users.netlink.co.uk
In-depth forecasts for the Midlands.

BBC Online Weather Centre
www.bbc.co.uk/weather
Forecasts for your postcode.

Meteorological Data From Sussex
http://cpesw3.mols.sussex.ac.uk/es/meteo
Let the Uni of Sussex help you out.

Scottish Weather Information
www.geo.ed.ac.uk/home/scotland/scotweather.html
North of the Border.

Stoke-On-Trent Weather Station
www.coyney.demon.co.uk
How specific do you want?

Weather Software
http://cirrus.sprl.umich.edu/wxnet/software.html
Stick out a wet thumb from the safety of your swivel chair.

Wild Weather
www.wildweather.com
http://australiasevereweather.com
www.nssl.noaa.gov
www.fema.gov/fema/trop.htm
Set your course into the eye of the storm.

World Climate
www.worldclimate.com
www.weatherbase.com
Off to Irkutsk next August? Here's what weather to expect.

the directory

World Meteorological Organization
www.wmo.ch
UN division that monitors global climate.

Webcams

Africam
www.africam.com
Go on a (virtual) safari without even leaving your armchair.

The Amazing Cooler Cam
www.coolercam.com
As if your workplace wasn't boring enough, watch Americans get drinks from the office water cooler.

Vote for us!

The Amazing MediaPlan

CoolerCam™

The first Water Cooler on the Web. Accept no substitutes!

Welcome to our office. This is our water cooler. Hang out for a while and you might see one of us get a drink from the cooler. In our new offices, we've set up the cam so that you can see us cool guys and gals as we move about the office.

This camera is LIVE 24 hrs a day, although we're usually only in the office Monday through Friday, 8 a.m. to 5 p.m. MST (-7 hours GMT). If nothing interesting is happening, click the *Random Castmember* link in the frame to the left to see some previously captured pictures.

How does it work?

CoolerCam
In the News

The Cast
The Camera Operator
Random Castmember
NEW Trailer Park Cam
An amazing

Beer Lover Cam
www.beerlovercam.com
Watch a couple of guys agonize over whether to grab a can of Bud or just go for the Miller.

Earth Cam

www.earthcam.com
Links to a vast array of webcams, usefully organized into categories and subcategories including Traffic, Arts & Entertainment, Metro, Weird and more. Also check Webcam Central and Webcam World:
www.camcentral.com
www.webcamworld.com

Fly on the Wall

www.flyonthewall.com
A portal dedicated to webcams and streaming video footage of movie premieres and showbiz parties, as well as Times Square, spacecraft landings and, umm, guinea pigs.

Jennicam

www.jennicam.org
The most celebrated webcam of 'em all. The enormous success of Jennicam is partially responsible for that most loathsome aspect of contemporary culture: reality television. But if you want to see where the phenomenon started, log on, pay your membership fee and watch Jenni get drunk and snog strangers...provided you're an adult.

Pavement Terror

www.backfire.co.uk
As if you needed more reason not to trust White Van Man, former delivery man Howard Stone has posted streaming videos of pedestrian horror when his van backfires.

Steve's Ant Farm

www.stevesantfarm.com
Watch blurry black punctuation marks build tunnels.

Telerobot

http://telerobot.mech.uwa.edu.au/testing.html
Control a robotic arm in Australia
from your Web browser.

Wearcam

www.wearcam.org
Your one-stop shop for information
on "photoborgs" and wearable computers.

ENGwear (Electronic News Gathering wear) student project: design and implementation of wearable wireless electronic newsgathering eyewear.

the directory

Weird

Absurd.org
www.absurd.org
Please do not adjust your set.

Aliens and Soul Abduction
www.cia.com.au/brough
Fact: spooky space dudes are stealing our souls. The Bible wouldn't lie:
http://aliensinthebible.com
If you think you may be one, see the Alien Counsel at:
www.angelfire.com/md/aliencounsel

American Pie and the Armageddon Prophecy
www.roytaylorministries.com
How Madonna testified against the descendants of Israel all the way to number
one. But what tragedy awaits her:
www.geocities.com/Athens/Atrium/3933/madonna.htm

Animal Mating Zone
www.matings.co.uk
Hardcore sex: the type you only get to see in wildlife documentaries.

Build a Better Batsuit
www.brotherhoodofthebat.com/batsuit_basics.htm
Take off on a caped crusade.

Entrances To Hell
www.entrances2hell.co.uk
Damnation is to be found in the strangest of places.

Celebrities in Distress
www.fortunecity.com/lavendar/mockingbird/472
What's sexier than being gassed, drowned, strangled or blown out into space?

Chemtrails Over America
http://home1.gte.net/quakker/Documents/Chemtrails_Over_America.htm
Those aren't clouds above your head.

Christian Guide to Small Arms
www.frii.com/~gosplow/cgsa.html
"He that hath no sword, let him sell his garment and buy one" – Luke 22:36. It's not
just your right; it's your duty, darnit.

the directory

Circlemakers
www.circlemakers.org
Create crop circles to amuse New Agers and the press.

A Citizen from Hell
www.amightywind.com/hell/citizenhell.htm
If Hell sounds this bad, you don't want to go there.

Clonaid
www.clonaid.com
Thanks to the Raelians, we now know all life on Earth was created in extraterrestrial laboratories. Here's where you can buy genuine cloned human livestock for the kitchen table. Ready as soon as the lab's finished.

Corpses for Sale
http://distefano.com
Brighten up your guestroom or spoil your pet with a life-sized chew-toy.

Corrugated Iron Club
www.corrugated-iron-club.info
It's metal. It's wavy. It rocks.

The Darwin Awards
www.darwinawards.com
Each year the Darwin Award goes to the person who drops off the census register in the most spectacular fashion. Here's where to read about the runners-up and er ... winners.

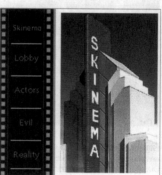

Deep Black Magic
www.mindspring.com/~txporter
Forty years of CIA research into mind control and ESP. For the perspective of a Finnish immigrant to Canada on mind control, see:
http://hackcanada.com/canadian/freedom/mylife.html

Derm Cinema
www.skinema.com
Know your celebrity skin conditions.

Dolphin Society
www.dolphinsociety.org
Driftnet-eating submarines rescue humans who've shape-shifted into dolphins.

the directory

weird

Dr MegaVolt
www.drmegavolt.com
The Doc sure sparked right up when they switched on the power, but could he cut it in the big league?
http://www3.bc.sympatico.ca/lightningsurvivor

English Rose Press
www.englishrosepress.com
Diana sends her love from Heaven.

Fetish Map
www.deviantdesires.com/map/map.html
Join the dots between piggy-players, fursuiters, inflators, crush freaks and where you're standing now.

Flatulence Filter
http://flatulence-filter.com
Because life wasn't meant to be a gas.

Fortean Times
www.forteantimes.com
Updates from the print monthly that takes the investigation of strange phenomena

more seriously than itself. See also:
www.bizarremag.com

Future Horizons
www.futurehorizons.net
Snap off more than your fair share through solid-state circuitry.

God Channel
www.godchannel.com
Relay requests to God via His official Internet channel.

Gum Blondes
www.gumblondes.com
Portraits of your favourite blondes lovingly fashioned from chewed bubblegum.

Great Joy In Great Tribulation
www.dccsa.com/greatjoy
Biblical proof that Prince Chuck is the Antichrist and key dates leading to the end
of the world. For more enlightenment, including how to debug the pyramids, see:
www.bibleprophecy.net

I Can Eat Glass Project
www.geocities.com/nodotus/hbglass.html
Deter excess foreign suitors and carpet dealers with the only words you know in
their language.

Illuminati News
www.illuminati-news.com
Storm into secret societies and thump your fist on the table.

I Love Leather Pants
www.geocities.com/westhollywood/heights/2828
Don't expect to get André out of his skintight black trousers.

International Ghost Hunters Society
www.ghostweb.com
www.ghostresearch.org
They never give up the ghost. Nab your own with:
www.maui.net/~emf/TriFieldNat.html

Itz Fun Tew Be Dat Kandie Kid
www.angelfire.com/ma/talulaQ/kandie.html
Mothers – don't let your babies grow up to be ravers.

the directory

Lego Death
www.legodeath.com
Unpleasant death scenes from the guillotine to Elvis dying on the crapper rendered with block toys. For Bible stories illustrated with plastic blocks, go to: www.thereverend.com/brick_testament

A Mathematical Survey of the English Language
www.geocities.com/garywaterbury
Plot your future through simple arithmetic.

Mind Control
www.mindcontrolmanual.com
www.psychops.com
www.raven1.net
Unpick Big Brother's evil scheme and then put it to work on the dance floor.

Mozart's Musikalisches Würfelspiel
http://sunsite.univie.ac.at/Mozart/dice
Compose a minuet as you play Monopoly.

Mudboy
www.mudboyuk.com
Some get their kicks from muddy boots.

Museum of Non-Primate Art
www.monpa.com
Become an aficionado of moggy masterpieces.

Neuticles
www.neuticles.com
Pick your pet's pocket but leave his dignity intact.

News of the Weird
www.newsoftheweird.com
www.thisistrue.com
www.weirdlist.com
Dotty clippings from the world press.

Nibiruan Council
www.nibiruancouncil.com
Stock your bar to welcome the heroic Starseeds, Walkins, and Lightworkers from the Battlestar Nibiru, who will finally usher in the fifth dimensional reality.

Nobody Here
www.nobodyhere.com
Sometimes things with the least purpose are the most enthralling.

Non-escalating Verbal Self Defence
www.taxi1010.com
Fight insults by acting insane.

PhobiaList
http://phobialist.com
So much to fear, it's scary.

Planetary Activation Organization
www.paoweb.com
Prevent inter-dimensional dark forces from dominating our galaxy by ganging up with the Galactic Federation of Light.

Professional Paranoid
www.proparanoid.com
For when nobody else will believe you.

Reincarnation.org
www.reincarnation-org.com
Stash your loot with this crowd, then come back to collect it in your next life.

Reptoids
www.reptoids.com
Was that an alien or merely the subterranean descendant of a dinosaur?

The Republic of Texas Provisional Government
www.republic-of-texas.net
Rednecks for liberty, fraternity and equality.

the directory

The Sacred Geometry Stories of Jesus Christ
www.jesus8880.com
How to decode the big J's mathematical word puzzle.

Scrambled Eggs
www.callnetuk.com/home/busted
Nothing a swift kick in the groin won't fix.

Sensoterapia
www.sensoterapia.com.co
Master the sex secret you'll never see revealed in this month's *Cleo*.

Sightings
www.rense.com
Fishy newsbreaks from talk radio truthferret Jeff Rense.

Streakerama
www.streakerama.com
Get to the bottom of the streaker phenomenon.

Sulabh International Museum of Toilets
www.sulabhtoiletmuseum.org
Follow the evolution of the ablution at the world's leading exhibition of bathroom
businessware. No need to take it sitting down:
www.restrooms.org

Terry J Hokanson lives under the Mafia
www.geocities.com/terry_tune
Mild-mannered inventor speaks out against the crime syndicate that controls his life
through government hypnotists.

Things My Girlfriend and I Have Argued About
http://homepage.ntlworld.com/mil.millington/things.html
Add this page to that list.

Time Travellers
http://time-travelers.org
Step back to a time that common sense forgot.

Toe Amputation Project
www.bme.freeq.com/spc/toecutter.htm
No big deal. He still has one left.

Toilet-train Your Cat
www.karawynn.net/mishacat
http://susandennis.com
How to point pusskins at the porcelain.

the directory

weird

Trapped Angels
www.cyberspaceorbit.com/april.html
Leading authorities point to evidence that angels may be alien frauds. Backed up at:
www.mt.net/~watcher

Why I will never have a girlfriend
www.nothingisreal.com/girlfriend
Derived from first principles, and confirmed by his nickname.

World Database of Happiness
www.eur.nl/fsw/research/happiness
Discover where people are happiest and statistically what they mean by that.

Xenophobic Persecution in the UK
www.five.org.uk
If you're below British standards, the MI5 will punish you by TV.

ZetaTalk
www.zetatalk.com
Nancy's guests today are those elusive aliens that frolic in the autumn mist at the
bottom of her garden.

353

notes

notes

notes

"WATER MY HORSE WILL YOU SON?"

"WATER YOUR HORSE, I'M NOT A STABLE BOY"

"I DON'T CARE ABOUT YOUR MENTAL CONDITION: WATER MY HORSE"

THE MONKEES

Rough Guides travel...

...music & reference

a & Middle East
Town
t
Gambia
n
a
akesh
RECTIONS
cco
Africa, Lesotho &
vaziland

ania
ia
Africa
bar
abwe

el Theme guides
Time Around the World
Time Asia
Time Europe
Time Latin America
g & Snowboarding in
rth America
l Online
l Health
s in London & SE England
en Travel

aurant guides
ch Hotels & Restaurants
on
York
Francisco

s
ve
erdam
ucía & Costa del Sol
ntina
ns
alia
California

Barcelona
Berlin
Boston
Brittany
Brussels
Chicago
Crete
Croatia
Cuba
Cyprus
Czech Republic
Dominican Republic
Dubai & UAE
Dublin
Egypt
Florence & Siena
Frankfurt
Greece
Guatemala & Belize
Iceland
Ireland
Kenya
Lisbon
London
Los Angeles
Madrid
Mexico
Miami & Key West
Morocco
New York City
New Zealand
Northern Spain
Paris
Peru
Portugal
Prague
Rome
San Francisco
Sicily
South Africa
South India
Sri Lanka
Tenerife
Thailand
Toronto
Trinidad & Tobago

Tuscany
Venice
Washington DC
Yucatán Peninsula

Dictionary Phrasebooks
Czech
Dutch
Egyptian Arabic
EuropeanLanguages (Czech,
    French, German, Greek,
    Italian, Portuguese, Spanish)
French
German
Greek
Hindi & Urdu
Hungarian
Indonesian
Italian
Japanese
Mandarin Chinese
Mexican Spanish
Polish
Portuguese
Russian
Spanish
Swahili
Thai
Turkish
Vietnamese

Music Guides
The Beatles
Bob Dylan
Cult Pop
Classical Music
Country Music
Elvis
Hip Hop
House
Irish Music
Jazz
Music USA
Opera
Reggae

Rock
Techno
World Music (2 vols)

History Guides
China
Egypt
England
France
India
Islam
Italy
Spain
USA

Reference Guides
Books for Teenagers
Children's Books, 0–5
Children's Books, 5–11
Cult Fiction
Cult Football
Cult Movies
Cult TV
Ethical Shopping
Formula 1
The iPod, iTunes & Music
    Online
The Internet
Internet Radio
James Bond
Kids' Movies
Lord of the Rings
Muhammed Ali
Man Utd
Personal Computers
Pregnancy & Birth
Shakespeare
Superheroes
Unexplained Phenomena
The Universe
Videogaming
Weather
Website Directory

so! More than 120 Rough Guide music CDs are available from all good book and record stores.
Listen in at www.worldmusic.net